CONTRIBUTORS

I0470720

The Federal Citizen Information Center would like to express its gratitude to the partners listed below who helped make possible the publication of the *2012 Consumer Action Handbook*:

American Cleaning Institute

American Express Company

American Financial Services Association Education Foundation

Bridgestone Retail Operations, LLC

The Colgate-Palmolive Company

Consumer Product Safety Commission

Department of Veterans Affairs

Federal Deposit Insurance Corporation

Federal Trade Commission

Financial Industry Regulatory Authority

General Services Administration

Government Printing Office

Kellogg Company

LeadingAge

Mozilla Firefox

National Futures Association

The Procter & Gamble Company

Securities and Exchange Commission

Society of Consumer Affairs Professionals International

THE WHITE HOUSE
WASHINGTON

December 9, 2011

Welcome to the Consumer Action Handbook.

Each day, families across America navigate complex decisions, from buying a home or
car to paying off a loan or using a credit card. That is why protecting American
consumers remains a top priority for my Administration. With new credit card rules and
the Dodd-Frank Wall Street Reform and Consumer Protection Act, we have taken
concrete steps to empower the American consumer. We understand how crucial it is for
consumers to be able to make the best choices for their families, and these common-
sense reforms will protect both consumers and our economy as a whole.

The annual handbook published by the General Services Administration provides clear
and practical information to help Americans make informed consumer decisions. From
information on using credit wisely and preventing identity theft to filing a consumer
complaint, this guide brings you the latest information about your consumer rights and
responsibilities.

I encourage you to take full advantage of this valuable resource.

 GSA

GSA Administrator

January 2012

Welcome to the 2012 edition of the Consumer Action Handbook. The U.S. General
Services Administration's (GSA) Office of Citizen Services and Innovative Technologies
updates this resource annually to help you be an informed consumer.

As we all become busier and balance more responsibilities, it's very important to get
reliable information quickly and easily. This Handbook helps you do just that, by
combining valuable consumer information from across many Government agencies into
one practical book. A variety of topics, such as retirement, funding college education,
online safety, and energy efficient appliances are all covered here. This same
information can also be found online at USA.gov.

The Handbook is just one way that GSA strives to make access to Government
information easy. To get answers to all your Government questions, visit USA.gov and
GobiernoUSA.gov, or phone 1-800-FED-INFO (333-4636). You can also download or
order this Handbook and other printed Government resources at the new
Publications.USA.gov.

Sincerely,

Martha Johnson
Administrator

TABLE OF CONTENTS

TIPS FOR USING THIS HANDBOOK

This everyday guide to being a smart shopper is full of helpful tips about preventing identity theft, understanding credit, filing a consumer complaint, and more. Use the margins to make notes, write questions, or record other useful information. The information and resources you'll need are arranged as follows:

PART I—BE A SAVVY CONSUMER

Read this section for advice before you make a purchase. To quickly locate specific topics and information, look in the Table of Contents and Index (p. 147).

PART II—FILING A COMPLAINT

Turn to this section for suggestions on resolving consumer problems. The sample complaint letter on page 57 will help you present your case.

PART III—KEY INFORMATION RESOURCES

Look here for a list of public resources and contact information.

PART IV—CONSUMER ASSISTANCE DIRECTORY

Here you'll find contact information for corporate offices, consumer organizations, trade groups, government agencies, and more.

VISIT US ONLINE

A searchable version of this *Handbook* is available online at USA.gov and in Spanish at GobiernoUSA.gov. You can also order or download an electronic version of th *Handbook* and hundreds of other consumer publications at Publications.USA.gov.

As a savvy consumer, you should always be on the alert for shady deals and scams. To avoid becoming a victim, keep these things in mind:

1. A deal that sounds too good to be true usually is! Be wary of promises to fix your credit problems, low-interest credit card offers, deals that let you skip credit card payments, work-at-home job opportunities, risk-free investments, and free travel.

2. Don't share personal information with someone you don't know or trust. Learn how to recognize fraud.

3. Beware of payday and tax refund loans. Interest rates on these loans are usually excessive. A cash advance on a credit card may be a better option.

4. Read and understand any contract or legal document you are asked to sign. Do not sign a contract with blank spaces or where the terms are incomplete.

5. Get estimates from several contractors for home or car repairs. Make sure the estimates are for the exact same repairs for a fair comparison.

6. When paying for your purchases, watch the cash register screen. If you think the price that has been charged is incorrect, speak up.

7. Before you buy, make sure you understand and accept the store's refund and return policies, especially for services and facilities that charge monthly fees.

8. Don't buy under stress. Avoid making big-ticket purchases during times of duress (e.g., coping with a death or debt).

9. When shopping online, look for the padlock icon in the bottom corner of your screen or a URL that begins with "https" to ensure that your payment information is transmitted securely.

10. If you are having difficulty making payments on loans, notify your lender immediately so that you can work out a payment plan.

BUYER BEWARE

BEFORE YOU BUY

To avoid problems and make better decisions, use this checklist BEFORE you make a purchase:

- Decide in advance exactly what you want and what you can afford.
- Do your research. Ask family, friends, and others you trust for advice based on their experience. Gather information about the seller and the item or service you are purchasing.
- Review product test results and other information from consumer experts. See general resources in Part III (p. 58) or check the *Handbook* index (p. 147) for specific information.
- Get advice and price quotes from several sellers.

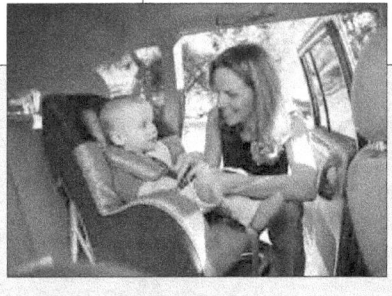

CHECK HERE FOR RECALLS

- www.recalls.gov lists government-initiated recalls from federal agencies.
- www.nhtsa.gov lists recalls and safety information on vehicles and equipment.
- www.fsis.usda.gov lists recalls that involve meat, poultry, or processed egg products.
- www.fda.gov lists recalls that involve food, medicines, medical devices, cosmetics, biologics, and pet food.
- Report incidents and safety concerns with consumer products, search for incidents, reported by others at Saferproducts.gov.

- Make sure that the seller has all appropriate licenses. Doctors, lawyers, contractors, and other service providers must register with a state or local licensing agency (p. 112).

- Check out a company's complaint record with your local consumer affairs office (p. 112) and Better Business Bureau (p. 66).
- Get a written copy of guarantees and warranties.
- Get the seller's refund, return, and cancellation policies.
- Ask whom to contact if you have a question or problem.
- Read and understand any contract or legal document you are asked to sign. Make sure there are no blank spaces. Insist that any extras you are promised be put in writing.
- Consider paying by credit card. If you have a problem, you can dispute a charge made on your credit card (p. 11).
- Don't buy on impulse or under pressure. This includes donating to charity.

SERVICE CONTRACTS AND EXTENDED WARRANTIES

Service contracts or "extended warranties" can add hundreds to your purchase price and are rarely worth the cost. Some duplicate warranty coverage you get automatically from a manufacturer or dealer. Ask these questions before you agree to one of these contracts:

- Does the dealer, the manufacturer, or an independent company back the service contract?
- How are claims handled? Who will do the work, and where will it be done?
- What happens to your coverage if the dealer or administrator goes out of business?
- Do you need prior authorization for repair work?
- Are there any situations when coverage can be denied? You may not have protection from common wear and tear, or if you fail to follow recommendations for routine maintenance.

PRODUCT SAFETY RECALLS

Before you buy a used vehicle or other second-hand product, check to be sure it hasn't been recalled for safety reasons. Some recalls ban the sale of an item, while others ask consumers to return the item for replacement or repair. Sometimes, a seller provides a part that reduces the danger of using the product.

If you're buying a product for a child, be especially vigilant. Each year, there are about 300 recalls of children's products such as toys, clothing, cribs, and costume jewelry. Visit the websites in the "Check Here for Recalls" box for the latest safety recalls. Download the app from Recalls.gov onto your mobile phone to stay informed about recalled products while you are on the go. You can also sign up for free e-mail notifications at www.cpsc.gov/cpsclist.aspx.

2 www.USA.gov

To contact an organization, use the directory beginning on page 62.

QUICK TIPS FOR AVOIDING FRAUD

There are many varieties of consumer frauds, but the most common ones are variations of fake check scams, credit repair, free trips offers, and sweepstakes. Here are some tips to help you avoid being a victim:

- **Don't give out personal information.** Be suspicious of anyone you don't know who asks for your Social Security number, birthdate, credit card number, bank account number, password, or other personal data.

- **Don't be intimidated.** Be suspicious of calls or e-mails that want you to provide or verify personal information immediately. Tell them you're not interested and hang up or don't reply to the e-mail.

- **Monitor your accounts.** Review bank and credit card statements carefully, and report unauthorized transactions to your financial institution immediately.

- **Use a shredder.** Tear or shred credit offers you receive in the mail, bank statements, insurance forms, and other papers with personal information.

IDENTIFYING AND STOPPING FRAUD

Look for these warning signs to avoid fraud:

- You are asked for your bank account or credit card number.
- Someone you don't know offers you the chance to receive a credit card, loan, prize, lottery, or other valuable item, but asks you for personal data to claim it.
- The solicitation looks like a government document and suggests that contest winnings or unclaimed assets are yours for a small fee. (The government doesn't solicit money from citizens.)
- Someone you don't know asks you to send money or money orders to claim a prize, lottery, credit card, loan, or other valuable offer.
- An unknown caller claiming to be a lawyer or in law enforcement offers to help you get your money back (for a fee).
- The deal is only good "for today" or a short time.
- A "repair person" suddenly finds a dangerous defect in your car or home.
- You are given little or no time to read a contract.
- A sale item is suddenly unavailable, but a "much better item" is available for slightly more money.
- Someone is trying to scare you into purchasing credit protection plans.

To learn more about avoiding identity theft and fraud, go to page 41.

AFTER YOU BUY

Even careful buyers can run into unforeseen problems later on. To minimize them, follow these steps after you buy:

- Save all papers that come with your purchase. Keep all contracts, sales receipts, canceled checks, owner's manuals, and warranty documents.
- Read and follow product and service instructions. The way you use or take care of a product might affect your warranty rights.

BANKING

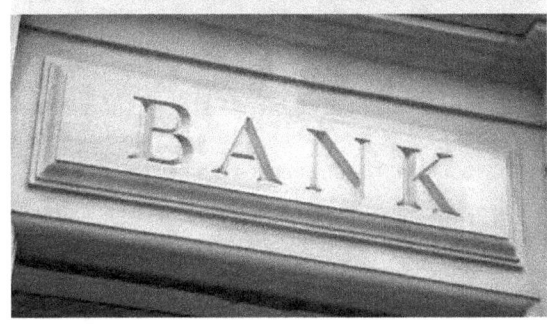

ATM/DEBIT CARDS

With a debit card and personal identification number (**PIN**), you can use an Automated Teller Machine (**ATM**) to withdraw cash, make deposits, or transfer funds between accounts. Some ATMs charge a fee if you are not a member of the ATM network or are making a transaction at a remote location.

Retail purchases can also be made with a debit card. You enter your **PIN** or sign for the purchase. Although a debit card looks like a credit card, the money for the purchase is transferred immediately from your bank account to the store's account. When you use a debit card, federal law does not give you the right to stop payment. You must resolve the problem directly with the seller.

If you suspect your debit card has been lost or

PROTECT YOUR PIN

Beware of "shoulder surfers." Be suspicious of anyone lurking around an ATM or watching over your shoulder while you use your card. Some thieves even put a device over the card slot of an ATM to read the magnetic strip and record your PIN; this is known as "skimming". If you suspect criminal activity, walk away and use a different ATM.

BEFORE YOU SWIPE YOUR DEBIT CARD

Although both credit cards and debit cards are easy ways to pay for your purchases, debit cards have some different levels of consumer protection and potential for consumer fees. Debit cards are directly connected to your bank account, so when you swipe your card, make sure that you have the money in your account to pay immediately. If you don't have enough money in your account,

your bank may "lend" you the money and pay the overage. However, it may charge you up to $35 for this courtesy, even if the dollar amount the bank covered was small. Some banks also charge you a monthly fee for making purchases with your debit card.

Debit cards don't offer as much protection against fraudulent use, or if your card is lost or stolen. Also, if you need to dispute a purchase, you are in a weaker position because the merchant already has the money and will only return it if you win the dispute.

Another fact to keep in mind is that when you use your debit card to make reservations for hotels or rental cars, a hold is placed on your card (and your checking account), which can affect your other pending transactions. Even if the hold is removed, it may take as long as a week until the funds are available to you again.

stolen, call the card issuer immediately. While federal law limits your liability for a lost or stolen credit card to $50, your liability for unauthorized use of your ATM or debit card can be much greater, depending on how quickly you report the loss.

- If you report a debit card missing before it is used, you are not responsible for any unauthorized withdrawals.

- Your liability is limited to $50 if you report the loss within two business days after you realize your debit card is missing and to $500 if you report the loss between two and 60 days.

- If you have not reported an unauthorized use of a debit or ATM card within 60 days after your bank mails the statement documenting the unauthorized use, you could lose all the money in your bank account as well as the unused portion of your line of credit established for overdrafts.

Check the policies of your card issuer. Some offer more generous limits on a voluntary basis.

Federal Reserve rules give debit and ATM card users additional protections covering overdrafts. Generally, banks cover your overdrafts by charging you a fee or offering an overdraft protection

plan, similar to a line of credit. If your bank pays overdrafts, you have the option to opt in to this service for most ATM and debit card transactions. Banks must disclose this option, the amount of the overdraft fee, and the customer's right to cancel this service. For more information, go to www.federalreserve.gov/consumerinfo.

PREPAID CARDS

Prepaid cards issued by banks and other government-regulated organizations offer consumers a way to make payments and conduct other financial transactions. There are plenty of situations where a prepaid card might be the most convenient choice, but be sure you understand the key terms and conditions BEFORE you buy.

Many cards carry protections similar to credit and debit cards. To obtain these benefits, you must follow the instructions for registering and activating your card. Be sure to record your card information, including the customer service telephone number listed on the back of the card in a separate place, so you can get a replacement if yours is lost or stolen.

If you have a problem with a prepaid card, first contact the customer service number. If the problem still isn't resolved, you may want to file a complaint with the proper authorities:

- For cards issued by retailers, contact the FTC (p. 106). You may also file a complaint with your local consumer protection office (p. 112).

- For cards issued by national banks, contact the Office of the Comptroller of the Currency (p. 104).

- For cards issued by state banks, contact the FDIC (p. 106) or state banking authority (p. 126).

SAVINGS AND CHECKING

When it comes to finding a safe place to put your money, there are a lot of options. Savings accounts, checking accounts, certificates of deposit (CD), and money market accounts are popular choices. Each has different rules and benefits that fit different needs. When choosing the one that is right for you, consider:

Minimum deposit requirements. Some accounts can only be set up with a minimum dollar amount. If your account goes below the minimum, the bank may not pay you interest on the money you deposited and you may be charged extra fees.

Limits on withdrawals. Can you take money out whenever you want? Are there any penalties for doing so?

Interest. How much (if anything) is paid and when? Daily, monthly, quarterly, yearly? To compare rates offered locally to those from financial institutions around the nation, visit www.bankrate.com.

Deposit insurance. Make sure your bank is a member of the Federal Deposit Insurance Corporation (FDIC). This agency protects the money in your checking and savings accounts, certificates of deposit (CDs), and IRA accounts up to $250,000. For more information, see page 106 or visit www.fdic.gov.

Credit unions. A credit union is a nonprofit, cooperative financial institution owned and run by its members. Like the FDIC does for banks, the National Credit Union Share Insurance Fund (NCUSIF) insures a person's savings up to $250,000.

Convenience. How easy is it to put money in and take it out? Are there branches or ATMs close to where you work and live? Can you bank by phone or Internet?

If you are considering a checking account or another type of account with check-writing privileges, add these items to your list of things to think about:

Number of checks. Is there a maximum number of checks you can write per month without incurring a charge?

Account and check fees. Is there a monthly fee for the account or a charge for each check you write?

Debit card fees. Are there fees for using your debit card?

Holds on checks. Is there a waiting period for checks to clear before you can withdraw the money from your account?

Overdrafts. If you write a check for more money than you have in your account, what happens? You may be able to link your checking account to a savings account to protect yourself.

Bounced checks. It's your responsibility to have sufficient funds in your account to cover checks that you write. Your bank will charge you for insufficient funds. Bounced checks can also blemish your credit record, so you may want to talk to your bank about overdraft protection.

UNSOLICITED CHECKS AND CREDIT OFFERS

If you cash an unsolicited check you've received in the mail, you could be agreeing to pay for products or services you don't want or need. In addition, those "guarantees" for credit cards or loans, without consideration of credit history, are probably a scam. Legitimate lenders never guarantee credit. For more information on how to identify fraudulent solicitations, visit www.ftc.gov.

Legitimate offers of credit often come in the form of "convenience checks," which credit card companies enclose with your monthly statement. However, these convenience checks may carry higher fees, a higher interest rate, and other restrictions. If you don't want the checks, be sure to shred them to protect yourself from "dumpster divers" and identity thieves.

Contact the proper regulatory agency below.

Dumpster divers sift through trash in search of your personal information.

Type of Institution	Regulatory Agency
State-chartered banks and trust companies	Federal Deposit Insurance Corporation (p. 106) and state banking authorities (p. 126)
Banks with National in the name or N.A. after the name	Office of the Comptroller of the Currency, U.S. Department of the Treasury (p. 104)
Federal savings and loans and Federal savings banks	Office of the Comptroller of the Currency, Department of the Treasury (p. 104)
Federally chartered credit unions	National Credit Union Administration (p. 107)
State-chartered banks that are members of the Federal Reserve System	Federal Reserve System (p. 106)

CARS

Whether you are buying or leasing a vehicle, these tips will help you get the best deal and avoid problems:

- Decide what kind of vehicle best suits your needs and budget.
- Check out the seller. For car dealers, check with your state or local consumer protection agency (p. 112) and Better Business Bureau (p. 66). If you're buying from an individual, check the title to make sure you're dealing with the vehicle's owner.
- Take a test drive. Drive at different speeds and check for smooth right and left turns. On a straight stretch, make sure the vehicle doesn't pull to one side.
- Handle trade-ins and financing separately from your purchase to get the best deal on each. Get a written price quote before you talk about a trade-in or dealer financing.
- Shop in advance and compare financing options at your credit union, bank, or finance company. Look at the total finance charges and the Annual Percentage Rate (APR), not just the monthly payment.
- Read and understand every document that you are asked to sign.
- Don't take possession of the car until all paperwork is final.
- Choose an auto insurance policy that is right for you (p. 28).

GOVERNMENT FUEL ECONOMY WEB PAGES

- **www.epa.gov/emissweb** is a green vehicle guide that can help you identify vehicles that are fuel-efficient and have clean-running engines.
- **www.fueleconomy.gov** compares the miles-per-gallon ratings of different vehicle models manufactured since the mid-1980s.
- **www.fueleconomy.gov/feg/savemoney.shtml** calculates annual fuel estimates.

Be wary of gas-saving automotive devices or gas or oil additives.

BUYING A NEW CAR

Do your research first and compare vehicles. Four key resources that offer vehicle performance, service, and safety information are: *Consumer Reports* (www.consumerreports.org), *Motor Trend* (www.motortrend.com), *Car and Driver* (www.caranddriver.com), and Edmunds automotive books and network (www.edmunds.com).

- Research the dealer's price for the car and options. It's easier to get the best price when you know what the dealer paid for a vehicle. The dealer invoice price is available on a number of websites and in printed pricing guides. *Consumer Reports* offers the wholesale price: this figure factors in dealer incentives from a manufacturer and is a more accurate estimate of what a dealer is paying for a vehicle.
- Find out whether the manufacturer is offering rebates that will lower the cost. For more information, visit www.carsdirect.com and www.autopedia.com/html/Rebate.html.
- Get price quotes from several dealers. Find out if the amounts quoted are the prices before or after rebates are deducted.
- Avoid low-value extras such as credit insurance, extended warranties, auto club memberships, rustproofing, and upholstery finishes. You do not have to purchase credit insurance in order to get a loan. See Service Contracts and Extended Warranties (p. 2).
- Hybrid-electric cars are becoming popular among consumers interested in fuel economy and reducing their negative impact on the environment. These cars combine the benefits of gasoline engines and electric motors and can be configured to achieve different objectives such as improved fuel economy, increased power, or additional auxiliary power. Tax breaks may also be available for qualifying vehicle purchases. For more information about hybrids, electric vehicles, alternative fuels, and tax incentives, visit www.fueleconomy.gov.

BUYING A USED CAR

- Learn what rights you have when buying a used car. Contact your state or local consumer protection office (p. 112).
- Find out in advance what paperwork you will need to register a vehicle. Contact your state's motor vehicle department. See www.usa.gov/Topics/Motor_Vehicles.shtml.
- Check prices of similar models using the NADA *Official Used Car Guide* (www.nadaguides.com) published by the National Automobile Dealers Association (p. 65) or the *Kelley Blue Book*

6   www.USA.gov

To contact an organization, use the directory beginning on page 62.

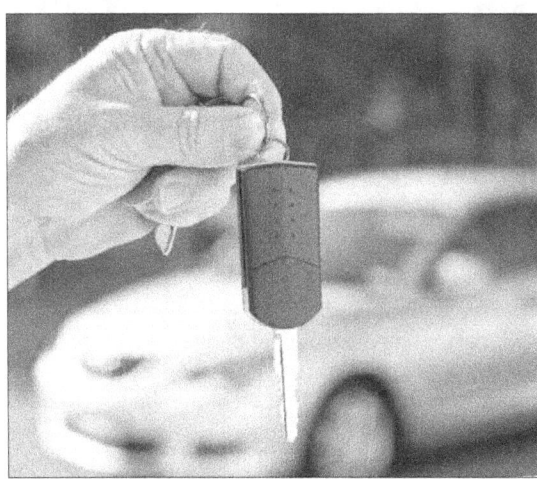

(www.kbb.com). These guides are usually available at local libraries.

- Research the vehicle's history. Ask the seller for details concerning past owners, use, and maintenance. Next, find out whether the car has been damaged in a flood, involved in a crash, been labeled a "lemon," or had its odometer rolled back. The vehicle identification number (VIN) will help you do this.

- Your state motor vehicle department can research the car's title history. Inspect the title for "salvage," "rebuilt," or similar notations.

- The National Highway Traffic Safety Administration's (NHTSA) website (www.nhtsa.gov) lists VINs of its crash-test vehicles and will let you search an online database of manufacturer service bulletins.

- The websites www.carfax.com and www.autocheck.com sell information on the history of vehicles gathered from state motor vehicle departments and other sources. These reports are helpful but do not guarantee that a vehicle is accident-free.

- The Center for Auto Safety (www.autosafety.org) provides information on safety defects, recalls, and "lemons" as well as service bulletins.

- Make sure any mileage disclosures match the odometer reading on the car.

- Check the warranty. If a manufacturer's warranty is still in effect, contact the manufacturer to make sure you can use the coverage.

- Ask about the dealer's return policy. Get it in writing and read it carefully.

- Have your mechanic inspect the car. Talk to the seller and agree in advance that you'll pay for the examination if the car passes inspection, but the seller will pay if significant problems are discovered. A qualified mechanic should check the vehicle's frame, tires, air bags, and undercarriage as well as the engine.

- Examine dealer documents carefully. Make sure you are buying—not leasing—the vehicle. Leases use terms such as "balloon payment" and "base mileage" disclosures.

DEALER VERSUS PRIVATE-PARTY PURCHASES

In general, buying a used car from a dealer is a safer option because you are dealing with an institution, which means you are better protected by law. The Federal Trade Commission (FTC) requires dealers to post a Buyer's Guide in the window of each used car or truck on their lot. This guide specifies whether the vehicle is being sold "as is" (in the current condition of the vehicle, without a warranty) or with a warranty, and what percentage of repair costs a dealer will pay under the warranty. Keep in mind that private sellers generally have less responsibility than dealers do for defects or other problems. FTC rules do not apply to private-party sales.

Expect to pay higher prices at a dealer than if you buy from an individual. Many dealers inspect their cars and provide an inspection report with each one. However, this is no substitute for your own inspection. Some dealers provide limited warranties, and most sell extended warranties. Watch out for dealer warranties that are "power train" warranties only, and not "bumper-to-bumper," full-coverage warranties. It's best to compare warranties that are available from other sources.

Some dealers provide "certified" cars. This generally means that the cars have had a more thorough inspection and come with a limited warranty. Prices for certified cars are generally higher. Be sure to get a list of what was inspected and what is covered under the warranty.

Purchasing a car from a private seller may save you money, but there are risks. The car could be stolen, damaged, or still under a finance agreement. If a private seller lies to you about the condition of the vehicle, you may sue the individual if you have evidence and you can find him or her. An individual is very unlikely to give a written warranty.

FINANCING

Most car buyers today need some form of financing to purchase a new vehicle. Many use direct lending, that is, a loan from a finance company, bank, or credit union. In direct lending, a buyer agrees to pay the amount financed, plus an agreed-upon finance charge, over a specified period. Once a buyer and a vehicle dealership enter into a contract to purchase a vehicle, the buyer uses the loan proceeds from the direct lender to pay the dealership for the vehicle.

Another common form is dealership financing, which offers convenience, financing options, and sometimes special, manufacturer-sponsored, low-rate deals. Before you make a financing decision, it's important to do your research:

- Decide in advance how much you can afford to spend and stick to your limit.

- Get a copy of your credit report and correct any errors before applying for a loan.

- Check buying guides to identify price ranges and best available deals.

More information about vehicle financing, deciding what you can afford, and consumer protections is available at www.ftc.gov/bcp/menus/consumer/autos/finance.shtm.

LEASING

When you lease, you pay to drive someone else's vehicle. Monthly payments for a lease may be lower than loan payments, but at the end of the lease you do not own or have any equity in the car. To get the best deal, follow these points of advice in addition to the general suggestions for buying a car (p. 6):

- To help you compare leasing versus owning, the Consumer Leasing Act requires leasing companies to give you information on monthly payments and other charges. Check out www.leaseguide.com and www.leasecompare.com for information on leases and current deals.

- Consider using an independent agent rather than the dealer; you might find a better deal. Most financial institutions that offer auto financing also offer leasing options.

- Ask for details on wear and tear standards. Dings that you regard as normal wear and tear could be billed as significant damage at the end of your lease.

- Find out how many miles you can drive in a year. Most leases allow 12,000 to 15,000 miles a year. Expect a charge of 10 to 25 cents for each additional mile.

- Check the manufacturer's warranty. It should cover the entire lease term and the number of miles you are likely to drive.

- Ask the dealer what happens if you give up the car before the end of your lease. There may be extra fees for doing so.

- Ask what happens if the car is involved in an accident.

- Get all of the terms in writing. Everything included with the car should be listed on the lease to avoid your being charged for "missing" equipment later.

The Federal Reserve System offers a consumer guide to auto leasing at www.federalreserve.gov/pubs/leasing.

RECALLS, "LEMON" LAWS, AND SECRET WARRANTIES

Sometimes a manufacturer makes a design or production mistake on a motor vehicle. A service bulletin notifies the dealer of the problem and how to resolve it. Because these free repairs are not publicized, they are called "secret warranties." The National Highway Traffic Safety Administration (www.nhtsa.dot.gov) maintains a database of service bulletins filed by manufacturers.

If you have a problem with a vehicle that is a safety hazard, check whether the manufacturer has recalled your vehicle. Go to www-odi.nhtsa.dot.gov/recalls/recallsearch.cfm or call NHTSA at 1-800-424-9393. You should report hazards that aren't listed to your dealer, the manufacturer of the vehicle (p. 63), and NHTSA. If a

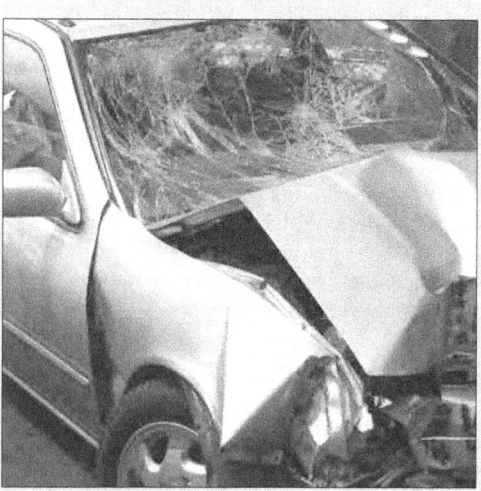

CHOOSE A SAFE VEHICLE

Crash tests can help you determine how well a vehicle will protect you in a crash. Here are different organizations that perform crash tests and rate vehicles:

- **The National Highway Traffic Safety Administration** Each year, NHTSA (www.nhtsa.gov) crashes vehicles head-on into a wall and bashes them broadside to test their ability to protect their occupants. NHTSA focuses on evaluating vehicle restraints such as air bags and safety belts.

- **The Insurance Institute for Highway Safety** A different test by the IIHS (www.hwysafety.org) uses offset-frontal car crashes to assess the protection a vehicle's structure provides.

- **Consumers Union** Published by CU, the annual auto issue of *Consumer Reports* (www.consumerreports.org) rates vehicles in terms of overall safety. Its safety score combines crash test results with a vehicle's accident avoidance factors—emergency handling, braking, acceleration, and even driver comfort.

To find out whether a manufacturer has recalled a car for safety defects, contact NHTSA (p. 104). If a vehicle has been recalled, ask the dealer for proof that the defect has been repaired. Used vehicles should also have a current safety inspection sticker if your state requires one.

safety-related defect exists, the maker must fix it at no cost to you—even if your warranty has expired.

If you have a vehicle with a unique problem that just never seems to get fixed, you may have a "lemon." Some states have laws concerning "lemons" that require a refund or replacement if a problem is not fixed within a reasonable number of tries or you haven't been able to use your vehicle for a certain number of days. Contact your state or local consumer protection office (p. 112) to learn whether you have such protections and what steps you must take to get your problem solved. If you believe your car is a "lemon":

- Give the dealer a list of the problems every time you bring it in for repairs.
- Get and keep copies of the repair orders listing the problems, the work done, and the dates that the car was in the shop.
- Contact the manufacturer, as well as the dealer, to report the problem. Check your owner's manual or the directory for the auto manufacturer (p. 63).

The Center for Auto Safety (p. 109) gathers information and complaints concerning safety defects, recalls, service bulletins, and state "lemon" laws.

RENTING

Federal law does not cover short-term car and truck rentals, but some state laws do. Contact your state or local consumer protection office (p. 112) for information or to file a complaint.

- Ask what the total cost will be after all fees are included. There may be an airport surcharge or drop-off fees, insurance fees, fuel charges, mileage fees, taxes, additional-driver fees, underage-driver fees, and equipment rental fees (for items such as ski racks and car seats).
- Ask whether the rental company checks the driving records of customers when they arrive at the counter. If so, you could be rejected, even if you have a confirmed reservation.
- Check in advance to be sure you aren't duplicating insurance coverage. If you're traveling on business, your employer may have insurance that covers accidental damage to the vehicle. You might also have coverage through your personal auto insurance, a motor club membership, or the credit card you use to reserve the rental.
- Carefully inspect the vehicle and its tires before renting.
- Check refueling policies and charges.
- Ask the rental company whether a deposit is required. If so, ask for a clear explanation of the deposit refund policies and procedures.

REPAIRS

Whenever you take a car to the repair shop:

- Choose a reliable repair shop. Family, friends, or an independent consumer-rating organization should be able to help you. Look for shops that display various certifications that are current. You should also check out the shop's record with your state or local consumer protection office (p. 112) or Better Business Bureau (p. 66).
- Describe the symptoms. Don't try to diagnose the problem.
- Make it clear that work cannot begin until you have an estimate (in writng, preferably) and you give your okay. Never sign a blank repair order. If the problem can't be diagnosed on the spot, insist that the shop contact you for authorization once the trouble has been found.
- Ask the shop to return the old parts to you.
- Follow the warranty instructions if a repair is covered under warranty.
- Get all repair warranties in writing.
- Keep copies of all paperwork.

Some states, cities, and counties have special laws that deal with auto repairs. For information on the laws in your state, contact your state or local consumer protection office (p. 112). A consumer guide to auto repair is available at www.ftc.gov/bcp/edu/pubs/consumer/autos/aut13.shtm.

CAR REPOSSESSIONS

When you borrow money to buy a car or truck, the lender can take your vehicle back if you miss a payment or in some other way violate the contract. You should also be aware that the lender:

- Can repossess with cause without advance notice.
- Can insist you pay off the entire loan balance in order to get the repossessed vehicle back.
- Can sell the vehicle at auction.
- Might be able to sue you for the difference between the vehicle's auction price and what you owe.
- Cannot break into your home or physically threaten someone while taking the vehicle.

If you know you're going to be late with a payment, talk to the lender to try to work things out. If you and the lender reach an agreement, be sure to get the agreement in writing. Contact your state or local consumer protection office (p. 112) to find out whether your state gives you any additional rights.

CREDIT

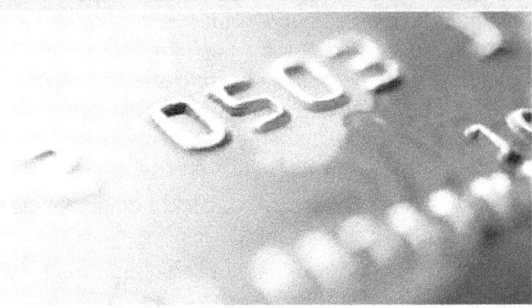

Like everything else you buy, it pays to comparison shop for credit. For up-to-date interest rate reports on mortgages, auto loans, credit cards, home equity loans, and other banking products, visit www.bankrate.com. The Equal Credit Opportunity Act protects you when dealing with anyone who regularly offers credit, including banks, finance companies, stores, credit card companies, and credit unions. When you apply for credit, a creditor may not:

- Ask about or consider your sex, race, national origin, or religion.
- Ask about your marital status or your spouse—unless you are applying for a joint account or relying on your spouse's income, or you live in a community property state (Arizona, California, Idaho, Louisiana, Nevada, New Mexico, Texas, Washington, or Wisconsin).
- Ask about your plans to have or raise children.
- Refuse to consider public assistance income or regularly received alimony or child support.
- Refuse to consider income because of your sex or marital status or because it is from part-time work or retirement benefits.

You Have the Right to:

- Have credit in your birth name, your first name and your spouse/partner's last name, or your first name and a combined last name.
- Have a co-signer other than your spouse if one is necessary.
- Keep your own accounts after you change your name or marital status or if you retire, unless the creditor has evidence that you are unable or unwilling to pay.
- Know why a credit application is rejected—the creditor must give you the specific reasons or tell you where and how you can get a copy of the credit report it used to determine its rejection, if you ask within 60 days.

- Have accounts shared with your spouse reported in both of your names.
- Know how much it will cost to borrow money.

For additional information on credit, see Buying a Home (p. 23) and Cars (p. 6). Other sources of information include the HUD Housing Counseling Clearinghouse at 1-800-569-4287, the FTC (p. 106), and the National Consumer Law Center (p. 110). You have the right to a FREE annual Credit Report (see "FREE CREDIT REPORTS" box, p. 13).

CREDIT CARDS

Chances are, you've received "pre-approved" credit card offers in the mail. Examine the fine print carefully before you accept any offer for a credit or charge card. Look for:

- **The Annual Percentage Rate (APR)**. If the interest rate is variable, how is it determined, and when can it change?
- **The periodic rate**. This is the interest rate used to figure the finance charge on your balance each billing period.
- **The annual fee**. While some cards have no annual fee, others expect you to pay an amount each year for being a cardholder.
- **The grace period**. This is the number of days you have to pay your bill before finance charges start. Without this period, you may have to pay interest from the date you use your card or the date the purchase is posted to your account.
- **The finance charges**. Most lenders calculate finance charges using an average daily account balance, which is the average of what you owed each day in the billing cycle. Look for offers that use an adjusted balance, which subtracts your payment from your beginning balance. This method usually has the lowest finance charges. Check whether there is a minimum finance charge.
- **Other fees**. Ask about fees when you get a cash advance, make a late payment, or go over your credit limit. Some credit card companies also charge a monthly fee.

CONSUMER FINANCIAL PROTECTION BUREAU

The Consumer Financial Protection Bureau (CFPB) is now up and running. This agency has authority to set clear rules for banks, mortgage companies, payday lenders, credit card lenders, and other financial service firms. Contact the CFPB to file credit card or mortgage complaints. For more information go to www.consumerfinance.gov.

The Fair Credit and Charge Card Disclosure Act requires credit and charge card issuers to include this information on credit applications. The Federal Trade Commission (p. 106) offers a wide range of free publications on credit and consumer rights at www.ftc.gov. The Federal Reserve Board (p. 106) provides a guide to choosing a credit card and credit protection laws at www.federalreserve.gov/consumerinfo.

Comparing Cards

- Bank Rate (www.bankrate.com) provides free credit card tips and information.
- Consumer Action (www.consumer-action.org) features credit card surveys of interest rates, fees, and other terms from dozens of credit cards as well as free brochures and guides on choosing and using credit cards.
- Card Trak (www.cardtrak.com) lists credit cards and offers e-mail newsletters for consumers, answers to frequently asked questions, and online credit card calculators.
- Card Ratings (www.cardratings.com) lists and reviews credit cards, and offers tips and credit card calculators.

Complaints

To complain about a problem with your credit card company, call the number on the back of your card or try to resolve it or with the CFPB (p. 96). If you fail to resolve the issue, ask for the name, address, and phone number of its regulatory agency. See the chart on page 5 to find the best federal or state regulatory agency to contact.

To complain about a credit bureau, a department store that offers credit, or other Federal Deposit Insurance Corporation (FDIC)-insured financial institution, write to the agency's Consumer Response Center (p. 106). You may also file a complaint with the FTC at www.ftc.gov.

Credit Card Billing Disputes

Under the Fair Credit Billing Act, you have the right to dispute charges on your credit card that you didn't make, are incorrect, or are for goods or services you didn't receive.

- Send a letter to the creditor within 60 days of the statement date of the bill with the disputed charge.
- Include your name and account number, the date and amount of the disputed charge, and a complete explanation of why you are disputing the charge.

  To ensure it's received, send your letter by certified mail, with a return receipt requested.
- The creditor or card issuer must acknowledge your letter in writing within 30 days of receiving it and conduct an investigation within 90 days. You do not have to pay the amount in dispute during the investigation.

- If there was an error, the creditor must credit your account and remove any fees.
- If the bill is correct, you must be told in writing what you owe and why. You must then pay it, along with any related finance charges.

If you don't agree with the creditor's decision, file an appeal with the Consumer Financial Protection Bureau (p. 96).

CREDIT REPORTS AND SCORES

A credit report contains information on where you work and live, how you pay your bills, and whether you've been sued or arrested, or have filed for bankruptcy. Consumer Reporting Agencies (CRAs) gather this information and sell it to creditors, employers, insurers, and others. The most common type of CRA is the credit bureau. There are three major credit bureaus: Equifax: 1-800-685-1111 or www.equifax.com or fraud alert 1-888-766-0008; Experian: 1-888-397-3742 or www.experian.com; TransUnion: 1-800-916-8800 or www.transunion.com or fraud alert 1-800-680-7289.

FICO

The information in your credit report is used to calculate your FICO score, a number generally between 300 and 850. The acronym stands for Fair, Isaac and Company. The higher your score, the less risk you pose to creditors. A high score, for example, makes it easier for you to obtain a loan, rent an apartment, or lower your insurance rate. Your FICO score is available from www.myfico.com for a fee. Free credit reports do not contain your credit score, although you can purchase it when you request your free annual credit report through www.annualcreditreport.com.

Tips for Building a Better Credit Score

- Pay your bills on time. Delinquent payments and collections negatively impact your score.
- Keep balances low on credit cards and other "revolving credit." High outstanding debt lowers your score.
- Apply for, and open, new credit accounts only as needed. Don't open an account just to have a better credit mix; it probably won't raise your score.
- Pay off debt instead of moving it around. Owing the same amount, but having fewer open accounts, may lower your score.

You don't rebuild your credit score; you rebuild your credit history. Time is your ally in improving credit. There is no "quick fix" for a bad credit score, so be suspicious of any deals that offer you a fast, easy solution.

CARD ACT PROTECTIONS FOR CONSUMERS

The Credit Card Accountability Responsibility and Disclosure (CARD) Act brought about sweeping protections for consumers. Among other things, your credit card company must comply with the rules below:

Fees

- Cannot change rates or fees without sending you a notice 45 days in advance in most cases.

- Must give you the option of rejecting a fee increase, but be aware that the credit card company may close your account if you reject the fee increase and may require a higher monthly payment.

- Cannot charge you a late payment fee of more than $25, regardless of how much you owe—unless one of your last six payments was late or the credit card company can justify a higher fee based on the cost of late payments.

- Cannot charge a late payment fee that is greater than your minimum payment.

- Cannot charge you an inactivity fee for not using your card.

- Cannot charge you more than one fee for a single late payment or any other violation of your cardholder agreement.

- Cannot charge you over-the-limit transaction fees unless you opt in, stating that you want to allow transactions that take you over your credit card limit. If the credit card company allows the transaction without your opt in, it cannot charge you a fee.

- Can impose only one fee per billing cycle for transactions that take you over your credit limit if you opt in to over-the-limit transactions. You can revoke your opt in at any time.

- Cannot impose annual fees, application fees, or other charges that total more than 25% of your initial credit limit; this does not apply to late fees or other penalties.

Payments

- Has to tell you how long it will take to pay off your balance if you make only minimum payments.

- Must mail or deliver your credit card bill at least 21 days before your payment is due.

- Must apply any payments above the minimum required amount to the balance with the highest interest rate, if you have more than one rate.

Interest Rates

- Cannot increase your rate for the first 12 months after you open an account unless you have a variable interest rate or an introductory rate; you are more than 60 days late paying your bill; or you are in a workout agreement and don't make payments as arranged.

- Cannot charge higher rates for purchases made before you receive notice of a new rate.

- Cannot use the double-cycle billing method when calculating interest; interest can only be charged on balances within the current billing cycle.

- Cannot increase your Annual Percentage Rate (APR) without explaining why it is doing so. If your credit card company increases your APR, it generally must re-evaluate that rate increase every six months. Under some circumstances, it may have to reduce your rate after the evaluation.

What's more, a credit card company can grant credit cards to consumers under age 21 only if they can show they are able to make payments or have a cosigner for the card. More information about CARD Act protections is available from www.federalreserve.gov/creditcard.

Negative Information in Your Credit Report

Negative information concerning your use of credit can be kept in your credit report for seven years. A bankruptcy can be kept for 10 years, and unpaid tax liens for 15 years. Information about a lawsuit or an unpaid judgment against you can be reported for seven years or until the statute of limitations runs out, whichever is longer. Inquiries remain on your report for two years.

Anyone who denies you credit, housing, insurance, or a job as a result of a credit report must give you the name, address, and telephone number of the credit reporting agency (CRA) that provided the report. Under the Fair Credit Reporting Act (FCRA), you have the right to request a free report within 60 days if a company denies you credit based on the report.

If there is inaccurate or incomplete information in your credit report:

- Contact the CRA and the company that provided the information.

- Tell the CRA in writing what information you believe is inaccurate. Keep a copy of all correspondence.

Under the Fair Credit Reporting Act, the information provider is required to investigate and report the results to the CRA. If the information is found to be incorrect, it must notify all nationwide CRAs to correct your file. If the investigation does not solve your dispute, ask that your statement concerning the dispute be included in your file. A notice of your dispute must be included whenever the CRA reports the negative item.

12   www.USA.gov

To contact an organization, use the directory beginning on page 62.

FREE CREDIT REPORTS

You can request a free credit report once a year from the three major credit reporting agencies—Equifax, Experian, and TransUnion. You may want to request your credit reports one at a time, every four months, so you can monitor your credit throughout the year without having to pay for a report. (If you ask the credit bureaus directly, they will charge you a fee to obtain your report.) To order your free report, you must go through www.annualcreditreport.com or call 1-877-322-8228.

If the information is accurate, only time, hard work, and a personal debt repayment plan will improve your credit report. Credit repair companies advertise that they can erase bad credit for a hefty fee. Don't believe it. Under the Credit Repair Organizations Act, credit repair companies can't require you to pay until they have completed promised services. They must also give you:

- A copy of the "Consumer Credit File Rights Under State and Federal Law" before you sign a contract.
- A written contract that spells out your rights and obligations.
- Three days to cancel without paying any fees.

Some credit repair companies promise to help you establish a whole new credit identity. You can be charged with fraud if you use the mail or telephone to apply for credit with false information. It is also a federal crime to make false statements on a loan or credit application, to give a false Social Security Number, or to obtain an Employer Identification Number from the Internal Revenue Service under false pretenses. If you have lost money to a credit repair scam, contact your state or local consumer affairs office (p. 112).

DEALING WITH DEBT

The Fair Debt Collection Practices Act applies to those who collect debts owed to creditors for personal, family, and household debts—these include car loans, mortgages, charge accounts, and money owed for medical bills. A debt collector is someone hired to collect money you owe.

Within five days after a debt collector first contacts you, the collector must send you a notice that tells you the name of the creditor, how much you owe, and what action to take if you believe you don't owe the money. If you owe the money or part of it, contact the creditor to arrange for payment. If you believe you don't owe the money, contact the creditor in writing and send a copy to the collection agency with a letter telling it not to contact you.

BE ALERT: 'CREDIT REPAIR' SCAMS

Beware! Before you sign up for fee-based credit repair services, beware. Many of the promised services are either illegal or are ones you can do for free by yourself. Before you sign up to work with these companies, here are some tidbits to keep in mind:

- A credit repair company must give you a copy of the "Consumer Credit File Rights under State and Federal Law" before you sign a contract.
- The company cannot perform any services until you have signed a written contract and completed a three-day waiting period, during which time you can cancel the contract without paying any fees.
- The company cannot charge you until it has completed the promised services, according to the Credit Repair Organizations Act.
- It is illegal to erase timely and accurate negative information contained in your credit history.
- Suggestions that you create a new credit history (also called file segregation) by requesting an Employer Identification Number from the IRS are also illegal.
- You can solve your own credit challenges by requesting a free copy of your credit report through www.annualcreditreport.com, and by working with creditors to dispute incorrect information.

A debt collector may not:

- Contact you at unreasonable times, for example, before 8 am or after 9 pm, unless you agree.
- Contact you at work if you tell the debt collector your employer disapproves.
- Contact you after you write a letter telling the collector to stop, except to notify you if the collector or creditor plans to take a specific action.
- Contact your friends, relatives, employer, or others, except to find out where you live and work.
- Harass you with repeated telephone calls, profane language, or threats to harm you.
- Make any false statement, or claim that you will be arrested.
- Threaten to have money deducted from your paycheck or to sue you, unless the collection agency or creditor intends to do so and it is legal.

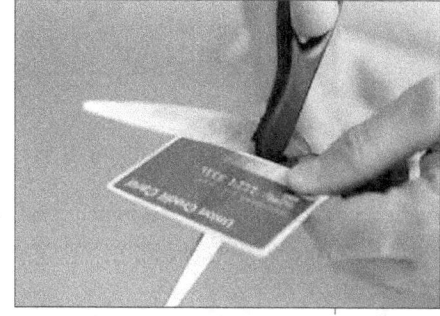

DEBT COLLECTION E-MAILS

Third party debt collection agencies can use e-mail as a means for contacting you to collect a debt. However, your privacy could be compromised if e-mails with sensitive information (social security number, account numbers) are intercepted. If you agree to accept e-mail from a debt collection agency, ask that all e-mails are encrypted.

To file a complaint, contact your state or local consumer protection agency (p. 112) and the Federal Trade Commission (p. 106).

Out-of-Control Debt

Counseling services are available to help people budget money and pay bills. Credit unions, extension offices, military family service centers, and religious organizations are among those that may offer free or low-cost credit counseling.

Local, nonprofit agencies that provide educational programs on money management and help in developing debt payment plans operate under the name Consumer Credit Counseling Service (CCCS). They are members of the National Foundation for Credit Counseling (NFCC), an organization that supports a national network of credit counselors.

Typically, a counseling service will negotiate lower payments with your creditors, and then make the payments using money you send to it each month. The cost of setting up this debt-management plan is paid by the creditor, not you. Ask these questions to find the best counselor for you:

- What services do you offer? Look for an organization that offers budget counseling and money management classes as well as a debt-management plan.

- Do you offer free information? Avoid organizations that charge for information or make you provide a lot of details about your problem first.

- What are your fees? Are there set-up and/or monthly fees? A typical set-up fee is $10. If you're paying a lot more, you could be the one being set up.

- How will the debt-management plan work? What debts can be included in the plan, and will you get regular reports on your accounts?

- Ask whether the counselor can get creditors to lower or eliminate interest and fees. If the answer is "yes," contact your creditors to verify this.

- Ask what happens if you can't afford to pay. If an organization won't help you because you can't afford to pay, go somewhere else for help.

- Will your counselor help you avoid future problems? Getting a plan for avoiding future debt is as important as solving the immediate debt problem.

- Ask for a contract. All verbal promises should be in writing before you pay any money.

- Are your counselors accredited or certified? Legitimate credit counseling firms are affiliated with the National Foundation for Credit Counseling (p. 145) or the Association of Independent Consumer Credit Counseling Agencies (p. 143).

Check with your local consumer protection agency (p. 112) and the Better Business Bureau (p. 66) to see whether any complaints have been filed about the counseling service you're considering.

If you have concerns about approved credit counseling agencies or credit counseling providers, please contact the U.S. Trustee Program, visit www.usdoj.gov/ust, or call 202-514-4100.

Personal Bankruptcy

Bankruptcy generally is considered the debt management option of last resort because the results are long-lasting and far-reaching. The Bankruptcy Abuse and Prevention Act of 2005 established more stringent rules for consumers and attorneys.

The filing process may be difficult for debtors:

- Debtors must file documents, including itemized statements of monthly net income, proof of income (pay stubs) for the last 60 days, and tax returns for the preceding year (four years for Chapter 13 bankruptcies).

- Debtors must take a pre-filing credit counseling and post-filing education course to have debts discharged.

- Debtors face increased filing fees, plus fees for credit counseling/education.

- The bankruptcy petition and process are complicated, so it's very difficult to file without an attorney.

LOST AND STOLEN CREDIT CARDS

Immediately call the card issuer when you suspect a credit or charge card has been lost or stolen. Once you report the loss or theft of a card, you have no further responsibility for unauthorized charges. In any event, your maximum liability under federal law is $50 per card.

BEWARE: OFFERS TO SKIP A PAYMENT

If your credit company invites you to skip a monthly payment without a penalty, it is not doing you a favor. You will still owe finance charges on your unpaid balance, and interest could be adding up on any purchases you make after the due date you skipped.

The filing process for lawyers:

- An attorney's signature on a petition certifies that the attorney has performed reasonable investigation into circumstances giving rise to the petition.
- Attorneys must carefully review documents such as tax returns and pay stubs as well as ask clients for credit reports.
- Attorneys are more apprehensive about sanctions.

LOANS

Home Equity Loans

A home equity loan could be a smart way to pay off high-interest debt or pay for home repairs. But consider carefully before taking out a home equity loan. If you are unable to make payments on time, you could lose your home.

Home equity loans can be either a revolving line of credit or a lump sum. Revolving credit lets you withdraw funds when you need them. A lump sum

PAYDAY AND TAX REFUND LOANS

Payday loans are illegal in some states. Changes in the law for payday lenders have also made payday loans illegal for members of the military. With a typical payday loan, you might write a personal check for $115 to borrow $100 for two weeks, until payday. The Annual Percentage Rate (APR) in this example is 390%! If you can repay the loan quickly, it may not appear such a bad deal. But if you can't pay off the loan quickly, that relatively small loan can grow into a major debt. At 390% interest, a $100 loan will become $490 in a year and $2,401 in two years.

Another high-cost way to borrow money is a tax refund loan. This type of credit lets you get an advance on a tax refund—for a fee. APRs as high as 774% have been reported. If you're short of cash, avoid both of these loans by asking for more time to pay a bill or seeking a traditional loan. A cash advance on your credit card may cost less.

is a one-time, closed-end loan for a particular purpose, such as remodeling or tuition. Apply for a home equity loan through a bank or credit union first. These loans are likely to cost less than those offered by finance companies.

Please see the Housing section (p. 23) for helpful information about buying, leasing, renting, or repairing a home.

Installment Loans

Before you sign an agreement for a loan to buy a house, a car, or other large purchase, make sure you fully understand all of the lender's terms and conditions, including:

- The dollar amount you are borrowing.
- The payment amounts and when they are due.
- The total finance charge, including all interest and fees you must pay to get the loan.
- The Annual Percentage Rate (APR), the rate of interest you will pay over the full term of the loan.
- Penalties for late payments.
- What the lender will do if you can't pay back the loan.
- Penalties if you pay the loan back early.

The Truth in Lending Act requires lenders to give you this information so you can compare different offers.

FINANCING YOUR EDUCATION

PAYING FOR COLLEGE 101

There's no way around it. A college education can be expensive. The cost of education after high school depends on several factors including the college you choose. Once you've narrowed your college choice, contact the school(s) to find out how much the total cost will be and what scholarships and types of financial aid are available.

High schools often hold free seminars on choosing and paying for college. The U.S. Department of Education's website, www.studentaid.ed.gov

BEWARE: SCHOLARSHIP AND FINANCIAL AID SCAMS

Scholarships and financial aid do not require up-front fees. While there are legitimate companies that will help guide you through the financial aid and college application process for a fee, disreputable companies may ask you for money up front and provide nothing in return. Red flags to watch out for include the following:

- A "money-back guarantee" to secure a scholarship. Don't believe it. Unscrupulous companies attach conditions that make it impossible to get the refund.
- "Secret scholarships." If a company claims to have inside knowledge of scholarship money, it's lying. Information on scholarships is freely available to the public. Ask your librarian or school counselor.
- Telling students they've been selected as "finalists" for awards. If a company asks for an up-front fee, head for the nearest exit.
- Asking for a student's checking account to "confirm eligibility." If a company wants bank account information or your credit card number to confirm or reserve a scholarship, it's a scam.
- Quoting a relatively small "monthly" or "weekly" fee, then asking for authorization to debit your checking account for an unspecified length of time. Ongoing fees are a sure sign of a scam.
- Unsolicited offers. Whether it's an e-mail or phone call, or it arrives in your mailbox, if you didn't request the information, ignore the offer.

provides information on preparing for and funding education beyond high school with details on the federal aid programs and how to apply for federal student aid. Another source of information on financial assistance is www.finaid.org. Both sites offer calculators to help you determine how much school will cost, how much you need to save, and how much aid you will need.

Many state governments have created programs to make it easier for families to save for their child's education. Visit www.collegesavings.org for links to information on the various state programs, such as 529 plans.

STUDENT FINANCIAL AID

Student financial aid is available from a variety of sources, including the federal government, individual states, colleges and universities, and other public and private agencies and organizations.

COLLEGE ACCREDITATION

You can check a school's accreditation with the Department of Education at www.ope.ed.gov/accreditation or search the Council for Higher Education Accreditation's database at www.chea.org/search.

FEDERAL STUDENT AID

- You can order many helpful publications at www.edpubs.gov, or by calling 1-800-433-3243.
- The U.S. Department of Education's federal student aid website, www.studentaid.ed.gov.
- The U.S. Department of Labor's *Occupational Outlook Handbook*, www.bls.gov/oco, provides information on various careers and their earning potential.
- The National Association of Student Financial Aid Administrators provides *Cash for College* with advice, tips, and information on financing your education at www.nasfaa.org.

The four basic types of college aid are:

- **Grants**. Gift aid that does not have to be repaid and is generally awarded according to financial need.
- **Work-Study**. The Federal Work-Study Program (FWS) is a federally funded source of financial assistance used to offset financial education costs. Students who qualify earn money by working while attending school. The money does not have to be repaid.
- **Loans**. Funds are borrowed and must be repaid with interest. As a general rule, federal student loans have more favorable terms and interest rates than traditional consumer loans.
- **Scholarships**. Offered by the school, local/community organizations, private institutions, and trusts. Scholarships do not have to be repaid and are generally awarded based on specific criteria.

Applying for Aid

You must complete and submit a *Free Application for Federal Student Aid* (FAFSA^SM) to apply for federal student aid. FAFSA on the Web^SM is the quickest and easiest method of applying. Go to www.fafsa.gov to apply.

Federal Student Aid Information Center

The Federal Student Aid Information Center (FSAIC) can answer your federal student financial aid questions and can give you all the help you need for free. You can also use the FSAIC automated response system to find out whether your FAFSA^SM has been processed and to request a copy of your Student Aid Report (SAR). For FSAIC contact information, see page 97.

Federal Loan Program Repayment Information

- **Public Service Loan Forgiveness Program**- offers forgiveness for outstanding federal loans

To contact an organization, use the directory beginning on page 62.

for individuals working full time in public service jobs.

- **Income-Based Repayment Plan**- helps to make repaying education loans more affordable for low-income borrowers.

Both programs offer generous benefits, but the rules may seem complex, so it is important to get all of the details. For more information on these programs as well as other repayment options:

- U.S. Department of Education/Federal Student Aid: www.studentaid.ed.gov/repaying.
- National Association of Student Financial Aid Administrators: www.nasfaa.org.

EMPLOYMENT

Times have changed for job searching, and numerous websites are now available that post jobs for private industry. Many companies also offer a way to apply online. However, these sites and new methods do not replace traditional and proven job-hunting approaches such as networking, personal contacts, business organizations, and interviewing.

EMPLOYMENT AGENCIES

If you're looking for a job, you may come across ads from employment agencies that promise wonderful opportunities. While some companies honestly want to help you, others are more interested in taking your money. Be wary of:

- Promises to get you a job and a guaranteed income.
- Up-front fees, even when you are guaranteed a refund if you are dissatisfied.
- Employment agencies whose ads read like job ads.
- Promotions of "previously undisclosed" government jobs. All federal jobs are announced to the public at www.usajobs.gov.

Get a copy of the employment agency contract and review it carefully before you pay any money. Check with your local consumer protection agency (p. 112) and the Better Business Bureau (p. 66) to see whether any complaints have been filed about a company.

The Federal Trade Commission (p. 106) investigates businesses that fraudulently advertise employment openings and guarantee job placement. Contact the FTC if you have a complaint.

WORK-AT-HOME COMPANIES

Not all work-at-home opportunities deliver on their promises. Some classic work-at-home schemes are medical billing, envelope stuffing, and assembly or craftwork. Ads for these businesses say, "Be part of one of America's Fastest-Growing Industries. Earn thousands of dollars a month from your home!" Legitimate work-at-home program sponsors should tell you, in writing, what's involved in the program they are selling. Here are some questions you might ask a promoter:

- What tasks will I have to perform? (Ask the program sponsor to list every step of the job.)
- Will I be paid a salary, or will my pay be based on commission?
- Who will pay me?
- When will I get my first paycheck?
- What is the total cost of the work-at-home program, including supplies, equipment, and membership fees? What will I get for my money?

The answers to these questions may help you determine whether a work-at-home program is appropriate for your circumstances and whether it is legitimate.

Multi-Level Marketing

Some multi-level marketing plans are legitimate; however, others are illegal pyramid schemes. In pyramids, commissions are based on the number of distributors recruited. Most of the product sales are made to these distributors, not to consumers in general. The underlying goods and services, which vary from vitamins to car leases, serve only to make the schemes look legitimate. Most people end up with nothing to show for their money except the expensive products or marketing materials they were pressured to buy.

If you're thinking about joining what appears to be a legitimate multi-level marketing plan, take time to learn about the plan:

- What is the company's track record?
- What products does it sell?
- Does it sell products to the public at-large?
- Does it have the evidence to back up the claims it makes about its product?

BEFORE YOU APPLY FOR A JOB

Are you in the market for a new job? If so, remember that potential employers aren't just reading your resumé; they are also reviewing your social media profiles, blogs, pictures, and videos. In 2011, the FTC ruled that background investigation companies can keep your social media history for as long as seven years. Even if you clean up your profiles, companies can still have access to older content that you posted publicly. To err on the side of caution:

- Use the privacy settings to manage who has access to your profile.

- Refrain from making defamatory comments about current or past employers.

- Avoid making statements that are discriminatory or demonstrate intolerance.

- Untag yourself in pictures or posts that are inappropriate.

- Is the product competitively priced?
- Is it likely to appeal to a large customer base?
- How much does it cost to join the plan?
- Are monthly minimum sales required to earn a commission?
- Will you be required to recruit new distributors to earn your commission?

Net-Based Business Opportunities

The Federal Trade Commission says that many Internet business opportunities are scams that promise more than they can possibly deliver. The companies lure would-be entrepreneurs with false promises of big earnings for little effort. Some tips for finding a legitimate opportunity:

- Consider the promotion carefully.

- Study the business opportunity's franchise disclosure document.

- Get earnings claims in writing and compare them with the experience of previous franchise and business opportunity owners.

- Visit previous franchise and business opportunity owners in person, preferably at their places of business.

- Check out the company with the local consumer protection agency (p. 112) and Better Business Bureau (p. 66). See whether there have been any complaints.

- If the business opportunity involves selling products from well-known companies, verify the relationship with the legal department of the company whose merchandise you would promote.

- Consult an attorney, accountant, or other business advisor before you put any money down or sign any papers.

- Take your time. Promoters of fraudulent business opportunities are likely to use high-pressure sales tactics to get you to buy in. If the business opportunity is legitimate, it will still be around when you're ready to decide.

UNEMPLOYMENT

The government's Unemployment Insurance Program provides benefits to eligible workers who become unemployed through no fault of their own and who meet other eligibility requirements. Each state administers its own program under federal guidelines. Eligibility requirements, benefit amounts, and length of benefits are determined by the states. For more information, go to www.dol.gov/dol/topic/unemployment-insurance/index.htm.

FOOD AND NUTRITION

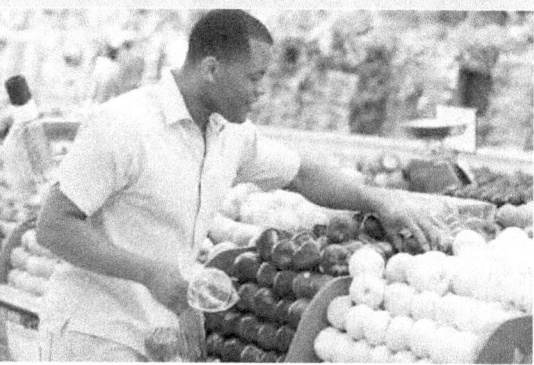

HEALTHY FOOD CHOICES

To help you make healthy food choices, the federal government posts dietary guidelines at www.health.gov/dietaryguidelines. Federal regulations also require many foods to identify fat content, fiber, and nutrients on their labels.

FOOD SAFETY

Food safety in the home revolves around three main functions: food storage, food handling, and cooking. Most experts agree that practicing a few simple rules focused on cleaning, separating, cooking, and chilling can prevent most food-borne illness in the home. The website www.foodsafety.gov is your gateway to government food safety information, including publications you can download or request. You can also visit www.recalls.gov for the latest food safety alerts and recalls.

18   www.USA.gov

To contact an organization, use the directory beginning on page 62.

For more information, here are some additional resources:

- Centers for Disease Control and Prevention (p. 99).
- FDA's Food Information and Seafood Hotline, 1-888-SAFEFOOD (723-3366).
- Partnership for Food Safety Education at www.fightbac.org.
- American Cleaning Institute at www.cleaninginstitute.org.
- U.S. Department of Health and Human Services (p. 98).
- USDA Food Safety and Inspection Service, www.fsis.usda.gov.
- USDA Meat and Poultry Hotline, 1-888-674-6854.

GROCERY SHOPPING

As the cost of food continues to rise, it can be a challenge to make healthy food choices and stay within your food budget. Here are some tips to help you get the most from your grocery budget:

- Take an inventory of the food you already have in your home. Plan your meals for the week, keeping in mind what you already have in your pantry.
- Make a shopping list and stick to it.
- Eat BEFORE going to the grocery store to avoid making impulse purchases. When you are hungry, everything looks good.
- Compare unit prices (cost per ounce or pound) to determmine if you are getting the best deal.
- Buy the generic store brand versions of foods.
- Take advantage of store loyalty savings programs, as well as clipping coupons and online discounts. Only take advantage of the deal if you know you will eat the discounted item. It's not a deal if the food goes to waste.
- Shop the perimeter of the store for nutrient dense foods. Processed and packaged foods tend to be more expensive.
- Visit your local farmer's market to find fresh produce. Arrive early to get the best selection or late to get the best deals. Fresh food spoils quickly so don't buy more than you can eat or freeze. Find your local farmers market at search.ams.usda.gov/farmersmarkets
- Shop for foods that are in season. When the supply is plentiful, the prices tend to be lower.
- Bring sturdy canvas bags and transport your food. Some stores offer discounts to customers for bringing their own bags.
- Reuse leftovers for lunch or casseroles.

For more grocery shopping tips visit www.extension.org and www.choosemyplate.gov.

FOOD FOR THOUGHT

Check out these resources for advice, tips, and information on food shopping and nutrition:

- U.S. Department of Agriculture (p. 96).
- U.S. Food and Drug Administration (p. 100).
- Nutrition.gov (www.nutrition.gov).
- MedlinePlus (click on F for Food or N for Nutrition at www.nlm.nih.gov/medlineplus).
- Center for Nutrition Policy and Promotion (www.choosemyplate.gov).

GOING GREEN

"Going Green," a relatively new term, means practicing an environmentally friendly and ecologically responsible lifestyle as well as making decisions to help protect the environment and sustain natural resources. There are lots of reasons to consider going green—too much trash, greenhouse gases, air and water pollution, damage to the ozone layer, and saving money. For example, switching all the light bulbs in a home from conventional incandescent light bulbs to compact fluorescent light (CFL) bulbs could save about $40 over the life of the bulb. Other examples include:

- Turning your thermostat down two degrees in winter and up two degrees in summer.
- Making sure your walls and ceilings are well insulated.
- Replacing bathroom and kitchen faucets with low-flow models.

BEWARE: GREEN MARKETING CLAIMS

You have probably seen products with labels claiming that they are "eco-friendly", "all-natural", or "made from recycled materials". The challenge with these statements is that there is no clear definition of these terms. Here are some tips to help you sort through green marketing:

- Look for specific (ex. "contains 75% post-consumer recycled materials") rather than vague statements about environmental impact.
- Determine whether the green marketing claims apply to the packaging, the product, or both.
- Beware of fake third-party certification. Visit Consumer Reports' website **www.greenerchoices.org/eco-labels** to find reliable environmental labels.

For more information about environmental advertising, contact the FTC (p. 106).

BUYING GREEN

Buying environmentally friendly products is also an important step in going green. Many such products can be identified by the Energy Star Logo at www.energystar.gov or the Green Good Housekeeping Seal of Approval at www. goodhousekeeping.com/product-testing/history.

You can also choose to buy organic or locally produced food and eco-friendly clothing. For more information about national standards covering organic food, go to the U.S. Department of

Agriculture's Agricultural Marketing Service at http://www.ams.usda. gov/AMSv1.0/nop. There are no national standards for organic clothing, but some fabrics to consider include organic cotton, bark cloth, bamboo, and organic wool.

REUSING AND RECYCLING

Other good ways to go green include reusing products, instead of throwing them away, and recycling items made of materials such as glass, metal, plastic, or paper.

It is estimated that 75% of our waste is recyclable, and most of the U.S. population has access to curbside or recycling programs. It is easy to safely dispose of many products. Others, such as car batteries, cell phones, televisions, paints, oils, and solvents, require special handling. Many of these products can be donated or recycled through local government recycling centers and hazardous household item collection days, charitable

organizations, or even electronics retailers. For more information about safely disposing of products that contain hazardous ingredients, visit the Environmental Protection Agency's (EPA) website: www.epa.gov/epawaste.

Many utility companies now offer curbside recycling programs that provide U.S. households with a responsible and convenient way to recycle materials. To locate information on recycling services and efforts in your area, call the Earth 911 toll free hotline, 1-800-CLEANUP (253-2687) or visit www.earth911.org.

HEALTH CARE

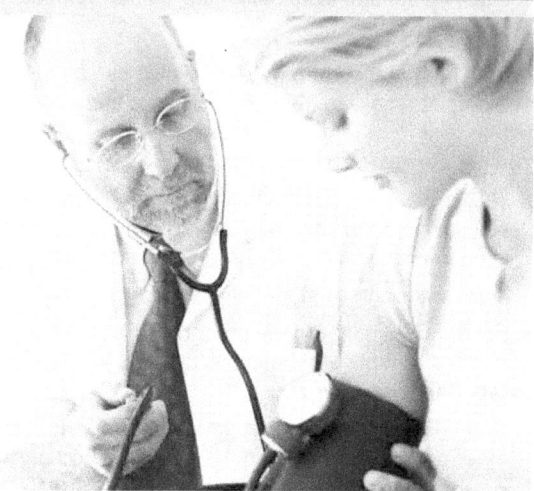

Thousands of resources are now available to help you make health care decisions. Be wary of websites sponsored by companies that are trying to sell you a particular treatment. It's better to contact reputable associations or visit sites run by government agencies and recognized organizations such as the Mayo Clinic or the American Medical Association (AMA). This information should complement, not replace, what you receive from a doctor. Here are some sites that are generally recognized as reliable information sources:

- **HealthFinder.gov** and **MedlinePlus** (www. medlineplus.gov) provide information on health issues, health care programs, and organizations.
- **Mayo Clinic** (www.mayoclinic.com) and **American Medical Association** (www.ama-assn.org) offer an index of diseases and much more.
- **Medical Library Association** (www.mlanet.org) links to websites suggested by librarians.
- **National Institute of Mental Health** (www.nimh.nih.gov) provides information on

To contact an organization, use the directory beginning on page 62.

research about understanding and treating mental illness.

- **Substance Abuse and Mental Health Services Administration** (www.samhsa.gov) provides information on prevention, treatment, and recovery from substance abuse or mental health issues.

For information on health care plans or the 2010 Affordable Care Act, see page 28.

CHOOSING A DOCTOR

When searching for a primary care doctor, dentist, specialist, or other health care professional:

- Find out whether the health care professional is licensed in your state. A state or local occupational and professional licensing board will be able to give you this information.

- Research whether the health care professional is board-certified in the appropriate specialty. Visit www.ama-assn.org and www.abms.org for more information.

- Ask how often the health care professional has done the procedure you need and his or her success rate. You may be able to find some of this information on the Internet. For example, the Centers for Disease Control and Prevention (CDC) reports the success rates and number of procedures performed by fertility clinics at www.cdc.gov. Some states also collect and post data on the success of heart-bypass surgery.

- Check whether there have been any complaints or disciplinary actions taken. Visit www.docboard.org and www.healthcarechoices.org for more information.

There are also pay-for-use sites with similar information, including www.Docinfo.org and www.checkbook.org.

Visit www.healthfinder.gov for more advice on identifying providers.

Filing a Complaint

If you have a complaint about the medical services you received from a physician, you may file a complaint with your State Medical Board. For a complete directory from the Federation of State Medical Boards, visit www.fsmb.org/directory_smb.html. You can also call the Federation at 817-868-4000 get the phone number of your state medical board.

CHOOSING A HEALTH CARE FACILITY

Report cards on the Internet can help you compare health care facilities. Three private websites that rate hospitals based on information collected from Medicare records and other sources are www.usnews.com, www.checkbook.org, and www.healthgrades.com.

The Joint Commission (p. 145) accredits hospitals as well as nursing homes and other health care organizations. Specially trained investigators assess whether these organizations meet set standards. At www.jointcommission.org you can check on a local facility, including how it compares with others. The Joint Commission also accepts consumer complaints. You can post a complaint on its website.

If you are looking for a nursing home or other assisted-living facility, these organizations can help:

- Nursing Home Compare, operated by the U.S. Department of Health and Human Services, will help you compare the facilities in many states. Go to www.medicare.gov/nhcompare/home.asp or call 1-800-MEDICARE (633-4227).

- Eldercare Locator (www.eldercare.gov) provides information and referral services for those seeking local and state support resources for the elderly (p. 99).

- LeadingAge (www.leadingage.org) is a trade group that represents many nonprofit facilities that serve and support the elderly (p. 145).

- The Assisted Living Federation of America (www.alfa.org) represents both for-profit and nonprofit assisted-living facilities; call 703-894-1805 (p. 143).

- The Commission on Accreditation of Rehabilitation Facilities (www.carf.org) gives its seal of approval to qualifying facilities; call 1-888-281-6531 (p. 143).

Naming a Durable Power of Attorney for Health Care

A durable power of attorney for health care (sometimes called a durable medical power of attorney) specifies the person you've chosen to make medical decisions for you. It is activated when you're unconscious or unable to make medical decisions, or when you have otherwise specified. You need to choose someone who meets the legal requirements in your state for acting as your agent. State laws vary, but most states disqualify anyone

---

EXAMINE YOUR LOCAL MEDICAL FACILITIES

Get statistics on medical facilities at these sources:

- **www.hcup.ahrq.gov** is a free online query system that provides access to national-, regional-, and state-level health statistics and information.

- **www.usa.gov** offers information on health facilities in your area and health by age group.

- **www.aha.org** is the website of the American Hospital Association.

MEDICAL IDENTITY THEFT

Medical identity theft can occur when someone steals your personal information number to obtain medical care, buy medication, or submit fake claims to your insurer or Medicare in your name. In order to prevent medical identity theft, you can:

- Guard your Social Security, Medicare and health insurance idenfication numbers. Only give your number to your physician or other approved health care providers.

- Review your explanation of benefits or Medicare Summary Notice to make sure that the claims match the services you received. Report questionable charges to your health insurance provider or Medicare.

- Request and carefully review a copy of your medical records for inaccuracies and conditions that you don't have.

If you believe that you have been a victim of medical identity theft, file a complaint with the FTC at 1-877- 438-4338 or https://ftccomplaintassistant.gov. If you suspect that you have been the victim of Medicare fraud, contact the Department of Health and Human Services' Inspector General at 1-800-447-8477 or by e-mail at HHSTips@oig.hhs.gov.

For more information about Medicare fraud, visit www.stopmedicarefraud.gov.

---

under the age of 18, your health care provider, or employees of your health care provider.

The person you name as your agent must:

- Be willing to speak and advocate on your behalf.
- Be willing to deal with conflict among friends and family members, if it arises.
- Know you well and understand your wishes.
- Be willing to talk with you about these issues.
- Be someone you trust with your life.

PRESCRIPTION DRUGS

Pharmacies may charge widely different prices for the same medicine, so it is a good idea to comparison shop:

- Ask your physician and pharmacist whether a generic drug may be appropriate. Generics usually cost less than brand-name drugs. Many insurance companies use a multi-tier co-payment plan for prescription drugs. Be sure to ask before filling the prescription.

- Consider using a mail-order or online pharmacy, especially if you will be taking a drug for a long time; they often charge less.

An increasing number of consumers are replacing a trip to the pharmacy with a trip on the Internet. While there are online pharmacies that provide legitimate prescription services, there are also some questionable sites that make buying medicines online risky. Do business only with a licensed U.S. pharmacy. Check with the National Association of Boards of Pharmacy to determine whether the site is licensed and in good standing. Visit www.nabp.net or call 847-391-4406.

An online pharmacy should offer you access to a registered pharmacist who can answer any questions you might have about drug interactions, side effects, and other safety precautions. Be wary of sites that:

- Sell medications without a prescription.
- Sell medications not approved by the FDA.
- Advertise quick cures.
- Tell stories of "amazing results."

If you suspect a site is not a licensed pharmacy, report it and any complaints to the Food and Drug Administration (p. 100) at www.fda.gov/Safety/ReportaProblem/ucm059315.htm.

Want to know the side effects of a particular medication? Curious whether a drug has been approved by the Food and Drug Administration? For answers to these questions and other information on approved prescription and over-the-counter and discontinued drugs, visit www.accessdata.fda.gov/scripts/cder/drugsatfda. For general drug information, you can also contact the FDA (p. 100).

MEDICARE PRESCRIPTION DRUG COVERAGE

Medicare offers prescription drug coverage to help you get the prescription drugs you need. Everyone with Medicare can join a drug plan to get this coverage. If you aren't sure whether a drug plan is approved by Medicare, call 1-800-MEDICARE (633-4227). Look for the "Medicare Approved" seal on drug discount cards to make sure you are getting the best deal.

Like other insurance, if you decide not to enroll in a drug plan when you are first eligible, you may pay a penalty if you choose to join later. If you have limited income and resources, you may get extra help to cover prescription drugs for little or no cost. For more information, contact the Centers for Medicare & Medicaid Services (p. 100).

HOUSING

The U.S. Department of Housing and Urban Development (HUD) funds housing counseling agencies throughout the country. These organizations can give you advice on buying a home, renting, defaults, foreclosures, credit issues, and reverse mortgages. To contact the agency nearest you, call 1-800-569-4287 or visit www.hud.gov. Homeowners with problems that could result in default of their mortgage or foreclosure on their property are encouraged to contact a HUD-approved housing counseling agency immediately.

If, in your housing search, you believe you are being discriminated against on the basis of your race, color, nationality, religion, sex, familial status, or disability, contact HUD's Office of Fair Housing and Equal Opportunity (p. 101).

BUYING A HOME

Buying a home is one of the most complex financial decisions you'll ever make. In addition to the financial and legal issues involved, real estate agents and lenders may not be acting in your best interest.

- Real estate agents represent the seller, not the buyer. Consider hiring a buyer's agent who works for you, not for the seller.
- Get prices on other homes. Knowing the price of other homes in a neighborhood will help you avoid paying too much.
- Have the property inspected. Use a licensed home inspector to carefully inspect the property before agreeing to buy it.

Mortgages
When shopping for a home mortgage, make sure you obtain all of the relevant information:
- Research current interest rates. Check the real estate section of your local newspaper, use the Internet, or call at least six lenders for information.
- Check the rates for 15-year, 20-year, and 30-year mortgages. You may be able to save thousands of dollars in interest charges by getting the shortest-term mortgage you can afford.
- Ask for details on the same loan amount, loan term, and type of loan from multiple lenders so that you can compare the information. Be sure to get the Annual Percentage Rate (APR), which takes into account not only the interest rate, but also points, broker fees, and other credit charges expressed as a yearly rate.
- Ask whether the rate is fixed or adjustable. The interest rate on adjustable-rate mortgages (ARMs) can vary a great deal over the lifetime of the mortgage. An increase of several percentage points might raise payments by hundreds of dollars per month.
- If a loan has an adjustable rate, ask when and how the rate and loan payment could change.
- Find out how much of a down payment is required. Some lenders require 20% of the home's purchase

BEFORE CHOOSING A LENDER, DO YOUR RESEARCH
- **Get recommendations:** Ask friends and family members for suggestions, especially if they've obtained a loan recently.
- **Check credentials:** Mortgage bankers are regulated by your state's department of banking or division of real estate. Check with the one appropriate to your state to see whether a lender is in good professional standing. Mortgage brokers may or may not be state regulated. If not, check with the local chapter of the Mortgage Bankers Association of America or the Better Business Bureau (p. 66) to see whether your mortgage banker's record is clean.
- **Do your homework:** Learn about typical mortgages and ask a question when something looks amiss; a broker may be trying to pad closing costs or other fees at your expense.
- **Be cautious online:** There are plenty of attractive deals online, but first make sure you're dealing with a reliable broker or lender.

price as a down payment. But many lenders now offer loans that require less. In these cases, you may be required to purchase private mortgage insurance (PMI) to protect the lender if you fall behind on payments.

- If PMI is required, ask what the total cost of the insurance will be. How much will the monthly mortgage payment be when the PMI premium is added, and how long you will be required to carry PMI?
- Ask whether you can pay off the loan early and whether there is a penalty for doing so.

There is a long list of sources for mortgages loans: mortgage banks, mortgage brokers, banks, thrifts and credit unions, home builders, real estate agencies, and Internet lenders.

For more information on home buying and mortgages, visit www.hud.gov. Other good sources include the Mortgage Bankers Association at www.homeloanlearningcenter.com and the National Association of Realtors at www.realtor.org.

Mortgage Transfers

CFPB rules help mortgage borrowers by requiring that mortgage companies notify them when their loans are transferred to another company. Before the new rules, if your loan was sold or transferred from your current lender to a new lender, the new lender did not have to tell you that it acquired your loan. The new rules ensure that you know who owns your loan, which is important information if you have questions or payment disputes or want to discuss loan modifications.

Under the new rules, the company that takes over your loan must send you a notice within 30 days of acquiring it. Even with a new loan owner, the company that "services" or handles your loan might not change and you might continue to send your mortgage payments to the same address. If that loan servicer changes, you will receive a separate notice.

For more information about servicing companies, read the Federal Trade Commission's publication, *Mortgage Servicing: Making Sure Your Payments Count* at www.ftc.gov/bcp/edu/pubs/consumer/homes/rea10.shtm.

AVOIDING FORECLOSURE

If you miss your mortgage payments, foreclosure may occur. This is the legal means your lender can use to repossess your home. If you owe more than your property is worth, a deficiency judgment is pursued. Both foreclosures and deficiency judgments have a negative impact on your future

Fixed-rate and adjustable-rate mortgages are the two main types of mortgages, but there is a wide variety of other mortgage products available. Below are pros and cons of some of the mortgage products you want to consider:

Type of Mortgage	Pros	Cons
Fixed-rate mortgage	No surprises. Interest rate stays the same over the entire term, usually 15, 20, or 30 years.	If interest rates fall, you could be stuck paying a higher rate.
Adjustable-rate (ARM) or variable-rate mortgage	Usually offers a lower initial rate of interest than fixed-rate loans.	After an initial period, rates fluctuate over the life of the loan. When interest rates rise, generally so do your loan payments.
FHA (Federal Housing Administration) loans	Allows buyers who may not qualify for a home loan to obtain one with a low down payment.	The size of your loan may be limited.
VA loan	Guaranteed loans for eligible veterans, active duty personnel, and surviving spouses. Offers competitive rates, low or no down payments.	The size of your loan may be limited.
Balloon mortgage	Usually a fixed-rate loan with relatively low payments for a fixed period.	After an initial period, the entire balance of the loan is due immediately. This type of loan may be risky for some borrowers.
Interest-only loan	Borrower pays only the interest on the loan in monthly payments for a fixed term.	After an initial period, the balance of the loan is due. This could mean higher payments, paying a lump sum, or refinancing.
Reverse mortgage	Allows seniors to convert equity in their homes to cash; you don't have to pay back the loan and interest as long as you live in the house.	Subject to aggressive lending practices and false advertising promises, particularly by lenders that prey on seniors. Check to make sure the loan is Federally insured.

MORTGAGE REFINANCING

Consider refinancing your mortgage if you can get a rate that is at least one percentage point lower than your existing mortgage rate and if you plan to keep the new mortgage for several years. When comparing mortgages, don't forget to include the extra fees you must pay for the new mortgage. You may be able to get some fees waived if you are able to refinance with your current mortgage holder.

credit. You should avoid foreclosure if at all possible.

These steps can help:

- Do not ignore the letters from your lender. If you're having problems making your payments, call or write to your lender's Loss Mitigation Department immediately. Explain your situation. Be prepared to provide financial information, such as your monthly income and expenses. Without this information, the lender may not be able to help.

- Stay in your home for now. You may not qualify for assistance if you abandon your property. For example, the Hope for Homeowners program offers 30-year, fixed-rate mortgages only to owner-occupiers.

- Contact a HUD-approved housing counselor. Call 1-800-569-4287 or TDD 1-800-877-8339 for the housing counseling agency nearest you. These agencies are valuable resources.

- Contact Making Home Affordable for help. Call 1-888-995-4673 to talk to a HUD-approved credit counselor who will guide you through your options for free.

HUD counselors frequently have information on services and programs offered by government agencies as well as private and community organizations that could help you. The housing counseling agency may also offer credit counseling. These services are usually free of charge.

For more information, resources are available at the following agencies:

- The U.S. Department of Housing and Urban Development (p. 101).

- The Federal Trade Commission (p. 106).

Additional advice, resources, and tips for homeowners can be found under Home Equity Loans (p. 15), Insurance (p. 29), and Home Improvement and Repairs (p. 25).

MOVING COMPANIES

Not all moving companies are the same. Although many are legitimate, some attempt to take advantage of their clients. Follow these guidelines to help you choose the right mover:

Get a written estimate from several movers. Be wary of very low estimates. Some companies use the low price to get a contract and later ask for more money before they will remove your belongings from their truck.

Make sure the mover has an operating license. For moves from one state to another, visit www.protectyourmove.gov to verify a mover's license. For moves within a state, check your state, county, or local consumer affairs agency (p. 112).

Make sure the mover has insurance. If furniture is damaged during the move, the mover's insurance should cover it. Ask how to file a complaint if there are limits to the coverage.

Check the mover's track record. Contact your state or local consumer protection agency (p.112) or Better Business Bureau (p. 66) to see whether there is a history of complaints.

If you have a dispute with a moving company, you can file a complaint with the Federal Motor Carrier Safety Administration by calling 1-800-832-5660 or by visiting www.fmcsa.dot.gov.

HOME IMPROVEMENT AND REPAIRS

Home improvements and repairs can cost thousands of dollars and are the subject of frequent complaints.

BEWARE OF FORECLOSURE RESCUE SCAMS—HELP IS FREE!

- Beware of anyone who asks you to pay a fee in exchange for a counseling service or modification of a delinquent loan.

- Scam artists often target homeowners who are struggling to meet their mortgage commitment or are anxious to sell their homes. Recognize and avoid common scams.

- Assistance from a HUD-approved housing counselor is free. Visit www.makinghomeaffordable.gov or call 1-800-569-4287.

- Beware of people who pressure you to sign papers immediately or who try to convince you that they can "save" your home if you sign or transfer the deed to your house over to them.

- Do not sign over the deed to your property to any organization or individual unless you are working directly with your mortgage company to forgive your debt.

MORTGAGE & FORECLOSURE SCAMS

- **Lease-back or rent-to-buy scams:** You are asked to transfer the title to your home "temporarily" to the scam artist who promises to obtain better financing for your mortgage and allow you to stay in your home as a renter with the option to purchase the home back. However, if you do not comply with the terms of the rent-to-buy agreement, you will lose your money and be evicted like any other tenant.

- **Fake "government" modification programs:** These scams claim to be affiliated with the government or require that you pay high fees in order to benefit from government modification programs. Remember that you do not have to pay any fees to participate in government-approved programs. Some frauds may even use words like "Federal" or "government-approved" or acquire website names that make consumers think they are associated with the government.

- **Refinance fraud:** The scam artist offers to be an intermediary between you and your mortgage lender to negotiate a loan modification. The scam artist may even instruct you to make payments directly to him or her, which the scammer will send to the lender. However, the scam artist will not forward the payments to your lender and you could still lose your home.

- **"Eliminate your debt" claims:** Some companies may make false legal claims that you are not required to repay your mortgage or that they know of "secret laws" that can eliminate your debt. Do not believe these claims.

- **Refinance scams:** You are encouraged to sign "foreclosure rescue" loan documents to refinance your loan. In reality, you have surrendered ownership of your home because the loan documents are actually deed transfer documents. You may falsely believe that your home has been saved from foreclosure until you receive an eviction notice months or even years later.

When selecting a contractor:

- Get recommendations and references. Talk to friends, family, and others who have used the contractor for similar work.
- Get at least three written estimates. Insist the contractors come to your home to evaluate what needs to be done. Be sure the estimates are based on the same work so that you can make meaningful comparisons.
- Check contractor complaint records with your state or local consumer protection agency (p. 112) or Better Business Bureau (p. 66).
- Make sure the contractor meets licensing and registration requirements. Your state or local consumer protection agency (p. 112) can help you find out what the necessary requirements are.
- Get the names of suppliers and ask them whether the contractor makes timely payments.
- Contact your local building inspection department to check for permit and inspection requirements. Be wary if the contractor asks you to get the permit; it could mean the firm is not licensed.
- Be sure your contractor is insured. The contractor should have personal liability, property damage, and workers' compensation insurance for workers and subcontractors. Also check with your insurance company to find out whether you are covered for any injury or damage that might occur.
- Insist on a written contract that states exactly what work will be done, the quality of materials that will be used, warranties, timetables, the names of any subcontractors, the total price of the job, and the schedule of payments.

- Try to limit your down payment. Some states have laws limiting the amount of down payment required.
- Understand your payment options. Compare the cost of getting your own loan versus contractor financing.
- Don't make a final payment or sign a final release until you are satisfied with the work and know that subcontractors and suppliers have been paid. Some state laws allow unpaid subcontractors and suppliers to put a lien on your home for bills the contractor failed to pay.
- Pay by credit card when you can. You may have the right to withhold payment to the credit card company until problems are corrected (see p. 11).

Be especially cautious if the contractor:

- Comes door-to-door or seeks you out.
- Just happens to have material left over from a recent job.
- Offers you discounts for finding other customers.
- Quotes a price that's out of line with other estimates.
- Pressures you for an immediate decision.
- Can only be reached by leaving messages with an answering service.
- Drives an unmarked van.
- Has out-of-state license plates.
- Asks you to pay for the entire job up front.

With most home improvements, federal law gives you three business days to cancel without penalty. See 3-Day Cooling-Off Rule (p. 43). Of course, you would be liable for any benefit already received.

26 www.USA.gov

To contact an organization, use the directory beginning on page 62.

State laws may also provide some protection. And remember, if you finance home improvements with a home equity loan (p. 15) and don't make your payments, you could lose your home.

RENTING/LEASING

A lease is an agreement that outlines the obligations of the owner and the tenants of a house or apartment. It is a legally binding document that courts will generally uphold in legal proceedings, so it is important for you to know the exact terms of the lease agreement before you sign it. Some things to look for in a lease:

- Clauses that allow the landlord to change the terms of the lease after it is signed.
- Requirements/responsibilities of the tenants to do routine repairs such as lawn maintenance, cleaning, or notification about repairs.
- Restrictions that would prevent you from living normally or comfortably in the home.
- Term of the lease and any important dates such as when the rent is due or garbage pickup days.

Read the lease carefully and discuss anything you don't understand or any issues you might have. All landlord responsibilities should be clearly stated. Always get a copy of the signed lease to keep in your records. Any clause or terms in the agreement affects ALL parties who sign.

Tenants who lease or rent property are protected by the Fair Housing Act. If you think your rights have been violated, you may write a letter to or call the HUD office nearest you (p. 101). You have one year after the alleged violation to file a complaint with HUD, but you should file as soon as possible.

Each state has its own set of tenant rights, laws, and protections. For a state-by-state directory, visit www.hud.gov/local. You can also find available public housing at www.hud.gov. The agency (p. 101) offers several housing assistance programs for tenants and landlords as well as information on rights of residents and displaced tenants.

Ten Tips for Renters

1. The best way to win over a prospective landlord is to be prepared by bringing a completed rental application with you; written references from previous landlords, employers, friends, and colleagues; and a current copy of your credit report.

2. Carefully review all of the important conditions of the tenancy before you sign.

3. To avoid disputes or misunderstandings with your landlord, get everything in writing.

4. Ask about your privacy rights before you sign the lease.

MAKING HOME AFFORDABLE

The Making Home Affordable Program offers opportunities to modify or refinance your mortgage to make your monthly payments more affordable. It also includes the Home Affordable Foreclosure Alternatives Program for homeowners who are interested in a short sale or deed-in-lieu of foreclosure. Visit www.makinghomeaffordable.gov or call 1-888-995-HOPE (4673).

5. Know your rights to live in a habitable rental unit—and don't give them up.

6. Keep communication open with your landlord.

7. Purchase renters' insurance to cover your valuables.

8. Make sure the security deposit refund procedures are spelled out in your lease or rental agreement.

9. Learn whether your building and neighborhood are safe, and what you can expect your landlord to do if they aren't.

10. Know when to fight an eviction notice and when to move. Unless you have the law and provable facts on your side, fighting an eviction notice is usually shortsighted.

INSURANCE

General sources of insurance information include the American Council of Life Insurers (p. 142), the Insurance Information Institute (p. 144), the National Association of Insurance Commissioners (p. 145), and your state insurance department (p. 130). You can also visit www.insure.com.

When buying insurance, whether it's home, life, auto, rental, or other:

- Find out whether your state insurance department (p. 130) offers any information concerning insurance companies and rates. This is a good way to get a feeling for the range of prices and the lowest-cost providers in your area.

- Check several sources for the best deal. Try getting quotes online, but be aware that many online services may provide prices for just a few companies. An independent insurance agent who works with several insurers in your local area may be able to get you a better deal.

- Make sure the insurance company is licensed and covered by the state's guaranty fund. The fund pays claims in case the company defaults. Your state insurance department (p. 130) can provide this information.

- Check the financial stability and soundness of the insurance company. Ratings from A.M. Best (www.ambest.com), Standard & Poor's (www.standardandpoors.com), and Moody's Investors Services (www.moodys.com) are available online and at most public libraries.

- Research the complaint record of the company. Contact your state insurance department (p. 130), or visit the website of the National Association of Insurance Commissioners (www.naic.org), which has a database of complaints filed with state regulators.

- Find out what others think about the company's customer service. Consumers can rate homeowner insurance companies at www.jdpower.com/insurance.

- Once you pay your first insurance premium, make sure you receive a written policy. This tells you that the agent forwarded your premium to the insurance company. If you don't receive a policy within 60 days, contact your agent and the insurance company.

If you suspect fraud, call the National Insurance Crime Bureau's hotline at 1-800-835-6422. For more information, check out www.insurancefraud.org.

AUTO INSURANCE

The requirements for auto insurance vary from state to state. Check with your state insurance regulator (p. 130) to learn more about individual requirements as well as insurers you may be considering for your policy.

To get the best coverage at the best price, get several quotes from insurance companies. It may save you hundreds of dollars a year. Other ways to reduce your insurance premium are:

- Raise your deductible on collision and comprehensive coverage. If you have an older car, you might want to drop this coverage altogether.

- Take advantage of discounts. You may be eligible for a discount based on the number of miles you drive; your age (turning 25 or 50); your good

grades if you are a student; your driving record (no moving vehicle violations or accidents in three years); or if you've taken a safe-driving course. You might also be able to get discounts if you insure more than one vehicle, insure your vehicle and your home with the same company, have anti-theft devices, or have safety features such as air bags or anti-lock brake system.

You can also find valuable information about car ownership in the Cars section (p. 6).

DISABILITY INSURANCE

Disability can be more disastrous financially than death. If you are disabled, you lose your earning power, but you still have living expenses and often huge expenses for medical care. When purchasing disability insurance, ask:

- **How is disability defined?** Some policies consider you disabled if you are unable to perform the duties of any job. Better plans pay benefits if you are unable to do the usual duties of your own occupation.

- **When do benefits begin?** Most plans have a waiting period after an illness before payments begin.

- **How long do benefits last?** After the waiting period, payments are usually available until you reach age 65, though shorter or longer terms are also available.

- **What dollar amount is promised?** Can benefits be reduced by Social Security disability and workers' compensation payments? Are the benefits adjusted for inflation? Will the policy provider continue making contributions to your pension plan so you have retirement benefits when the disability coverage ends?

For more information on disability insurance, visit www.iii.org and www.ahip.org.

HEALTH INSURANCE

More Coverage, More Choices

The 2010 Affordable Care Act puts in place comprehensive health insurance reforms that will roll out over several years. Some new provisions are already in place; most changes will take affect by 2014. The law puts into place comprehensive health insurance reforms that will hold insurance companies more accountable and will lower health care costs, guarantee more health care choices, and enhance the quality of health care for all Americans. Major provisions affecting consumers include:

- Coverage for seniors who hit the Medicare Prescription Drug "donut hole," including a rebate for those who reach the gap in drug coverage;

- Expanded coverage for young adults, allowing

28   www.USA.gov

To contact an organization, use the directory beginning on page 62.

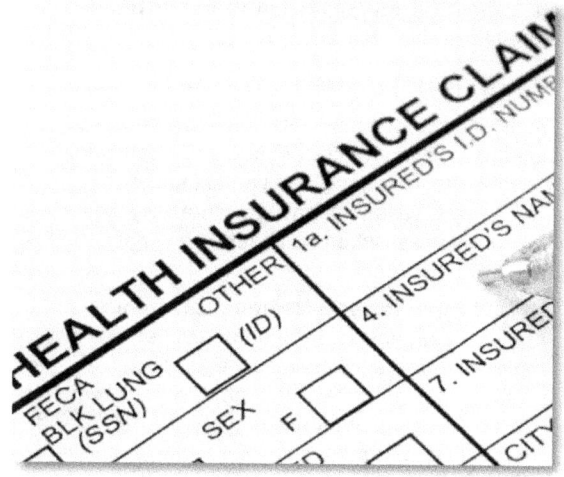

MEDICARE BENEFICIARIES

Medicare beneficiaries can compare HMO programs at www.medicare.gov and www.medicarenewswatch.com.

them to stay on their parents' plan until they turn 26 years old;

- Small-business tax credits to help these companies provide insurance coverage to their workers; and

- Providing access to insurance for uninsured Americans with pre-existing conditions.

For more information about the law, go to www.healthcare.gov.

Group Policies

Many consumers have health care coverage from their employers. Others have medical care paid through a government program such as Medicare (p. 100), Medicaid (p. 100), or the Veterans Health Administration (p. 104).

If you have lost your group coverage from an employer as the result of unemployment, death, divorce, or loss of "dependent child" status, you may be able to continue your coverage temporarily under the Consolidated Omnibus Budget Reconciliation Act (COBRA). You, not the employer, pay for this coverage. When one of these events occurs, you must be given at least 60 days to decide whether you wish to purchase the coverage.

Some states offer an insurance pool to residents who are unable to obtain coverage because of a health condition. To find out if a pool is available in your state, check with your state department of insurance (p. 130).

Most states also offer free or low-cost coverage for children who do not have health insurance. Visit www.insurekidsnow.gov or call 1-877-KIDS-NOW (543-7669) for more information.

HEALTH CARE PLANS

When purchasing health insurance, your choices will typically fall into one of three categories:

- **Traditional** fee-for-service health insurance

plans are usually the most expensive choice, but they offer you the most flexibility when choosing health care providers.

- **Health Maintenance Organizations (HMOs)** offer lower co-payments and cover the costs of more preventive care, but your choice of health care providers is limited. The National Committee for Quality Assurance evaluates and accredits HMOs. You can find out whether one is accredited in your state by calling 1-888-275-7585. You can also get this information, as well as report cards on HMOs, by visiting www.ncqa.org.

- **Preferred Provider Organizations (PPOs)** offer lower co-payments like HMOs, but give you more flexibility when selecting a provider. A PPO gives you a list of providers you can choose from.

WARNING: If you go outside the HMO or PPO network of providers, you may have to pay a portion or all of the costs.

When choosing among different health care plans, you'll need to read the fine print and ask lots of questions, such as:

- Do I have the right to go to any doctor, hospital, clinic, or pharmacy I choose?

- Are specialists such as eye doctors and dentists covered?

- Does the plan cover special conditions or treatments such as pregnancy, psychiatric care, and physical therapy?

- Does the plan cover home care or nursing home care?

- Will the plan cover all medications my physician may prescribe?

- What are the deductibles? Are there any co-payments?

- What is the most I will have to pay out of my own pocket to cover expenses?

- If there is a dispute about a bill or service, how is it handled? In some plans, you may be required to have a third party decide how to settle the problem.

HOMEOWNERS'/RENTERS' INSURANCE

You may be able to save hundreds of dollars a year on homeowners' insurance by shopping around. You can also save money by following these tips:

- Consider a higher deductible. Increasing your

deductible by just a few hundred dollars can make a big difference in your premiums.

- Ask your insurance agent about discounts. You may be able to get a lower premium if your home has safety features such as dead-bolt locks, smoke detectors, an alarm system, storm shutters, or fire-retardant roofing material. Persons over 55 years of age or long-term customers may also be offered discounts.

- Insure your house, NOT the land under it. After a disaster, the land is still there. If you don't subtract the value of the land when deciding how much homeowners' insurance to buy, you will pay more than you should.

- Don't wait until you have a loss to find out whether you have the right type and amount of insurance.

- Make certain you purchase enough coverage to replace what is insured. "Replacement" coverage gives you the money to rebuild your home and replace its contents. An "Actual Cash Value" policy is cheaper but pays the difference between your property's worth at the time of loss minus depreciation for age and wear.

- Ask about any special coverage you might need. You may have to pay extra for computers, cameras, jewelry, art, antiques, musical instruments, stamp collections, etc.

- Remember that flood and earthquake damage are not covered by a standard homeowners' policy. The cost of a separate earthquake policy will depend on the likelihood of earthquakes in your area. Homeowners who live in areas prone to flooding should take advantage of the National Flood Insurance Program (p. 101).

- If you are a renter, do not assume your landlord carries insurance on your personal belongings. Purchase a separate policy for renters.

LIFE INSURANCE

Your need for life insurance will change with changes in your life. For example, the arrival of children usually triggers a sharp increase in the amount you will need. As children grow older and leave the nest, you will probably need less protection.

Term life insurance policies are the least costly. They pay death benefits but have no cash value if you decide to stop making payments. As the word "term" suggests, these policies are in effect for a specific period—one year, or until you reach a certain age are common. Visit www.accuquote.com for online comparisons of term life insurance.

Whole life, universal life, and other cash value policies combine a long-term savings and investment product with life insurance. Canceling these policies after only a few years can more than double your life insurance costs.

LONG-TERM CARE INSURANCE

Medical advances have resulted in an increased need for nursing home care and assisted living. Most health insurance plans and Medicare severely limit or exclude long-term care. Here are some questions to ask when considering a separate long-term care insurance policy:

- **What qualifies you for benefits?** Some insurers say you must be unable to perform a specific number of the following activities of daily living: eating, walking, getting from bed to a chair, dressing, bathing, using the restroom, and remaining continent.

- **What type of care is covered?** Does the policy cover nursing home care? What about coverage for assisted-living facilities that provide less client care than a nursing home? If you want to stay in your home, will it pay for care provided by visiting nurses and therapists? What about help with food preparation and housecleaning?

- **What will the benefit amount be?** Most plans are written to provide a specific dollar benefit per day. The benefit for home care is usually about half the nursing home benefit, but some policies pay the same for both forms of care. Other plans pay only for your actual expenses.

- **What is the benefit period?** It is possible to get a policy with lifetime benefits, but this can be very expensive. Other options for coverage are from one to six years. The average nursing home stay is about 2.5 years.

- **Is the benefit adjusted for inflation?** If you buy a policy prior to age 60, you face the risk that a fixed daily benefit will not be enough by the time you need it.

- **Is there a waiting period before benefits begin?** A 20- to 100-day period is not unusual.

OTHER INSURANCE

- **Travel Insurance.** There are four kinds of travel insurance: Travel Cancellation Insurance, Baggage or Personal Effects Coverage, Emergency Medical Coverage, and Accidental Death. One helpful website is www.insuremytrip.com. See page 47 for additional insight on travel concerns and problems.

- **Identity Theft Insurance.** This type of insurance provides reimbursement to crime victims for the cost of restoring their identity and repairing credit reports. Some companies now include this as part of their homeowners' insurance policy. Others sell it as a stand-alone policy. Ask your homeowner policy company for information.

30 www.USA.gov

To contact an organization, use the directory beginning on page 62.

- **International Health Care Insurance**. A policy that provides health coverage no matter where you are in the world. The policy term is flexible so you can purchase it only for the time you will be out of the country. Contact your current health care provider for coverage information.
- **Liability Insurance**. Insurance for what the policyholder is legally obligated to pay because of bodily injury or property damage caused to another person. Search online or ask your personal insurance agent for more information.
- **Umbrella Insurance**. A policy that supplements the insurance you already have for home, auto, and other personal property. Umbrella insurance can help cover costs that exceed the limits of other policies.

INTERNET

CHOOSING SERVICE PROVIDERS

To connect your computer to the Internet, you'll need an Internet Service Provider (ISP). Some ISPs are large and well known, while others are literally one-person operations. Some companies limit their service to providing Internet access only. Others, such as a telephone or cable company, may offer Internet access as part of a larger package of services. You may also have access to fiber-optic service in your community. It is important to compare service providers and options to make sure you are getting what you want and the best deal possible to meet your needs.

If you have limited Internet expertise, you may want to start with one of the well-known ISPs. They usually offer user-friendly startup software. This software often includes features such as a browser, instant messaging, parental controls, and pop-up blockers. Many also offer 24-hour tech support. Of course, all of this convenience results in higher monthly user fees. Once you are comfortable with how the Internet works, you may decide you don't need the "extras" and can switch to a lower-cost ISP.

Whatever your present level of expertise, you will want to consider these factors when selecting a provider:

- **Speed**. If all you want to do is check e-mail and read web pages, a dial-up connection may be enough. But most people also want to download music or television shows or watch videos. For these, you will need a faster connection with broadband access, such as a digital subscriber line (DSL), a cable modem, or satellite.
- **Availability**. For dial-up service, is there a local phone number or a toll free number for access?
- **Wireless access**. Can you get a wireless connection for other computers in your home?
- **E-mail**. How many e-mail accounts come with the service? What will be the storage limit on your mailbox? How many days does the ISP keep your mail before deleting it?
- **Website space**. Do you want to create a personal website? If so, find out whether your provider offers web space and software to create your page.
- **Software**. Is any software required to activate the service? How do you get it? What is the capacity of this software? Can you use whatever browser or e-mail program you'd like?

BUNDLING AND OTHER PROMOTIONS

Do you want to get Internet, telephone, and TV service from the same provider? Buying a bundle of services from one provider can be a good deal, but it could make it more difficult to change providers for any one service if you're tied into a long-term contract.

Special promotions such as introductory pricing may be enticing, but read the fine print. The promotion price probably does not include taxes or the cost of extra equipment or fees. Ask the provider to explain all the one-time, recurring, and special charges, including taxes and fees. Get all promises in writing. Ask when the special promotions end and what the post-promotion cost will be. Also find out whether you have to install any special equipment and whether the provider will help troubleshoot on the phone if you have any problems.

Some deals are available only online or by phone. Even if you have to order online, call the provider first to ask questions. When you are online, review any frequently asked questions, minimum system requirements, and fine-print terms and conditions. Read the entire customer service agreement and print a copy for your records. For more information, go to www.ftc.gov/bcp/consumer.shtm. For help deciding on the best values from Internet, telephone, and TV service providers; filing a complaint; or learning more about consumer protections, go to www.reboot.fcc.gov/consumers.

PROTECTING CHILDREN ONLINE

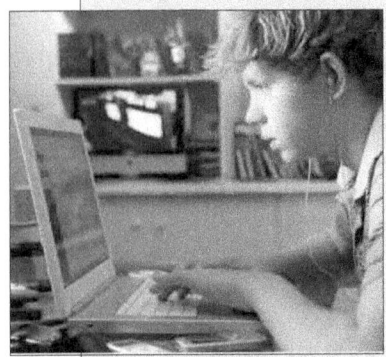

The Children's Online Privacy Protection Act requires commercial websites to obtain parental consent before collecting, using, or disclosing personal information from children under age 13. For more information, contact the FTC (p. 106) or visit www.ftc.gov.

- **Support**. What kinds of support are available—phone, e-mail, chat, etc.? What are the hours of support? Are there any additional charges for support?
- **Special features**. What services are provided for spam blocking, virus protection, instant messaging, and chat rooms?
- **Terms of service**. Is there a limit to the number of hours per month you can use the service?
- **Cost**. What is the monthly fee for the service? Are there any additional equipment or set-up fees?

WIRELESS COMPUTING

Going wireless provides you with freedom to use your computer in multiple locations, without dragging cables and cords with you. However, the privilege of increased freedom comes with the danger of increased vulnerability. Wireless internet requires that you have access to a wireless network via a wireless router. It is important that you secure your network so that strangers can't use your network without your knowledge (also known as "piggybacking"). In addition, computer hackers could use your network to access personal information you save or send from your computer. This is particularly important if you conduct financial transactions online. These reasons highlight the importance of taking steps to secure your wireless network. If you use the wireless ("Wi-Fi") network at bookstores, airports or other public places, there are other precautions you should take to protect your privacy.

At home:

- **Turn on encryption.** When you buy a wireless router, it is important to turn on the encryption feature. This scrambles information that you send over the Internet so that other people cannot access it.
- **Rename your router.** Change the name from the default to something only you would know.

- **Change the password.** Routers come with a standard password. Create a new smart one with a mix of letters, numbers, and special characters. For help creating passwords, see page 41.
- Turn off your router when you are not using it.

On public wireless networks:

- **Don't assume that the network is secure.** Most public wireless networks don't encrypt information you send. Avoid sending private information from public locations.
- **Use encrypted websites.** If you must send sensitive information from a public network, make certain that URL starts with "https" ("s" means secure). Look for that on every page you visit.
- **Log out** of sites after you finish using them rather than using "remember me" features. It is better to deal with the hassle of logging in again than giving away your login credentials to someone else on the network.

For more information about wireless computing visit www.onguardonline.gov.

ONLINE FILE SHARING

Every day, millions of computer users share files online. Whether it's music, games, video, or software, peer-to-peer (P2P) file sharing allows users to share all kinds of content. To share files, you download special software that connects your computer to an informal network of other computers running the same software. The software is often free and easy to access.

However, file sharing can have a number of risks. For example, when you are connected to file sharing programs, you could unknowingly allow others to copy private files you never intended to share. You could download material that is protected by copyright laws and find yourself mired in legal issues; you could download a virus or facilitate a security breach; or you could unwittingly download pornography labeled as something else.

BEWARE: SCAREWARE

If you've ever received a "security alert" stating that malicious software was found on your computer it may have been scareware. These messages will persuade you that your computer is infected with a virus that you can only eliminate by purchasing and installing specific software. Don't follow that advice; shut down your browser without clicking in the message. If you believe that your computer is infected, you should run a scan using a known anti-virus software. For more information about scareware and protecting your computer, visit www.onguardonline.gov.

32 www.USA.gov

To contact an organization, use the directory beginning on page 62.

SOCIAL NETWORKING

Social networking sites such as Facebook, Twitter, LinkedIn, craigslist, and others continue to gain popularity. These sites make it easy to re-connect, stay in touch, and even do business. But recent reports involving privacy concerns and crimes should make users more careful about the information they share. Some tips to consider to protect your privacy and safety include:

- Make your contact information private.
- Limit who can search your profile from Internet search engines.
- Manage who can view your images; untag photos if necessary.
- Create separate lists to manage who can see the information you've posted.
- Be careful about who can see your status updates.
- Refrain from telling people where you are at any specific time.
- Be cautious about arranging meetings in person with online acquaintances.

For more information go to:

- Federal Communications Commission: www.reboot.fcc.gov/consumers
- Federal Trade Commission: www.onguardonline.gov
- GetNetWise: www.getnetwise.org
- Internet Keep Safe Coalition: www.ikeepsafe.org
- i-SAFE: www.i-safe.org
- National Center for Missing & Exploited Children: www.missingkids.com.
- National Crime Prevention Council: www.ncpc.org; www.mcgruff.org
- National Cyber Security Alliance: www.staysafeonline.org
- Wired Safety: www.wiredsafety.org

To file a complaint about fraudulent, deceptive, or unfair business practices, or for additional information, visit www.ftc.gov or call 1-877-382-4357; TTY: 1-866-653-4261.

See page 51 for tips to write a social media will.

To secure the personal information stored on your computer, the FTC suggests that you:

- Set up the file-sharing software very carefully.
- Be aware of spyware. Use a good anti-spyware program.
- Close your connection when you're not using it.
- Use an effective anti-virus program and update it regularly.
- Talk with your family about file sharing.

For more information on P2P, visit www.onguardonline.gov.

ONLINE COPYRIGHT ISSUES

Quite simply, it's illegal to make or download unauthorized copies of software. Whether you are casually making a few copies for friends, lending disks, distributing and/or downloading pirated software via the Internet, or buying a single software program and then installing it on 100 computers, you are committing a copyright infringement. It doesn't matter whether you make money doing it or not. If you or your company is caught copying software, you may be held liable under both civil and criminal law.

If the copyright owner brings a civil action against you, the owner can seek to stop you from using its software immediately and can also request monetary damages. The copyright owner can sue

for as much as $150,000 for each program copied. In addition, the government can prosecute you criminally for copyright infringement. If convicted, you can be fined up to $250,000, or sentenced to jail for up to five years, or both.

For more information, visit www.cybercrime.gov, a site sponsored by the U.S. Department of Justice (p. 102), or www.bsa.org, a site on online piracy issues managed by the Business Software Alliance.

PREVENTING ONLINE FRAUD

The Internet gives you easy access to information, entertainment, financial offers, and countless other services. The flip side, however, is that it can leave you vulnerable to online scammers, identity thieves, and criminals. To guard against Internet fraud, follow these tips:

- **Know your seller.** If you don't, do some research.
- **Company websites** often provide information in a section called "About Us." Some online sellers participate in programs, such as BBB*OnLine*, that help resolve problems. Look for a logo or endorsement seal on the company website; this is an indication, but not a guarantee, of the seller's reliability.
- **Check with state** and/or local consumer offices.
- Another way to check online sellers is to look for **other consumers' comments**. Some Internet auction sites post ratings of sellers based on

comments from buyers. Beware of too many glowing stories that might have been placed by sellers themselves.

- **Protect your personal information**. Don't provide it in response to an e-mail, a pop-up, or a website you've linked to from an e-mail or web page.

- **Take your time** and resist any urge to "act now" to keep your account open or take advantage of a special offer.

- **Use anti-virus and anti-spyware software**, as well as a firewall, and update them all regularly. Make sure your operating system and web browser are set up properly, and update them regularly as well.

- **Protect your passwords**. Don't share your passwords with anyone. Memorize them.

- **Back up important files**. Copy them onto another computer or a removable hard drive such as a flash memory stick.

Learn whom to contact if something goes wrong online. Report suspected fraud to your bank, credit card company, or relevant authority.

The FTC (p. 106) provides tips to help secure your computer, guard against Internet fraud, and protect your personal information. Visit www.onguardonline.gov for more information. To keep up to date with the latest computer threats, sign up for alerts from the Department of Homeland Security at www.uscert.gov.

Here are some other sources on protecting yourself and your family while using the Internet:

- **GetNetWise** (www.getnetwise.org) is a public service sponsored by Internet industry corporations and public interest organizations to help ensure that Internet users have safe, constructive, and educational or entertaining online experiences.

- **Internet Keep Safe Coalition** (www.ikeepsafe.org) is a coalition of governors/ first spouses, law enforcement, the American Medical Association, the American Academy of Pediatrics, and other associations dedicated to helping parents, educators, and caregivers by providing tools and guidelines to teach children the safe and healthy use of technology.

- **National Cyber Security Alliance** (www.staysafeonline.org) is a nonprofit organization that provides tools and resources to empower home users, small businesses, and schools, colleges, and universities to stay safe online.

- **Staysafe** (www.staysafe.org) is an educational site intended to help consumers understand the positive aspects of the Internet and how to manage a variety of safety and security issues that exist online.

- **Wired Safety** (www.wiredsafety.org) is an Internet safety and help group comprised of unpaid volunteers around the world that provides education, assistance, and awareness on all aspects of cybercrime and abuse, privacy, security, and responsible technology use. Wired Safety is the parent group of www.teenangels.org, FBI-trained teens and preteens who promote Internet safety.

Phishing Continues to Be a Problem

"Phishing" is the use of fraudulent e-mail designed to steal identities as well as vital personal information such as credit card numbers, bank account PINs, and passwords. Phishing e-mails often ask you to verify this type of information. Legitimate companies never ask for your password or account number via e-mail. If you're not sure, call the company directly.

Don't Take the Bait

Don't reply to e-mail messages that claim your credit card information or other personal information needs to be updated. They may even threaten to disable your account. Don't believe it!

SPAM

E-mail spam is not just unwanted; it can be offensive. Pornographic spam causes many consumer complaints. Decrease the number of spam e-mails you receive by making it difficult for spammers to get and use your e-mail address:

- Don't use an obvious e-mail address, such as JaneDoe@isp.com. Instead use numbers or other digits, such as Jane4oe6@isp.com.

- Use one e-mail address for close friends and family and another for everyone else. Free addresses are available from Yahoo!, Gmail, and Hotmail. You can also get a disposable forwarding address from www.spammotel.com. If an address attracts too much spam, get rid of it and establish a new one.

- Don't post your e-mail address on a public web page. Spammers use software that harvests text addresses. Substitute "janedoe at isp.com" for the "janedoe@isp.com," or display your address as a graphic image, not text.

- Don't enter your address on a website before you check its privacy policy.

- Uncheck any checked boxes. These often grant the site or its partners permission to contact you.

- Don't click on an e-mail's "unsubscribe" link unless you trust the sender. This action tells the sender you are there.

To contact an organization, use the directory beginning on page 62.

- Never forward chain letters, petitions, or virus warnings. All could be a spammer's trick to collect addresses.

- Disable your e-mail "preview pane." This stops spam from reporting to its sender that you've received it.

- Choose an Internet Service Provider (ISP) that filters e-mail. If you get lots of spam, your ISP may not be filtering effectively.

- Use spam-blocking software. Web browser software often includes free filtering options. You can also purchase special software that will accomplish this task.

- Report spam. Alert your ISP that spam is slipping through its filters. The Federal Trade Commission also wants to know about "unsolicited commercial e-mail." Forward spam to spam@uce.gov. For more information, visit www.ftc.gov/spam.

INVESTING

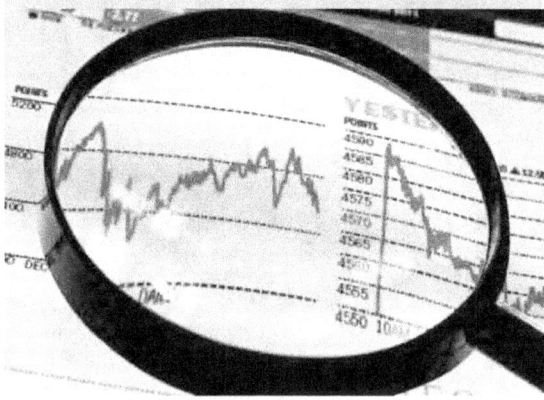

If you have a financial goal in mind, such as saving for retirement, paying for college, or buying a new house, then you have some homework to do before you invest your money. What is your tolerance for risk? What do you want to invest in: stocks, bonds, mutual funds? Do you want to open an IRA or buy an annuity? Does your employer offer a 401(k)? You must investigate before you invest—and remember, every investment involves some degree of risk. Most securities are not insured by the Federal government if they lose money or fail, even if you purchase them through a bank or credit union that offers Federally insured savings accounts. Make sure you have answers to all of these questions before you invest:

- **How quickly can you get your money back?** Stocks, bonds, and shares in mutual funds usually can be sold at any time, but there is no guarantee you will get back all the money you paid for them. Other investments, such as limited partnerships,

certificates of deposit (CDs), or IRAs, often restrict your ability to cash out your holdings.

- **What can you expect to earn on your money?** While bonds generally promise a fixed return, earnings on most other securities go up and down with market changes. Keep in mind that just because an investment has done well in the past, there is no guarantee it will do well in the future.

- **What type of earnings can you expect?** Will you get income in the form of interest, dividends, or rent? Some investments, such as stocks and real estate, have the potential for earnings and growth in value. What is the potential for earnings over time?

- **How much risk is involved?** With any investment, there is always the risk that you won't get your money back or the earnings promised. There is usually a trade-off between risk and reward—the higher the potential return, the greater the risk. The Federal government insures bank savings accounts and backs up U.S. Treasury securities (including savings bonds). See FDIC on page 106 and the chart on page 5 for regulatory information. Other investment options are not protected.

- **Are your investments diversified?** Some investments perform better than others in certain situations. For example, when interest rates go

BEWARE: INVESTMENT FRAUD

Deceptive pitches for investments often misrepresent or leave out facts in order to promote fantastic profits with little risk. No investment is risk-free, and a high rate of return means greater risk. Before investing, get written information such as a prospectus or annual report. Beware if a salesperson:

- Encourages you to borrow money or cash in retirement funds to invest.

- Pressures you to invest immediately.

- Promises quick profits.

- Says the disclosure documents required by Federal law are just a formality.

- Tells you to write false information on your account form.

- Sends material with typos or misspellings or not printed on letterhead.

- Does not send your money promptly.

- Offers to share inside information.

- Uses words such as "guarantee," "high return," "limited offer," or "as safe as a CD."

- Uses the phrase, "this investment is IRA-approved."

- Claims that "off-shore investments are tax-free and confidential."

up, bond prices tend to go down. One industry may struggle while another prospers. Putting your money in a variety of investment options can help to reduce your risk.

- **Are there any tax advantages to a particular investment?** U.S. Savings Bonds are exempt from state and local taxes. Municipal bonds are exempt from Federal income tax and, sometimes, state income tax as well. For special goals, such as paying for college and retirement, tax-deferred investments are available that let you postpone or even eliminate paying income taxes.

For more information about investing, check out the Securities and Exchange Commission's (SEC) website: www.investor.gov. Be sure to note specific tips at http://investor.gov/avoid-fraud/get-the-facts-the-secs-roadmap-to-saving-and-investing. The SEC requires public companies to disclose financial and other information to help you make sound decisions. View the text of these files at www.sec.gov/edgar.shtml, or call the SEC toll free Investor Information Service at 1-800-732-0330 to obtain free publications and investor alerts, or to learn how to file a complaint.

The Financial Industry Regulatory Authority (FINRA) also provides up-to-date market data and information for a wide range of stocks, bonds, mutual funds, and other securities through its Market Data Center at www.finra.org/marketdata.

The following companies rate the financial condition of corporations and municipalities issuing bonds. Their ratings are available online and at many public libraries:

- Standard & Poor's (www.standardandpoors.com)
- Moody's Investors Services (www.moodys.com)

For ratings of mutual funds, consult personal finance magazines such as *Kiplinger's Personal Finance*, *Money*, *Consumer Reports*, *Smart Money*, and *Worth*. To compare expenses, use the Financial Industry RegulatoryAuthority (FINRA) Mutual Fund Expense Analyzer at https://apps.finra.org/fundanalyzer/1/fa.aspx.

ONLINE TRADING

Stocks can now be bought and sold with a mouse click from a wide range of online brokers, often with low transaction fees. However, the price of some stocks can instantly go from high to low. Online trading is quick and easy, but online investing takes time. Before you trade, ask questions and learn how to limit losses in this fast-moving marketplace by:

- Knowing what you're buying.
- Understanding why you're buying or selling.

Type of Investment	What is It?	Risk Level
Traditional IRA	Traditional IRA is a personal savings plan that gives tax advantages for savings for retirement. Investments may include variety of securities. Contributions may be tax-deductible; earnings are not taxed until distributed.	Risk levels vary according to the holdings in the IRA.
Roth IRA	A personal savings plan where earnings that remain in the account are not taxed. Investments may include a variety of securities. Contributions are not tax-deductible.	Risk levels vary according to the holdings in the IRA.
Money Market Funds	Mutual funds that invest in short-term bonds. Usually pay better interest rates than a savings account but not as much as a certificate of deposit (CD).	Low risk.
Bonds and Bond Funds	Also known as fixed-income securities because the income they pay is fixed when the bond is sold. Bonds and bond funds invest in corporate or government debt obligations.	Low risk.
Index Funds	Invest in a particular market index such as the S&P 500 or the Russell 2000. An index fund is managed passively and mirrors the performance of the designated stock or bond index.	Risk level depends on which index the fund uses. A bond index fund involves a lower risk level than an index fund of emerging markets overseas.
Stocks	Stocks represent a share of a company. As the company's value rises or falls, so does the value of the stock.	Medium to high risk.
Mutual Funds	Invest in a variety of securities, which may include stocks, bonds, and/or money market securities. Costs and objectives vary.	Risk levels vary according to the holdings in the mutual fund.

To contact an organization, use the directory beginning on page 62.

- Being aware of how quickly trading changes during fast markets.

FINANCIAL BROKERS AND ADVISORS

When selecting a broker or investment advisor, research the person's education and professional history as well as the firm the person works for. Ask:

- Has the person worked with others who have circumstances similar to yours?

- Is the person licensed in your state? Your state securities regulator (p. 134) lists individuals and firms that are registered in your state. Ask if the regulatory office has any other background information. You can find out how to reach your state securities regulator by visiting www.nasaa.org.

- Has the person had any run-ins with regulators or received serious complaints from investors? Call your local state securities regulator or the SEC (p. 107). You can also check out www.finra.org/brokercheck or call FINRA at 1-800-289-9999 to find licensing, employment, and disciplinary information.

- How is the person paid? Is it an hourly rate, a flat fee, or a commission that depends on the investments you make? Does the person get a bonus from his or her firm for selling you a particular product?

- What are the fees for setting up and servicing your account?

Additional organizations that could be helpful are:

- The Commodity Futures Trading Commission (CFTC) provides consumer alerts and advisories. Visit www.cftc.gov/ConsumerProtection. The Commission oversees the Reparations Program that resolves disputes between commodity customers and commodity professionals. You can institute "reparations" proceedings against commodity professionals registered with the Commission if they violate the anti-fraud or other provisions of the Commodity Exchange Act. To ask a question, report information, or submit a complaint, contact the CFTC (p. 108).

- Both the North American Securities Administrators Association and the National Futures Association (p. 146) can offer helpful information.

INVESTING IN GOLD

Many financial experts recommend buying gold as part of a balanced portfolio. Some suggest buying only a small amount because values can fluctuate; others recommend heavier investments.

There are a number of ways to invest in gold; common ones include bullion, certificates, and coins. Most people depend on an investment advisor or company to help them choose. Make sure the person or company you choose is licensed with your state securities administrator (p. 134).

Also be aware that the U.S. Mint's American Eagle Gold Bullion Coins are the only gold coins guaranteed by the U.S. government in terms of purity, weight, and content. They're available from precious metal or collectible coin dealers, certain banks, and brokerage houses. If you're considering investing in gold, do your homework first. Check the U.S. Mint website at www.usmint.gov.

Another useful source for information on protecting yourself against scam artists touting coins and precious metals as safe investments to hedge against bad economic times is www.ftc.gov/bcp/edu/pubs/consumer/alerts/alt186.shtm.

> If you need more information or have an investment advisor problem that you are unable to resolve directly, you can contact the SEC (p. 107) or FINRA (p. 144).

RETIREMENT PLANNING

Part of smart investing is planning for retirement. The average American spends 20 years in retirement, but less than half of Americans calculate how much they need to save for their retirement years. Regardless of your age, it's never too early or too late to start.

The three major components of a retirement portfolio are generally benefits from pensions, savings and investments, and Social Security.

If you are still working and your employer offers a plan, find out how it works. If your employer has a 401(k) type plan and offers to put some money in if you do (called a match), this should be the first place that you save. Make sure you understand how a job change might affect your employer-based retirement plan and what your options are for saving that money. If you switch jobs before you are fully vested, you may lose a significant amount of money.

As you approach retirement, there are many factors to consider. Experts advise that you will need about 80% of your pre-retirement income in your retirement years. The exact amount, of course, depends on your individual needs. For example:

- How old do you plan to be when you retire?

- Will your spouse or partner retire when you do?

- Where do you plan to live? Will you downsize, own, or rent?

- Do you expect to work part time?

- Will you have the same medical insurance you had while working? Will coverage change?

- Do you want to travel or pursue a new hobby that might be costly?

- If you have a financial advisor, talk to him or her about your plans.

For more information go to:

- AARP: www.aarp.org
- American Savings Education Council: www.asec.org
- Certified Financial Planner Board of Standards: www.cfp.net
- Investopedia: www.investopedia.com/university/retirement
- Department of Labor: www.dol.gov/ebsa
- The Investor's Clearinghouse: www.investoreducation.org
- MyMoney.gov: www.mymoney.gov
- Securities and Exchange Commission: www.sec.gov
- Social Security Administration: www.socialsecurity.gov

PHONES

The choices for phone service have never been greater. Most consumers are now able to buy local and long-distance phone service from their telephone company, cable or satellite TV provider, or Internet service provider. Services such as voice mail, call waiting, caller ID, and wireless service may be offered as a package deal or sold separately. Before you buy, compare services and prices, and think about what you really need:

- Whom do you call most often?
- What time of day or day of the week do you call?
- Do you want to get messages? If so, do you need voice mail or will an answering machine do?
- Do you want call waiting and/or caller ID?
- How important is it for you to have your phone with you when you are away from home?

Find out how each company prices its services. Are there minimum use, time-of-day, or distance requirements; flat monthly fees; or special plans?

BEWARE: CALLER ID SPOOFING

Scammers have adopted the practice of Caller ID spoofing to obtain personal information from consumers. In this fraud, someone calls you using a false name and phone number for the Caller ID screen. During the call, the scammer describes an urgent scenario, such as the cancellation of an account. The caller may say you can avoid the cancellation if you provide your bank account or credit card number to pay the company. If you give the sensitive information, he can use it to steal your identity, or use your bank accounts.

You can prevent being a victim of caller ID spoofing. Don't give out personal information on an incoming call. Hang up and call the customer service phone number printed on your statement, the company's website or in the phonebook.

Report caller ID spoofers to the Federal Communications Commission at fcc.gov/complaints or 1-888-225-5322.

For example, wireless service may be cheaper than regular local service if you don't make many calls. Make sure you're comparing prices on similar plans and features. Understand that many service providers offer contracts for specific periods. Read the fine print and ask questions if there is anything you're not clear about.

The FCC (p. 105) offers consumer information about choosing a long-distance carrier, understanding new phone fees and taxes, and more at www.fcc.gov/cib. The National Consumers League also maintains a web page (http://nclnet.org/technology/88-telecommunications/228-understanding-your-phone-bill) to help you understand phone charges and recognize fraud.

SLAMMING AND CRAMMING

"Slamming" occurs when a phone company illegally switches your phone service without your permission. If you notice a different company name on your bill or see phone charges that are higher than normal, take action:

- Contact the company that slammed you and ask to be switched back to your original company. Tell the company you are exercising your right to refuse to pay charges.
- Report the problem to your original company and ask to be enrolled in your previous calling plan. If you're unable to resolve your complaint, contact the FCC (p. 105).

To contact an organization, use the directory beginning on page 62.

"Cramming" occurs when companies add charges to your phone bill without your permission. These charges may be for services such as voice mail, ringtones, or club memberships. You may not notice these monthly charges because they are relatively small, $5 to $30, and look like your regular phone charges.

Take These Steps to Avoid Slammers and Crammers:

- **Block changes to your phone service.** Ask your telephone service provider if it offers a blocking service, which usually requires the company to notify you before making any changes to your service.

- **Read the fine print** on contest entry forms and coupons. You could be agreeing to switch your phone service or to buy optional services.

- **Watch out for impostors.** Companies could falsely claim to be your regular phone company and offer some type of discount plan or change in billing. They may also say they are taking a survey or they may pretend to be a government agency.

- **Beware of "negative option notices."** You can be switched or signed up for optional services unless you say "NO" to telemarketers.

- **Examine your telephone bill** carefully, including pages that show the details, and look for suspicious charges.

Your phone service cannot be shut off for refusal to pay for unauthorized services. For help, contact your local or state consumer protection agency (p. 112), state public utilities commission (p. 138), or the FCC (p. 105).

CELL PHONES

Before you sign a contract and choose a plan and a company that meets your needs, you should ask these types of questions:

Where can you make and receive calls? Most providers now offer a choice of local, regional, or national plans. A local plan offers low-cost options if most of your calls are near your home. Regional plans cover a larger geographic area—sometimes several states. If you call outside the area covered by these plans, you will pay long-distance and roaming charges in addition to the airtime used. National plans are the most expensive, but they let you use your phone anywhere in the country for a single per-minute price.

How frequently will you use the phone? If you just want a phone for emergencies, an economy plan with a few minutes a month may be all you need. On the other hand, if you are going to be a heavy user, a plan with several free hours and the lowest airtime rate is a wiser choice. If you plan to use texting, pick

---

APPS FOR YOUR SMARTPHONE

"Apps", short for applications, are tools that help you accomplish tasks or find information when you are on the go. Apps are designed to work on smart phones and may be downloaded or accessed using your phone's web browser. Some apps are designed for specific platforms (Android, Blackberry, or iPhone), so make sure that you purchase apps that are compatible with your phone's software requirements.

While some apps are free, many of them do charge a small fee. Before you click "download", keep in mind that the cost of your purchases are automatically deducted from your bank account or charged to your credit card or phone bill. Keep track of the amount of money that you spent on apps, to avoid shock when you receive your bill.

Visit **Apps.usa.gov** to download free apps from the government. Look for some of the consumer apps for product recalls, fuel economy, food safety, nutrition, and health information.

---

a plan that will meet your needs and avoid surprises on your bills. Most services allow you to upgrade a plan without an added one-time charge.

Is a family plan option available? Instead of individual cell phone plans for each member of the family, you can share one cellular service plan and a pool of monthly usage minutes among several phones. The cost of the additional numbers per month is usually less than if you purchased individual accounts.

Is there a trial period? Many people experience "dead spots" where a cell phone doesn't work. A trial period lets you test your service and try the features of the phone without incurring a termination fee.

Know your options. Make sure you are only buying the options or features you really need. It is always easier to upgrade a plan later if you feel you need another feature.

What if you want to cancel your service? Most providers have a penalty. This is a concern if you have to move out of the area covered by your plan.

BUNDLING, PROMOTIONS, AND DEALS

For information about bundling Internet, telephone, and TV service, along with special promotions and deals, see Bundling and Other Promotions on page 31.

SMART PHONES

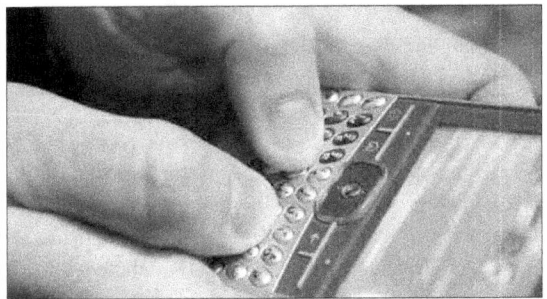

Smart phones are like miniature computers; they provide basic phone functions, along with advanced features, including browsing the Internet, accessing e-mail, interacting on online social networks, listening to music, watching videos, uploading pictures, and managing your calendar. They also allow use of a QWERTY keyboard to facilitate texting and e-mailing. (The keys are arranged the same way they would be on your computer keyboard.)

When shopping for a smart phone, consider these tips:

• Consider the shape and size of the phone.

• Make sure you can easily use the keypad to make calls or send messages.

• Do you need to access the Internet with your phone? If so, ask whether a data plan is required and how much it costs; compare options carefully. Data plans govern use and costs associated with mobile access for e-mail, text messaging, web browsing, social networking, and other applications.

• Take advantage of special pricing and promotions.

• Learn the return and cancellation policies.

• Be wary of buying phone insurance, which may sound tempting, but consumer groups generally advise against it.

Since smart phones are like miniature computers, many of the same privacy and safety concerns apply; however, unlike computers, these devices do not have anti-virus software to protect your phone from malware attacks. For more information on how to protect yourself from these concerns, see the Online Privacy (p. 42) and Internet (p. 31) sections.

PAY-AS-YOU-GO PLANS

If you want cell phone service only for emergencies or aren't sure how much you will actually use a cell phone once you get it, you may want to consider a prepaid cell phone before you commit to a long-term wireless contract. With a prepaid cell phone, there is no contract to sign and no monthly bill to worry about. You will know exactly how much you spend. The downside of prepaid plans is that you pay more

BEWARE: GPS ENABLED APPS

GPS enabled apps on mobile phones make it easy to share your fun adventures through social media. Some apps let others know your general vicinity, while others allow you to virtually "check in" at your favorite places so that you can earn free merchandise. Beware: this same information in the wrong hands can make you vulnerable to stalking, home burglary, or worse. Take advantage of the privacy settings on these apps and only share your location with people that you know and trust.

per minute, and, if you don't use the phone for an extended period, you may lose the money in your account.

VoIP

Voice over Internet Protocol (VoIP) phone service is an option for anyone with a broadband Internet connection. Most telephone and cable companies offer VoIP service, as do private companies. Some VoIP services only work using special phones, while other services allow you to use a traditional phone through an adaptor. For more information on whether VoIP is right for you, visit www.ftc.gov.

For help deciding on the best values from telephone, TV, and Internet service providers; filing a complaint; or learning more about consumer protections, go to www.reboot.fcc.gov/consumers.

PRIVACY PROTECTION & IDENTITY THEFT

Identity thieves steal your personal information to commit fraud. They can damage your credit status and cost you time and money to restore your good name. To reduce your risk of becoming a victim, follow these tips:

40   www.USA.gov

To contact an organization, use the directory beginning on page 62.

Tips for Preventing Identity Loss

- **Don't carry your Social Security card** in your wallet or write your number on your checks. Only give out your SSN when absolutely necessary.

- **Protect your PIN. Never write a PIN** on a credit/debit card or on a slip of paper kept in your wallet.

- **Watch out for "shoulder surfers."** Use your free hand to shield the keypad when typing your passwords on computers and at ATMs.

- **Collect mail promtptly.** Ask the post office to put your mail on hold when you are away from home for more than a day or two.

- **Pay attention to your billing cycles.** If bills or financial statements are late, contact the sender.

- **Keep your receipts.** Ask for carbons and incorrect charge slips as well. Promptly compare receipts with account statements. Watch for unauthorized transactions.

- **Tear up or shred** unwanted receipts, credit offers, account statements, expired cards, etc., to prevent "dumpster divers" (see page 5) from getting your personal information.

- **Store personal information in a safe place** at home and at work. Don't leave it lying around.

- **Don't respond to unsolicited requests** for personal information in the mail, over the phone, or online.

- **Install firewalls** and virus-detection software on your home computer.

- **Check your credit report once a year.** Check it more frequently if you suspect someone has gained access to your account information. See Credit Reports (p. 11).

REPORTING IDENTITY THEFT

If you suspect or become a victim of identity theft, follow these steps:

- **Report it to your financial institution.** Call the phone number on your account statement or on the back of your credit or debit card.

- **Report the fraud to your local police.** Keep a copy of the police report, which will make it easier to prove your case to creditors and retailers.

- **Contact the credit-reporting bureaus** (p. 11) and ask them to flag your account with a fraud alert, which asks merchants not to grant new credit without your approval.

If your identity has been stolen, you can use an ID Theft affidavit to report the theft to most of the parties involved. All three credit bureaus and many major creditors have agreed to accept the affidavit. Request a copy of the document by calling toll free 1-877-ID-THEFT (438-4338) or visit www.ftc.gov/idtheft. You can also use this website to file a complaint with the FTC.

The FTC also publishes a series of publications about the importance of personal information privacy. To download copies, go to www.ftc.gov or request free copies of brochures by calling 1-877-FTC-HELP (382-4357).

PROTECTING YOUR PRIVACY

Getting a credit card approved, transferring money from one account to another, renewing your driver's license, getting a prescription from your doctor at your local pharmacy: think about how easily and quickly you can do these things today. A downside of this convenience is that there are more opportunities for your personal information to be changed, stolen, or reported inaccurately. To help protect your privacy, follow these tips:

- Look for privacy statements on websites, sales materials, and forms you fill out. If a website claims to follow a set of established voluntary standards, read the standards. Don't assume it provides the level of privacy you want.

- Ask what information will be collected and how it may be used.

- Be selective in what you put on warranty

See page 22 for tips to prevent medical identity theft.

CREATE SECURE PASSWORDS

In an effort to protect your privacy and personal information, many websites require you to login with a username and password to access your account. The number of passwords that you need on a daily basis can be overwhelming. It is tempting to use the same password across several sites. However to get the most protection available, you should use different passwords on each site and change your passwords periodically. The goal for creating passwords is to strike a balance between being something that is easy to remember, yet random and unique.

Some general tips for creating a secure password include:

- Use a mix of uppercase and lowercase letters, numbers, and special characters.

- The longer the password, the better it is.

- Don't use your name, birthday, license plate, favorite sports teams or other facts that are easily guessed.

- Create a password based on a phrase. For example "A stitch in time saves nine" can be translated into the password "Ast!Ts9", where each character represents a word in the phrase.

- If you must use the same password on several websites, add a prefix or suffix. For example, use "Ast!Ts9:4bnk" for your bank account and "Eml: Ast!Ts9" for your email account.

BEWARE: E-MAIL BREACH

Do you ever share your e-mail address with your favorite retailer to be notified of sales, coupons, and new arrivals? What happens if the company's e-mail database is hacked? You should receive a notice from the company to let you know about the data breach. After that, you may see an increase in phishing e-mail you receive. Your best advice is to "do nothing": don't respond or verify personal information. For more detailed information, see the "Phishing Continues to Be a Problem" section (p. 34).

registration forms. The company only needs the purchase date, model/serial numbers, and how you can be contacted if there is a product recall. You can ignore questions not related to your purchase, such as your income and hobbies.

- Discuss privacy with others in your home. Everyone, even children, should understand what information is not appropriate to share on the phone, while using a computer, and in other situations.

Check with your state or local consumer agency (p. 112) to find out whether any state laws help protect your privacy. Some companies and industry groups have also adopted voluntary policies that address privacy concerns.

FINANCIAL PRIVACY

The Federal Deposit Insurance Corporation (p. 106) and other federal regulators require banks, insurance companies, brokerage firms, and certain businesses that share financial information to tell you their privacy policies. They must give you this information when you open an account and at least once every year. This includes:

- The kinds of information being collected.
- How the confidentiality and security of this information will be protected.
- What types of businesses may be provided this information.

If a business is going to share the information with anyone outside its corporate family, it must also give you the chance to "opt out" or say no to information sharing. Even if you don't opt out, your account numbers may not be shared with third parties for marketing purposes.

Your credit information has additional privacy protections under the Fair Credit Reporting Act. Only people with a legitimate business need can get a copy of your report. An employer can only get your report with your written consent. For more information on your rights under this federal law

and to find out how you can get a copy of your credit reports, see Credit Reports and Scores on page 11.

MEDICAL PRIVACY

Personal information you give to your doctor is shared with insurance companies, pharmacies, researchers, and employers based on specific regulations. The privacy of your health records is protected by federal law (the Health Insurance Portability and Accountability Act, also known as HIPAA), which:

- Defines your rights over your health information.
- Sets rules and limits on who is allowed to receive and/or see your health information.

The U.S. Department of Health and Human Services, Office for Civil Rights (www.dhhs.gov/ocr or 1-800-368-1019) is an excellent resource for complete details and advice about the HIPAA ruling. Along with fact sheets and educational materials, the Office for Civil Rights provides a listing of resources for consumers, providers, and advocates.

The Medical Information Bureau (MIB) is a data bank used by insurance companies that collects and shares information. You can request a copy of your file by writing to MIB, Inc., 50 Braintree Hill Park, Suite 300, Braintree, MA 02184-8734 or call toll free 1-866-692-6901 (TTY: 1-866-346-3642). There is a fee to obtain a copy of your file.

If you believe that a person, agency, or organization covered under the HIPAA Privacy Rule violated your health information privacy rights or committed another violation of the Privacy Rule, you may be able to file written complaints with the Department of Health and Human Services, Office for Civil Rights (p. 98).

For more information on how the federal government protects your personal health information, visit the Department of Health and Human Services, Office for Civil Rights website at www.hhs.gov/ocr/privacy.

ONLINE PRIVACY

In addition to following the general advice on protecting your privacy, make sure you only use websites with acceptable privacy policies.

- Look for a privacy policy statement or seal that indicates the site abides by privacy standards. Take time to read how your privacy is protected.
- Look for signals that you are using a secure web page. A secure site encrypts or scrambles personal information so it cannot be easily intercepted. Signals include a screen notice that says you are on a secure site, a closed padlock or unbroken key in the bottom corner of your screen, or the first letters of the Internet address you are viewing changes from "http" to "https."

Another threat to your privacy is spyware, which is sneaky software that rides its way onto computers when you download screensavers, games, music, and other applications. Spyware sends information about what you're doing on the Internet to a third party, usually to target you with pop-up ads. Browsers like Internet Explorer and Firefox, and search engines like Google and Bing, enable you to block pop-ups. You can also install anti-spyware to stop this threat to your privacy. For more information, see the Internet section on page 31.

SMART HOME SHOPPING

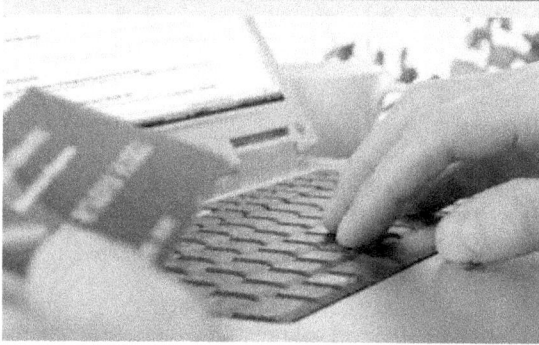

Late delivery, shipment of wrong or damaged items, and hidden costs are common home shopping complaints. To avoid problems and resolve them more easily, follow the advice in the "Before You Buy" checklist (p. 2). In addition:

- **Be wary of post office boxes** and sellers in other countries. It may be difficult to find the seller to resolve a problem later.
- **Know the total price.** Make sure it includes all charges, shipping, handling, insurance, and taxes. Coupons and other discounts should be properly deducted.
- **Make sure you are clear on what you are buying.** Watch for words such as "refurbished," "reconditioned," "closeout," or "discontinued."
- **Use your credit card**, debit card, or bank account number for payment only, never to prove your identity.
- **Keep a record of your purchase.** Save any information the seller gives you, such as product description, delivery date, cancellation policy, privacy policy, warranties, and order confirmation numbers.
- **Keep track of your order.** If it's late, you have the right to cancel and demand a refund.

YOUR RIGHTS: SHOPPING FROM HOME

When you order something by mail, phone, fax, or computer, the Federal Trade Commission (FTC) requires the company to:

- Ship the merchandise within the time promised, or if no specific delivery time was stated, within 30 days of receiving your order.
- Notify you if the shipment cannot be made on time and give you the choice of waiting longer or getting a refund.
- Cancel your order and return your payment if the new shipping date cannot be met, unless you agree to another delay.

If you cancel, your money must be refunded within seven days (or your account must be credited within one billing cycle if you charged the order). The company can't substitute a store credit. If you applied for a charge account with the merchant at the same time that you placed your order, the company has an extra 20 days to ship the merchandise to allow time for processing your application.

These FTC rules only apply to the first shipment of magazine subscriptions or other merchandise that you receive repeatedly. Orders for services (for example, photo finishing), sale of seeds and growing plants, collect-on-delivery (C.O.D.) orders, and transactions, such as books and music clubs, are covered by a different FTC rule. There could also be laws or regulations in your state that apply. Report suspected violations to your state or local consumer protection agency (p. 112) and to the FTC (p. 106).

YOUR RIGHTS: 3-DAY COOLING-OFF RULE

This federal law, which dates back to 1972, was intended to protect consumers in their homes during door-to-door sales pitches or at sales in temporary business locations. According to the FTC, the 3-Day Cooling-Off Rule does NOT apply to the purchase of new automobiles or items sold online. It only applies when a company is selling something that costs $25 or more at a location other than its regular place of business.

To comply with the 3-Day Cooling-Off Rule, a seller must inform buyers of their right to cancel the sale and receive a full refund within three business days.

Be aware that there are situations in which the Cooling-Off Rule does not apply:

- You made the purchase entirely by mail or telephone.
- The sale was the result of prior contact you had at the seller's permanent business location.
- You signed a document waiving your right to cancel.

- Your purchase is not primarily for personal, family, or household use.
- You were buying real estate, insurance, securities, or a motor vehicle.
- You can't return the item in a condition similar to how you received it.
- You bought arts or crafts at a fair, shopping mall, civic center, or school.

Remember, if you paid by credit card and are having difficulty getting your refund, you may also be able to dispute the charge with your credit card company under the Fair Credit Billing Act. See Credit Card Billing Disputes (p. 11).

ONLINE SHOPPING

Online shopping websites often offer great deals, variety, and convenience. But consumers need to be careful and make informed decisions about their purchases. Some tips for shopping safely online:

- Stick to websites that are known or recommended.
- Compare prices and deals, including free shipping, extended service contracts, or other offers.
- Search for online coupons, known as promo codes, which may offer discounts or free shipping. Some sites offer promo codes for coupons to be used in bricks-and-mortar stores.
- Get a complete description of the item and parts included, and the price, including shipping, delivery time, warranty information, return policy, and complaint procedure.
- Before you finalize the order, make sure the quantity and total price are correct; don't buy 11 items when you only meant to buy one.
- Pay with a credit card. Federal law protects you if you need to dispute charges, but it doesn't apply to debit cards, checks, cash, money orders, or other forms of payment.

- Use a secure browser. Look for an address that starts with "https" rather than "http." Also look for a closed padlock icon, usually in the lower right-hand corner of the screen.
- Print your purchase order with details of the product and your confirmation number.

For more information, go to www.onguardonline.gov.

ONLINE AND GROUP COUPONS

In addition to the traditional coupons found in newspapers, coupons can also be found online. Online coupons come in a variety of forms; they can be found on manufacturers' websites and on dedicated coupon websites. Coupons are also available on social media websites for becoming a fan of a product, or for sharing your email address with the company.

Group coupons are another online saving tool. Here's how they work: local companies offer reduced prices for things like spa services, gourmet meals, and outdoor adventures through a third party company. If interested, you pay the third party company to take advantage of the deal. Group coupons allow you to try new experiences, by reducing the trial cost. Since your ultimate goal when using a coupon is to save money, follow some guidelines to that you get your money's worth from group coupons. Ask yourself "Am I really going to use this?" If the answer is "no", don't buy it. A coupon isn't really a deal if you don't use it. Read the terms and conditions of the deal for expiration dates and scheduling appointments with the actual business.

ONLINE AUCTIONS AND SELLERS

Many people sell items on the Internet through auctions, classified ads, news groups, and chat rooms. Review the Internet section (p. 31) for safe shopping online as well as the general tips on shopping from home (p. 43).

- Check how the auction works. Can you cancel a bid? Don't assume that the rules used by one auction site apply to another. Some sites offer step-by-step instructions that will take you through the bidding process.
- Find out what protections you have. Does the site provide free insurance or guarantees for items that are not delivered or are not what the seller claimed?
- Follow the strategies used in any auction. Learn the value of the item before you begin bidding, then establish your top price and stick to it.
- Don't bid on an item you don't intend to buy. If you're the highest bidder, you have bought it. Auction companies often bar those who back out of a deal from future bidding.
- If the seller can't accept payment by credit card, use an escrow service. A third party holds your money until you get your purchase and approve

44   www.USA.gov

To contact an organization, use the directory beginning on page 62.

release of your payment to the seller. There is a small fee, but the peace of mind is worth it.

For more tips, check out the Federal Trade Commission's *Internet Auctions: A Guide for Buyers and Sellers* at http://ftc.gov/bcp/edu/pubs/consumer/tech/tec07.shtm.

TELEMARKETING & UNWANTED MAIL

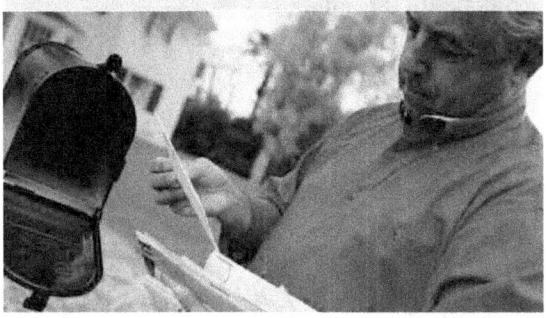

What can you do about the growing pile of unwanted mail in your mailbox and unwelcome telemarketers on your phone? Actually, there's a lot you can do:

- Tell companies you do business with to remove your name from customer lists they rent or sell to others. Look for information on how to opt out of marketing lists on sales materials, order forms, and websites.

- Use the services provided by the Direct Marketing Association (p. 144) to remove your name from most national telemarketing, mail, and e-mail lists.

- Call the credit reporting agencies' notification system at 1-888-567-8688. This will reduce the number of unsolicited credit and insurance offers you get. All three major credit bureaus participate in this program.

- Under U.S. Postal Service (USPS) rules, it is illegal to send mail that looks like it is from a government agency when it isn't. It is also illegal to send mail that looks like a bill when nothing was ordered, unless it clearly states that it is not a bill. Report violations of this rule to the USPS (p. 108).

NATIONAL DO NOT CALL REGISTRY

The federal government's Do Not Call Registry allows you to permanently restrict telemarketing calls by registering your phone number at www.donotcall.gov or by calling 1-888-382-1222. If you receive telemarketing calls after your number has been in the national registry for three months,

you can file a complaint using the same web page and toll free number.

Placing your number on this national registry will stop most telemarketing calls, but not all of them. Calls that are still permitted include those from political organizations, charities, telephone surveyors, and some organizations with which you have a relationship.

PRE-RECORDED MESSAGES

Pre-recorded sales calls or robocalls are illegal. Companies cannot transmit these messages to consumers who have not agreed, in writing, to accept such messages. Pre-recorded calls may only be made to residential telephone numbers in the following cases:

- Emergency calls needed to ensure your health and safety.
- Non-commercial calls.
- Calls that don't include any unsolicited advertisements.
- Calls by, or on behalf of, tax-exempt nonprofit organizations.
- Calls for which you have given prior consent.
- Calls from entities with which you have an established business relationship.

If you receive pre-recorded telemarketing calls but have not agreed to get them, file a complaint with the FTC at www.donotcall.gov or by calling 1-888-382-1222.

TELEMARKETING SALES CALLS

A Federal Trade Commission rule defines what telemarketers can and cannot do when making a sales call. Callers must:

- Provide the seller's name.
- Disclose that the call is a sales call.
- Tell you exactly what they're trying to sell.
- Disclose the total cost and other terms of sale

OPTING OUT

Tired of unwanted e-mail filling up your inbox? You can opt out of most unsolicited e-mail lists by going to the "unsubscribe" button, usually found at the bottom of the message. Some senders make the button difficult to find, so you may have to do some searching.

In addition, the Direct Marketing Association lets you opt out of receiving unsolicited commercial mail from many national companies for three years. You can register with this service for a small fee, but your registration only applies to organizations that use the association's Mail Preference Service. To register go to www.dmachoice.org.

before you make any payment for goods or services.

- Tell you if they don't allow refunds, exchanges, or cancellations.

If a prize is involved, the caller must give you the odds of winning, inform you that no purchase is necessary, and tell you how to get instructions for entering without buying anything.

It's illegal for telemarketers to:

- Misrepresent what they're offering.
- Call before 8 am or after 9 pm.
- Threaten, intimidate, or harass you, or call again if you ask them not to.

This FTC rule applies even when you receive a call from a telemarketer in another state or country. It also applies when you make a call to a company in another state or country in response to a mail solicitation.

The rule generally does not apply when you call to order from a catalog or in response to an ad on television or radio, or in a magazine or newspaper. It also does not apply to solicitations you receive by fax or e-mail. Beware that certain types of businesses, including nonprofit organizations, investment brokers and advisors, and banks and financial institutions, are exempt from the rule.

In addition, telemarketers are not allowed to use auto dialers to reach cell phones.

If you get a phone call from someone who says he or she is with your bank and/or credit company and the person asks you to provide or confirm any personal information:

- Do NOT answer any questions.
- Hang up immediately.
- Call your bank or credit company directly and describe what happened.

TRAVEL

Flight Information

Whether reserving a hotel room, buying plane tickets, or making other travel arrangements, these tips will help you get the deal you've been promised:

- **Plan as far ahead as you can.** Special deals on hotel rooms and airline seats often sell out very quickly.

- **Be flexible in your travel plans.** Hotels usually offer better rates on days when they expect fewer guests. Once you get a fare quote from an airline, ask if you can save money by leaving a day earlier or later, by taking a different flight on the same day, or by using a different airport. Changing planes during your trip is sometimes cheaper than a nonstop flight.

- **Check out the seller.** Ask tour operators and travel agents whether they belong to a professional association, then check to see if they are members in good standing. Contact your state or local consumer protection agency (p. 112) and the Better Business Bureau (p. 66) to find their complaint history.

- **Comparison shop.** Determine the complete cost of the trip in dollars, including all service charges, taxes, processing fees, etc.

- **Beware of unusually cheap prices and freebies.** It could be a scam, and you could end up paying more than the cost of a regular package tour.

- **Make sure you understand the terms of the deal.** If you hear you've won a free vacation, ask if you have to buy something in order to get it. If the destination is a beach resort, ask the seller how far the hotel is from the beach. Then ask the hotel.

- **Ask about cancellation policies.** You may want to look into trip insurance for added protection. The website www.insuremytrip.com offers pricing and policy information on plans from different companies and describes the different forms of policies available.

- **Insist on written confirmations.** Ask for written proof of reservations, rates, and dates.

- **Pay by credit card.** It's not unusual to make a deposit or even pay in full for travel services before the trip. A credit card gives you the right to dispute charges for services that were misrepresented or never delivered. If a travel agent or service provider says you can't leave for at least two months, be very cautious—the deadline for disputing a credit card charge is 60 days and most scam artists know this. (See Credit Card Billing Disputes, page 11).

In some states, travel sellers must be registered and insured. Advance payments for travel must be placed in an escrow account until services are provided. Prizes or "free" gifts may also be regulated. Contact your state or local consumer protection agency (p. 112) to find out about your rights and how to file complaints. The American Society of Travel Agents (p. 143) will also help resolve disputes with member agents.

RESOLVING AIR TRAVEL PROBLEMS

No matter how well you plan, you might encounter these common air travel hassles.

Delayed and Canceled Flights

Airline delays caused by bad weather, traffic control problems, and mechanical repairs are hard to predict. If your flight is canceled, most airlines will rebook you on the earliest flight possible to your destination, at no additional charge. If you're able to find a flight on another airline, ask the first airline to endorse your ticket to the new carrier. This could save you a fare increase, but there is no rule requiring the airline to do this.

Each airline has its own policies about what it will do for delayed passengers; there are no federal requirements. If your flight is delayed or canceled, ask the airline whether it will pay for meals or a phone call. Contrary to what many people believe, airlines are not required to do so.

Delayed or Damaged Bags

If your bags aren't on the conveyor belt when you arrive, file a report with the airline before you leave the airport:

- Insist the airline fill out a form and give you a copy, even if personnel say the bag will be on the next flight.
- Get the name of the person who filled out the form and a phone number.
- Confirm that the airline will deliver the bag to you without charge when it's found.

Some airlines will give you money to purchase a few necessities. If they don't provide you with cash, ask what types of articles are reimbursable and keep all receipts.

If a suitcase arrives damaged, the airline will usually pay for repairs. If an item can't be fixed, the airline will negotiate to pay you its depreciated value. The same is true for belongings packed inside a suitcase. Of course, airlines may refuse to pay for damage if it was caused by your failure to pack something properly rather than by the airline's handling.

Lost Bags

If your bag is declared officially lost, you will have to submit a second, more detailed form within a time period set by the airline. The information on the form is used to estimate the value of your lost belongings. Airlines can limit their liability for delay, loss, and damage to baggage; however, they must prominently display a sign that explains the limit.

AIRLINE FEES

Many airlines charge extra fees for checked baggage, advance seat assignments, meals, and other services. The Department of Transportation has ruled that an airline must prominently disclose all potential fees on their websites. The airline must also refund baggage fees if they lose your baggage. Airlines are also required to include all government taxes and fees in the advertised price. For more information, go to airconsumer.dot.gov/subjects.htm.

According to the Office of Aviation Consumer Protection and Enforcement (http://airconsumer.ost.dot.gov/SA_Baggage_Limits.htm), the maximum an airline pays on lost bags and their contents is limited to $3,300 per passenger on domestic flights, and approximately $1,500 per passenger for unchecked baggage on international flights. See www.thetravelinsider.info/travelaccessories/lostbaggagerights.htm for more information on maximum liability, including special rates that change on a daily basis.

If the airline's offer doesn't fully cover your loss, check your homeowners' or renters' insurance to see if it covers losses away from home. Some credit card companies and travel agencies also offer optional or even automatic supplemental baggage coverage.

On those trips when you know you're carrying more than the liability limits, you may want to ask about purchasing "excess valuation" from the airline when you check in. Of course, there is no guarantee the airline will sell you this protection. The airline may refuse, especially if the item is valuable or breakable.

Overbooked Flights

Selling more tickets than there are seats is not illegal. Most airlines overbook their flights to compensate for "no-shows." If there are more passengers than seats just before a plane is scheduled to depart, you can be "bumped" or left behind against your will. Whether you are bumped or not may depend on when you officially checked in for your flight, so try to arrive early. The U.S. Department of Transportation requires airlines to ask people to give up their seats voluntarily, in exchange for compensation. Airlines decide what to offer volunteers, such as money, a free trip, food, or lodging.

Federal rules protect you if you are "bumped" on most flights within the United States and on outbound international flights. Passengers who are involuntarily bumped are protected under Federal Aviation Administration guidelines (www.faa.gov). If you volunteer to be bumped, your agreement with the airline is not regulated and will depend on negotiating at the gate.

The airline must give you a written statement describing your rights, as well as the airline's boarding priority rules and criteria. If the airline is not able to get you to your final destination within two hours of your original arrival time, you may be entitled to a maximum of $800 compensation if they are delayed (i.e. over two hours for domestic and over four hours for international) from their original arrival time. The amount depends on the price of the ticket and the length of the delay. To receive this payment, you must have a confirmed reservation. You must also meet the airline's deadlines for ticketing and check-in. An airline may offer you a free ticket on a future flight in place of a check, but you have the right to insist on a check.

Tarmac Delays

Under new federal rules, U.S. airlines operating domestic flights must allow passengers to deplane after a tarmac delay of three hours. The only exceptions allowed are for safety or security, or if air traffic control advises the pilot otherwise. Carriers are also required to provide adequate food and drinking water within two hours of being delayed on the tarmac; they must also maintain operable lavatories and, if necessary, provide medical attention.

There are other protections as well, such as prohibiting airlines from scheduling chronically delayed flights. For more information, go to www.airconsumer.ost.dot.gov, and search for Airline Passenger Protections.

CHECK BUS SAFETY RECORDS

Some travelers have turned to commercial buses as an inexpensive option for traveling long distances. Before planning a trip on a commercial bus or hired motorcoach, you should research the company's record. The Federal Motor Carrier Safety Administration (FMCSA) recommends that you contact the company and ask these questions:

- Do the drivers hold valid Commercial Driver's Licenses with a "passenger" endorsement?
- Does the company comply with the Department of Transportation's drug and alcohol testing requirements for drivers?
- Does the company conduct safety inspections of their buses?

You can find more information on interstate travel safety and use the FMCSA's (p. 104) bus safety database at **www.fmcsa.dot.gov/safety-security/pcs/Index.aspx.** If you would like to file a safety complaint call 1-888-368-7238.

PASSPORTS

A valid U.S. passport is required to enter and leave most foreign countries. The Passport Services Office provides information and services to American citizens about how to obtain, replace, or change a passport. To obtain a passport for the first time, you need to go in person to one of 7,000 passport acceptance facilities located throughout the United States with:

- Two photographs of you taken within the last six months.
- Proof of U.S. citizenship.
- A valid form of photo identification (such as a driver's license).

Acceptance facilities include many federal, state, and probate courts; post offices; some public libraries; and a number of county and municipal offices. There are also 24 regional passport agencies, and one Gateway City Agency, that serve customers who are traveling within two weeks (14 days), or who need foreign visas for travel. Appointments are required in such cases.

All American citizens must now have a valid U.S. passport to re-enter the country, regardless of what nations they have been visiting while traveling. For more information on how to get a new passport, visit www.travel.state.gov/passport.

TRAVEL SAFETY

Several federal agencies offer advice and information on the Internet that can help you have a safe trip. For advice on:

- **Airline, highway, and rail safety information**: Check out the U.S. Department of Transportation (p. 103) at www.dot.gov. Look up crash-safety reports on cars or find out how weather is affecting air travel and road conditions.
- **Safe travel by air, land, and sea**: Contact the Transportation Security Administration (p. 101) at www.tsa.gov/travelers. It posts tips on dealing with airline security checks, traveling with kids, and warnings on prohibited items.
- **What to do before, during, and when you return from a trip overseas**: Visit the U.S. Department of State (p. 103) at www.state.gov/travel. You can also get warnings on locations to avoid and what to do in an overseas emergency.
- **Health-related travel information**: Consult the Centers for Disease Control and Prevention (p. 99) at www.cdc.gov/travel. Research vaccination requirements, find information on how to avoid illnesses caused by food and water, and review inspection scores on specific cruise ships.

TV

Many changes have taken—and are continuing to take—place in the industry. Savvy consumers need to keep up with new rules, products, and services to make sure they are getting the best quality and taking advantage of the best offers.

CABLE

You can start with a basic lineup of channels and go from there. The more channels you want, the more it will cost. You may want to consider video on demand so you can order movies and sports events and watch them when you like (usually within a 24-hour window). You can also buy a bundle of services that includes digital TV, digital phone, and broadband Internet access at discounted rates. Bear in mind, however, that you may be asked to sign a contract for bundled services.

SATELLITE

This requires a dish that's mounted outside (service requires an unobstructed view of the satellite) and a receiver that's placed by your television. Satellite TV may offer more channels than cable TV, and you can add a digital video recorder to record shows for viewing later. One downside to satellite TV is occasional interference during periods of rain or snow. Check with your satellite TV provider for channel options and prices. As with cable TV, you may be asked to sign a contract for a package of services.

INTERNET TV

If you have a high-speed Internet connection, you're already able to watch thousands of videos on your computer. But movies and TV shows are also available and becoming more prevalent as large online companies start distributing TV programming.

TV OPTIONS

There are many choices for consumers looking to buy new televisions today.

BUNDLING, PROMOTIONS, AND DEALS

For information about bundling Internet, telephone, and TV service, along with special promotions and deals, see Bundling and Other Promotions on page 31.

Before buying a new TV, do your homework. Visit stores and online sites to compare prices, models, and features. It is important to see the monitors in person before buying to make sure the one you select will meet your needs. For independent ratings and reviews, check out *Consumer Reports* at www.consumerreports.org. Additional information is also available at www.energystar.gov/index. cfm?c=home_elec_details.fap_tv_whatelse.

UTILITIES

In many states, consumers can choose their telephone and energy service provider. Contact your state utility commission (p. 138) to find out whether you have a choice. Some commissions will provide a list of service providers and advice on making a choice. Most state utility commissions will also take any complaints you have concerning utility sales and service.

ELECTRICITY AND NATURAL GAS

If you have a choice of suppliers, ask:

- **How much will it cost?** How long can I depend on this rate? Will I be charged any other fees?

- **Are there any other terms or conditions?** For example, is there a fee if I cancel my agreement before the service period is up?

- **Whom do I contact if I have a problem?** Do you have a local customer service office?

For advice on how to save money on your energy bills, visit the U.S. Department of Energy at www.energysavers.gov or www.energystar.gov. You'll find information to help save energy at home and work. The Energy Savers site also provides

ENERGY STAR APPLIANCES

ENERGY STAR-qualified appliances use about 33% less energy than standard units.

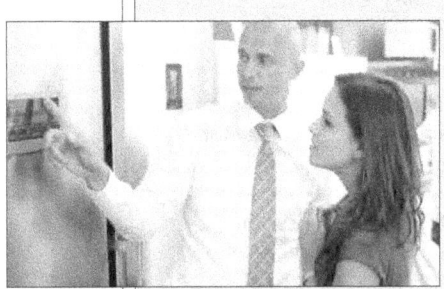

You can find the ENERGY STAR logo on TVs, clothes washers and dryers, water heaters, furnaces and many other products.

Home electronics that have earned the ENERGY STAR rating deliver exceptional features, while using less energy. Saving energy helps you save money on utility bills and helps to protect the environment by reducing greenhouse gas emissions to counter climate change. For more information, go to www.energystar.gov.

the latest updates on efficient, EPA-approved, and renewable energy, with links that take you directly to available federal resources.

WATER

The majority of consumers rely on local utilities to provide a safe and ample supply of water. Your local water agency is responsible for sending you an annual Consumer Confidence Report that should list the source of your water, what contaminants may be in the water, and information on the safety levels of contaminants and their effects on health. For more information, call the Environmental Protection Agency's Safe Drinking Water Hotline at 1-800-426-4791 or visit EPA's website at www.epa.gov/safewater.

WATERSENSE MAKES SENSE

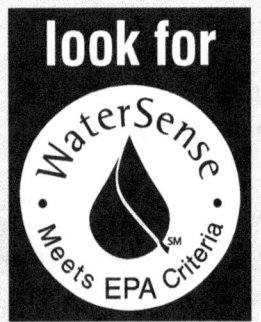

The EPA WaterSense program can help protect the future of our nation's water supply by promoting water-efficiency and enhancing the market for water-efficient products, programs, and practices. To learn more and see what you can do to conserve water, visit www.epa.gov/watersense.

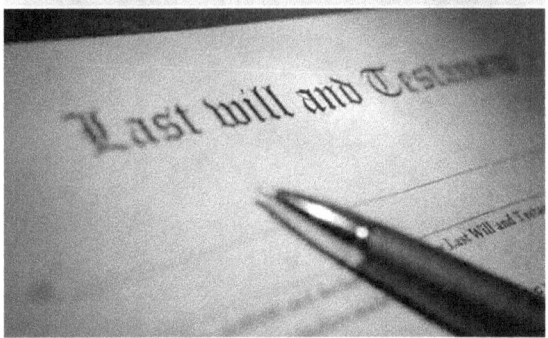

PLANNING FOR THE END OF LIFE

It's unfortunate how many people believe that estate planning is only for the wealthy. People at all economic levels benefit from an estate plan. Upon death, an estate plan legally protects and distributes property based on your wishes and the needs of your family and/or survivors with the fewest tax consequences.

Advance Medical Directives

We all face the possibility that sometime during our lifetime, we may become incapacitated. This often happens when nearing death, but it can also be the result of a temporary condition. Many people assume their spouses or children will automatically be allowed to make financial and/or medical decisions for them, but this is not necessarily true.

Advance directives are written documents that tell your doctors what kind of treatment you'll want if you become unable to make medical decisions (for example, if you're in a coma). Forms and laws vary from state to state, so it's a good idea to understand the laws of the state where you live when you write advance directives. It's also a good idea to make them before you are very ill. Federal law requires hospitals, nursing homes, and other institutions that receive Medicare or Medicaid funds to provide written information regarding advanced care directives to all patients upon admission.

A living will is one type of advance directive that goes into effect when a person is terminally ill. A living will does not give you the opportunity to select someone to make decisions for you, but it does allow you to specify the kind of treatment you want in specific situations. For example, you might choose to specify that you do not want to be treated with antibiotics if death is imminent. You can, if you choose, include an advance directive that you do not wish to be resuscitated if your heart stops or if you stop breathing. In this case, a Do Not Resuscitate (DNR) order would be entered on your medical chart.

To contact an organization, use the directory beginning on page 62.

WILLS

A will is the most practical first step in estate planning. It makes clear how you want your property to be distributed after you die.

Writing a will can be as simple as typing out how you want your assets to be transferred to loved ones or charitable organizations after your death. If you don't have a will when you die, your estate will be handled in probate, and your property could be distributed differently from what you would like.

It may help to get legal advice when writing a will, particularly when it comes to understanding all the rules of the estate disposition process in your state. For information about legal issues, see page 55. Some states, for instance, have community-property laws that entitle your surviving spouse to keep half of your wealth after you die no matter what percentage you leave him or her. Fees for the execution of a will vary according to its complexity.

CHOOSE AN EXECUTOR

An executor is the person who is responsible for settling the estate after death. Duties of an executor include:

- Taking inventory of property and belongings.
- Appraising and distributing assets.
- Paying taxes.
- Settling debts owed by the deceased.

Most important, the executor is legally obligated to act in the interests of the deceased, following the wishes provided by the will. Here again, it could be helpful to consult an attorney to help with the probate process or offer legal guidance. In most states, any person over the age of 18 who hasn't been convicted of a felony can be named executor of a will. Some people choose a lawyer, accountant, or financial consultant based on his or her professional experience. Others choose a spouse, adult child, relative, or friend. Since the role of executor can be demanding, it's often a good idea to ask the person if he or she is willing to serve.

If you've been named executor in someone's will but are not able or do not want to serve, you need to file a "declination," which is a legal document that declines your designation as an executor. The contingent executor named in the will then assumes responsibility. If no contingent executor is named, the court will appoint one.

FUNERALS

One of the most expensive purchases many consumers will ever make is the arrangement of a funeral. A traditional burial, including a casket and vault, costs about $7,000. Extras such as flowers, obituary notices, cards, and limousines can add

---

RULES TO REMEMBER WHEN WRITING A WILL

- In most states, you must be 18 years of age or older.
- To be valid, a will must be written when you are of sound judgment and have adequate mental capacity.
- The document must clearly state that it is your will.
- An executor of your will, who ensures your estate is distributed according to your wishes, must be named.
- It is not necessary to notarize or record your will, but doing so can safeguard any claims that it is invalid. To be valid, you must sign a will in the presence of at least two witnesses.

---

thousands of dollars more. At such a highly emotional time, many people are easily swayed to believe that their decisions reflect how they feel about the deceased and wind up spending more than may be necessary.

Most funeral providers are professionals who work to serve their clients' needs and best interests. Unfortunately, some do not. They may take

---

WRITE A SOCIAL MEDIA WILL

Social media is a part of daily life, so what happens to the online content that you created once you die? If you are active online you should consider creating a statement of how you would like your online identity to be handled, like a social media will. You should appoint someone you trust as an online executor. This person will be responsible for the closure of your email addresses, social media profiles, and blogs after you are deceased. Take these steps to help you write a social media will:

- Review the privacy policies and the terms and conditions of each website where you have a presence.
- State how you would like your profiles to be handled. You may want to completely cancel your profile or keep it up for friends and family to visit. Some sites allow users to create a memorial profile where other users can still see your profile but can't post anything new.
- Give this person a document that lists all the websites where you have a profile, along with your usernames and passwords.
- Stipulate in your will that the online executor should have a copy of your death certificate. The online executor may need this as proof in order for websites to take any actions on your behalf.

---

advantage of clients by insisting on unnecessary services and overcharging consumers. That's why there is a federal law, called the Funeral Rule, that regulates the actions of funeral directors, homes, and services.

Many funeral providers offer a variety of package plans that include products and services that are most commonly sold. Keep in mind, you are not obligated to buy a package plan; you have the right to buy the individual products and services you prefer.

As outlined by the Funeral Rule:

- You have the right to choose the funeral goods and services you want (with some exceptions).

- The funeral provider must state this "Rule" in writing on the general price list.

- If state or local law requires you to buy any particular item, the funeral provider must disclose it on the price list, with a reference to the specific law.

- The funeral provider may not refuse, or charge a fee, to handle a casket that you bought elsewhere.

- A funeral provider who offers cremations must make alternative containers available.

- For more information about the Funeral Rule, visit www.ftc.gov/bcp/edu/microsites/funerals.

Planning ahead is the best way to make informed decisions about funeral arrangements. An advance plan also spares your family from having to make choices in the middle of grief and under time constraints. Every family is different, and funeral arrangements are influenced by religious and cultural traditions, budgets, and personal preferences.

You are not legally required to use a funeral home to plan and conduct a funeral, but most people find that the services of a professional funeral home make it easier.

Comparison shopping, either in person or by phone, can save you money and is much easier when done in advance. Many funeral homes will also send you a price list by mail, but this is not required by law. If you have a problem concerning funeral matters, it's best to try to resolve it first with the funeral director. If you are dissatisfied, the Funeral Consumers Alliance (p. 110) may be able to advise you on how best to resolve your issue. You can also contact your state or local consumer protection agencies (p. 112) or the Funeral Service Consumer Assistance Program at 1-800-662-7666. Most states have a licensing board that regulates the funeral industry. You can contact the board in your state for information or help.

THE FUNERAL RULE

A federal law makes it easier for you to choose only the goods and services you want or need when planning a funeral, and to pay only for those you select. The Funeral Rule, enforced by the Federal Trade Commission, requires funeral directors to give you itemized prices in person and, if you ask, over the phone.

VETERANS CEMETERIES

All veterans are entitled to a free burial in a national cemetery and a grave marker. This eligibility also applies to some civilians who have provided military-related service and some Public Health Service personnel. Spouses and dependent children also are entitled to a lot and marker when buried in a national cemetery. There are no charges for opening or closing the grave, for a vault or liner, or for setting the marker in a national cemetery. For more information, visit the Department of Veterans Affairs (p. 104) at www.cem.va.gov.

52   www.USA.gov

To contact an organization, use the directory beginning on page 62.

FILING A COMPLAINT

Even the savviest consumer has problems with a good or service at one time or another. It is your right to complain if you have a genuine consumer problem. It is also your responsibility. A problem can't be fixed if no one knows it exists.

CONTACT THE SELLER

The first step in resolving a consumer problem is contacting the seller. You can solve most consumer problems by talking to a salesperson or customer service representative. Do this as soon as possible because some retailers have time limits on returns and refunds. If this doesn't work, ask for a supervisor or manager. If this fails, try going higher up, to the national headquarters of the seller or the manufacturer of the item. Many companies have a special customer relations or consumer affairs division whose primary function is solving consumer problems. Many companies provide a toll free number or address for this office on the product label, warranty, or other papers, you received at the time of purchase. If this is not the case:

- Check the Corporate Consumer Directory portion of this *Handbook* for the contact information of several hundred corporations (p. 71).

- Visit the company's website, and look for a "Contact Us" link.

- Dial the directory of toll free numbers at 1-800-555-1212 to see whether the company has a toll free number listed.

- Ask your local librarian to assist you. Most public libraries have reference books with contact information.

- As you do your search, keep in mind that the name of the manufacturer or parent company is often different from the brand name. The *Thomas Register of American Manufacturers*, a book available at many public libraries, lists the manufacturers of thousands of products.

- With each person you contact, calmly and

accurately explain the problem and what action you would like to be taken. A written letter is a good strategy because you will have a record of your communication with the company. The sample letter (p. 57) will help you prepare a written complaint.

- Be brief and to the point. Note all important facts about your purchase, including what you bought, serial or model numbers, the name and location of the seller, and when you made the purchase.

- State exactly what you want done about the problem and how long you are willing to wait for a response. Be reasonable.

- Don't write an angry, sarcastic, or threatening letter. The person reading your letter probably was not responsible for your problem but could be very helpful in resolving it.

- Send your letter as certified mail or request delivery confirmation.

- Include copies of all documents regarding your problem. Keep the originals.

- Provide your name, address, and phone numbers. If an account is involved, be sure to include the account number.

- Keep a record of your efforts to contact the seller; include the name of the person with whom you spoke and what was done, if anything.

STEPS TO FOLLOW TO RESOLVE A COMPLAINT

- Before starting, start a file or log to record all contacts and documents.
- Contact the seller.
- Contact the manufacturer.
- Contact industry trade associations.
- Contact local and state consumer protection/regulatory/licensing officers.
- Contact the local BBB.

CONTACT THIRD PARTIES

Don't give up if you are not satisfied with the seller's response to your complaint. Once you have given the seller a reasonable amount of time to respond, consider filing a complaint with one or more of these outside organizations:

State or local consumer protection offices (p. 112). These government agencies mediate complaints, conduct investigations, and prosecute those who break consumer laws.

State regulatory agencies that have jurisdiction over the business. For example, banking (p. 126), securities (p. 134), insurance (p. 130), and utilities (p.138) are regulated at the state level.

Local politicians. Your local and state politicians may be able to help you get your complaint addressed.

Call for Action, Inc.
11820 Parklawn Dr., Suite 340
Rockville, MD 20852
Phone: 240-747-0229
Web: www.callforaction.org

Call for Action, Inc., is a nonprofit network of consumer hotlines that educate and assist consumers with consumer problems. Listed below are hotlines in major markets staffed with trained volunteers who offer advice and mediate complaints at no cost to consumers. Consumers in locations not listed should call the Network Hotline at 240-747-0225 (T, W, F 10 am–2 pm).

WTAJ–TV Altoona, PA 814-944-9336 M–F 1–3 pm	WJW–TV Cleveland, OH 216-578-0700 M, W, Th 10 am–1:00 pm M 5:30–6:30 pm	KSHB–TV Kansas City, MO 816-932-4321 T–Th 10 am–1 pm	KPNX–TV & KNAZ–TV & *The Arizona Republic* Phoenix, AZ 602-260-1212 or 1-866-260-1212 M–F 11 am–1 pm
WAGA–TV Atlanta, GA 404-879-4500 M–F 11 am–1 pm	KKTV–TV Colorado Springs, CO 719-457-8211 M–Th 11 am–1 pm	KTNV–TV Las Vegas, NV 702-368-2255 M–F 11 am–1 pm	WPRI–TV Providence, RI 401-228-1850 M–Th 11 am–1 pm
WRDW–TV Augusta, GA 803-442-4550 T–Th 11 am-1 pm	WSYX–TV Columbus, OH 614-821-9799 T–Th 11 am-1 pm	WKOW–TV Madison, WI 608-661-2727 M–F 11 am–1 pm	KTVI–TV St. Louis, MO 636-282-2222 1-800-782-2222 (IL) M–Th 11 am–1 pm
WBRC–TV Birmingham, AL 205-583-4321 M-F 11 am- 1 pm	WXYZ–TV Detroit, MI 248-827-3362 M–Th 11 am–1 pm	WTMJ–TV Milwaukee, WI 414-967-5495 M–Th 11 am–1 pm	WTOL–TV Toledo, OH 419-255-2255 T–Th 11 am–1 pm
WBZ Radio Boston, MA 617-787-7070 M–F 11 am–1:30 pm	WINK–TV Fort Myers, FL 239-334-4357 T–Th 11 am–1 pm	WQAD–TV Moline, IL 309-764-2255 M–F 11 am–1 pm	WTOP AM & FM Washington, DC 301-652-4357 T–F 11 am–1 pm
WIVB–TV Buffalo, NY 716-879-4900 M–F 11 am–1 pm	WHTM–TV Harrisburg, PA 717-214-9187 T–Th 11 am–1 pm	WTAE–TV Pittsburgh, PA 412-244-4698 T–Th 9 am–1 pm	

State and local licensing agencies. Doctors, lawyers, home improvement contractors, auto repair shops, debt collectors, and child care providers are required to register or be licensed. The board or agency that oversees this process may handle complaints and have the authority to take disciplinary action. Your state or local consumer protection office (p. 112) can help you identify the appropriate agency.

Better Business Bureaus (p. 66). This network of nonprofit organizations supported by local businesses tries to resolve buyer complaints against sellers. Records are kept on unresolved complaints as a source of information for the seller's future customers. The umbrella organization for the BBBs assists with complaints concerning the truthfulness of national advertising and helps to settle disputes with automobile manufacturers through the BBB AUTO LINE program (p. 65).

Trade associations. Companies selling similar products or services often belong to an industry association that will help resolve problems between its members and consumers (p. 142).

National consumer organizations. Some of these organizations assist consumers with complaints. Others may be unable to help individuals but are interested in hearing about problems that could influence their education and advocacy efforts (p. 109).

Media programs. Local newspapers, radio stations, and television stations often have Action Lines or Hotline services that try to resolve consumer complaints they receive. To find these services, check with your local newspapers or broadcast stations. See the "Call for Action" box above.

To contact an organization, use the directory beginning on page 62.

DISPUTE RESOLUTION PROGRAMS

Some companies and industries offer programs to address disagreements between buyers and sellers. The auto industry (p. 65) has several of these programs . The Financial Industry Regulatory Authority (FINRA) offers a program to resolve investment-related disputes (p. 144). Some small claims courts also offer a dispute resolution program as an alternative to a trial.

Mediation, arbitration, and conciliation are three common types of dispute resolution. During mediation, both sides involved in the dispute meet with a neutral third party and create their own agreement jointly. In arbitration, the third party decides how to settle the problem. Conciliation is similar, however you and the other party would meet with the conciliator separately (not a group meeting). Request a copy of the rules of any program before making a decision to participate. You will want to know beforehand whether the decision is binding; some programs do not require both parties to accept the decision. Also ask whether participation in the program places any restrictions on your ability to take other legal action. The American Bar Association (p. 142) publishes a directory of state and local dispute resolution programs.

SMALL CLAIMS COURT

Small claims courts resolve disputes over small amounts of money. While the maximum amount that can be claimed differs from state to state, court procedures are generally simple, inexpensive, quick, and informal. Court fees are minimal, and you often get your filing fee back if you win your case. Typically, you will not need a lawyer—some states do not permit them. If you live in a state that allows lawyers, and the party you are suing brings one, don't be intimidated. Most judges make allowances for consumers who appear without lawyers. Even though the court is informal, the judge's decision must be followed.

If you file a case and win, the losing party should give you what the court says you are owed without further action on your part. But some losers refuse to follow the court's decision. When this happens, you can go back to court and ask for the order to be enforced. Depending on local laws, law enforcement officials might sell a person's property or take money from a bank account or business cash register. If the person who owes the money receives a salary, the court might order an employer to garnish (deduct money from) each paycheck to pay you.

Check your local telephone book under the municipal, county, or state government headings for small claims court offices. Ask the clerk how to use

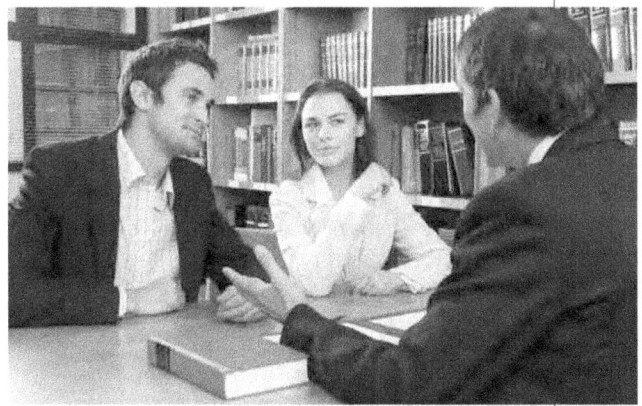

the small claims court. Before taking your own case to court, observe a small claims court session and ask the court if it has information that will help you prepare your presentation to the judge.

LEGAL HELP AND INFORMATION

If you need an attorney to advise or represent you, ask friends and family for recommendations. You can also contact the Lawyer Referral Service of your state, county, or city bar association listed in your local phone directory. Websites such as www.abalawinfo.org (American Bar Association) and www.nolo.com can help you with answers to general legal questions.

Tips for Choosing an Attorney

Many lawyers who primarily serve individuals and families are general practitioners with experience in frequently needed legal services, such as divorce and family matters, wills and probate, bankruptcy and debt problems, real estate, and criminal and/or personal injury. Some have a narrower focus. Be sure the lawyer you are considering has experience in the area for which you are seeking help.

Once you've identified some candidates:

- Call each attorney on the telephone, describe your legal issue, and find out if he or she handles your situation.
- Ask if you will be charged for an initial consultation.
- Ask for an estimate of what the lawyer usually charges to handle your kind of case.

FILE A COMPLAINT USING SOCIAL MEDIA

Social media offers an alternative to filing a formal consumer complaint. The customer relations staff at many major corporations monitor posts and complaints about their company's service. Someone may respond to your problem quiickly, to avoid negative perceptions of their performance by other potential customers. While there is no guarantee that you'll get your problem resolved, it can be a worthwhile effort.

- Ask whether there are hourly charges or your attorney accepts a percentage of the settlement as a fee contingency.

The initial consultation is an opportunity for you and the lawyer to get to know each other. After listening to the description of your case, the lawyer should be able to outline your rights and liabilities as well as alternative courses of action. The initial consultation is the lawyer's opportunity to explain what he or she can do for you and how much it will cost. You should not hesitate to ask about the attorney's experience in handling matters such as yours. Also, do not hesitate to ask about the lawyer's fees and the likely results. If you are considering going beyond the initial consultation and hiring the lawyer, request a written fee agreement before proceeding.

What If You Can't Afford a Lawyer?

If you cannot afford a lawyer, you may qualify for free legal help from a Legal Aid or Legal Services Corporation (LSC) office. These offices generally offer legal assistance for such things as landlord-tenant relations, credit, utilities, family matters (for example, divorce and adoption), foreclosure, home equity fraud, Social Security, welfare, unemployment, and workers' compensation. If the Legal Aid office in your area does not handle your type of case, it may refer you to other local, state, or national organizations that can provide help. Additional resources may be found at www.lawhelp.org or www.freeadvice.com.

- To find the Legal Aid office nearest to you, check a local telephone directory or contact:

  National Legal Aid and Defender Association
  1625 K St., NW, 8th Floor
  Washington, DC 20006
  Phone: 202-452-0620
  ✉: info@nlada.org
  www.nlada.org

- To find the LSC office nearest you, check a local telephone directory or contact:

  LSC Public Affairs
  3333 K St., NW, 3rd Floor
  Washington, DC 20007
  Phone: 202-295-1500
  www.lsc.gov

Free assistance could also be available from a law school program where students, supervised by attorneys, handle a variety of legal matters. Some of these programs are open to all, others limit their service to specific groups, such as senior citizens or low-income persons. Contact a law school in your area to find out whether such a program is available.

REPORT FRAUD & SAFETY HAZARD

If you suspect a law has been violated, contact your local or state consumer protection agency (p. 112). This agency may take action or refer you to another state organization that has authority where you live. A local law enforcement officer could also be able to provide advice and assistance.

Violations of federal laws should be reported to the federal agency responsible for enforcement. While federal agencies are rarely able to act on behalf of individual consumers, complaints are used to document patterns of abuse, allowing the agency to take action against a company.

Throughout Part I of this *Handbook*, you will find references to federal agencies you can contact for more information, which is usually the same agency to contact with your complaint. You can also find the appropriate federal agency by using the Federal Agency Directory (p. 96).

People who have no intention of delivering what is sold, misrepresent items, send counterfeit goods, or otherwise try to trick you out of your money are committing fraud. If you suspect fraud, there are some additional steps to take:

- Contact the Federal Trade Commission (p. 106).
- Scams that use the mail or interstate delivery service should also be reported to the U.S. Postal Inspection Service (p. 108). It is illegal to use the mail to misrepresent or steal money.

Reporting fraud promptly improves your chances of recovering what you have lost and helps law enforcement authorities stop scams before others are victimized.

If you suspect you have a product that poses a safety hazard, report the problem to the appropriate federal agency:

- **Animal Products.** Food and Drug Administration (p. 100**)**
- **Automobiles.** National Highway Traffic Safety Administration (p. 104)
- **Consumer Household Products.** U.S. Consumer Product Safety Commission (p. 97)
- **Drugs, Cosmetics, and Medical Devices.** Food and Drug Administration (p. 100)
- **Food.** Food and Drug Administration (p. 100), U.S. Department of Agriculture (p. 96)
- **Household Chemicals.** Environmental Protection Agency (p. 105)
- **Seafood.** Food and Drug Administration (p. 100), U.S. Department of Commerce (p. 97)
- **Toys, Baby, and Play Equipment.** U.S. Consumer Product Safety Commission (p. 96)

To contact an organization, use the directory beginning on page 62.

Keep copies of all of your letters, faxes, e-mails, receipts and related documents.

Your Address
Your City, State, ZIP Code
Date

Name of Contact Person, if available
Title, if available
Company Name
Consumer Complaint Division (if you have no specific contact)
Street Address
City, State, Zip Code

Dear (Contact Person):

Re: (account number, if applicable)

On (date), I (bought, leased, rented, or had repaired) a (name of the product, with serial or model number or service performed) at (location, date and other important details of the transaction).

Unfortunately, your product (or service) has not performed well (or the service was inadequate) because (state the problem). I am disappointed because (explain the problem: for example, the product does not work properly, the service was not performed correctly, I was billed the wrong amount, something was not disclosed clearly or was misrepresented, etc.).

To resolve the problem, I would appreciate your (state the specific action you want—money back, charge card credit, repair, exchange, etc.). Enclosed are copies (do not send originals) of my records (include receipts, guarantees, warranties, canceled checks, contracts, model and serial numbers, and any other documents).

I look forward to your reply and a resolution to my problem and will wait until (set a time limit) before seeking help from a consumer protection agency or Better Business Bureau. Please contact me at the above address or by phone at (home and/or office numbers with area code).

Sincerely,

Your name

Enclosure(s)

- describe purchase
- name of product, serial number
- include date and place of purchase

- state problem
- give history

- ask for specific action
- enclose copies of documents

- allow time for action
- state how you can be reached

Download a copy of the sample complaint letter at:
www.usa.gov/topics/consumer/complaint/complaint-letter.shtml

KEY INFORMATION RESOURCES

Federal Citizen Information Center (FCIC)

FCIC is a one-stop source that provides government information and services directly to the public. FCIC offers information across various channels, including websites USA.gov and GobiernoUSA.gov (in Spanish), telephone at 1-888-333-4636, print publications available through the *Consumer Information Catalog* and at Publications.USA.gov, and via social media on Facebook at: facebook.com/USAgov and Twitter: @USAgov.

SERVICES AND RESOURCES FOR CONSUMERS WITH DISABILITIES

Relay Services: Telecommunications relay services link telephone conversations between individuals who use standard voice telephones and those who use text telephones (TTYs). Calls can be made from either type of telephone to the other type through the relay service.

Local Relay Services: States provide relay services for local and long-distance calls. Consult your local telephone directory for information on use, fees (if any), services, and dialing instructions for that area.

Federal Relay Service: The FRS, a program of the U.S. General Services Administration (GSA), provides access to TTY users who wish to conduct official business nationwide with and within the Federal government. The toll free number is 1-866-377-8642. For more information on relay communications or to obtain a brochure on using the FRS, call 1-800-877-0996.

Other Services: Consumers who are deaf or hard of hearing, or who have speech impairment, and use a TTY may receive operator and directory assistance for calls by calling 1-800-855-1155. Check the introductory pages of your local telephone directory for additional TTY services.

Center for the Study of Services

www.checkbook.org Evaluates quality and price for local services in major metropolitan areas. See page 109.

Consumers Union (CU)

www.consumerreports.org Researches and tests goods and services such as automobiles, appliances, food, clothing, luggage, and insurance. See page 110.

Consumer World

www.consumerworld.org A public service website with links to hundreds of consumer resources, corporations and government agencies.

National Institute of Food and Agriculture (NIFA)

Programs cover food and nutrition, housing, gardening, budgeting, using credit, saving for retirement, and more. Visit www.nifa.usda.gov or www.extension.org. See page 96.

Libraries

Publications from many of the organizations mentioned on this page are available at your local public library or by visiting www.publiclibraries.com.

EMERGENCY PREPAREDNESS

Disasters can strike in many forms—fires, floods, hurricanes, tornadoes, and even national emergencies. Protecting yourself, your family, your pets, and your home or your business requires advance planning. It is equally important to know where to turn for help and information. You may even be eligible for government assistance.

There are numerous sources of information to help you prepare. To get started, check out these sites:

- www.disasterassistance.gov
- www.fema.gov/areyouready
- www.ready.gov
- www.redcross.org

FOR TEACHERS

Teachers often use the *Consumer Action Handbook* to teach essential information about credit, insurance, major purchases, complaint letters, saving and investing, and other consumer topics. For classroom copies of the *Handbook*, e-mail action.handbook@gsa.gov; include the name and address of your school and the number of copies you would like to receive.

To contact an organization, use the directory beginning on page 62.

FOR PERSONS WITH DISABILITIES

National Council on Disability

www.ncd.gov A federal agency whose mission is to improve the quality of life for Americans with disabilities and their families; see page 107.

National Disability Rights Network

www.ndrn.org Provides legally based advocacy services for people with disabilities.

Department of Education

www.ed.gov Provides training and information to parents of disabled children and to people who work with them; see page 97.

Department of Housing and Urban Development

www.hud.gov/offices/fheo/disabilities Learn more about the housing rights of people with disabilities, and the responsibilities of housing providers and building and design professionals; see page 101.

National Library Service for the Blind and Physically Handicapped

www.loc.gov/nls Administers a free loan service of recorded and Braille books and magazines, music scores in Braille and large print, plus specially designed playback equipment.

FOR MILITARY PERSONNEL

Today's military families face many common consumer challenges as well as the additional stress associated with frequent separation. To ease such difficulties, Family Centers, along with the other programs described below, provide help and support for military families.

U.S. Military Family Centers

Located on most military installations, Family Centers provide information, life skills education, and support services to military members and their families. One key function of the Family Center is to link customers with appropriate services available in the local community and/or through state and federal assistance programs such as those related to health and human services, school systems, employment assistance, law enforcement, and recreation.

If you cannot locate a Family Center, please contact your respective military branch's headquarters office listed below. The designation "DSN," preceding some of the phone numbers, refers to the military phone system and does not apply to the civilian sector.

Air Force Community Readiness and Family Support

AF/A1SF 4E235
Force Sustainment Division
1040 Air Force Pentagon
Washington, DC 20330-1040
Phone: 703-697-0067
www.afcrossroads.com
Air Force Crossroads is a comprehensive resource for Air Force members and their families relating to nearly every aspect of personal and professional life. With topics that cover, among others, health and wellness, finances, family matters, and recreation, the network includes access to the Air Force Spouse Forum, chat rooms, an employment forum, and a flea market, and links to news sources.

Marine Corps Community Services (MCCS)

3280 Russell Rd.
Quantico, VA 22134-5103
703-784-0275
DSN: 278-0275
Toll free: 1-800-627-4637
www.usmc-mccs.org
The Personal and Family Readiness Division (MR) provides a number of Marine Corps personnel service programs, such as Casualty Assistance, DEERS Dependency Determination, Voting Assistance, Postal Services, and Personal Claims.

BETTER BUSINESS BUREAU MILITARY LINE

The BBB Military Line, www.military.bbb.org, offers consumer education and advocacy to service members and their families. Five service-specific sites contain current military-related consumer news as well as links to local BBBs and other sites with useful consumer information:

www.bbb.org/us/Military/Army

www.bbb.org/us/Military/Navy

www.bbb.org /us/Military/Air-force

www.bbb.org/us/Military/Marine

www.bbb.org/us/Military/Coast-guard

Users may request reports, file complaints, and sign up for a custom consumer newsletter. At the local level, area BBBs provide educational briefings for military personnel and their families, and work with local businesses to promote ethical treatment of military consumers.

Fleet and Family Support Programs

Commander, Navy Installations Command
2713 Mitscher Rd., SW, Suite 300
Washington, DC 20373-5802
Toll free: 1-800-372-5463
www.nffsp.org

The Fleet and Family Support Program delivered by Commander, Navy Installations Command, provides support, references, information, and a wide range of assistance for members of the Navy and their families to meet the unique challenges of the military lifestyle. Up-to-date news, messages, links, and resources are provided, including assistance with relocation, employment, career and benefits, healthy lifestyles, casualties, domestic violence, and retirement.

PREDATORY LENDING RESTRICTIONS

As of October 1, 2007, the Talent-Nelson Amendment to the John Warner National Defense Authorization Act allows the Department of Defense to regulate the terms of payday loans, vehicle title loans, and tax refund loans to active-duty service members and their dependents. These three products have high interest rates, coupled with short payback terms.

The rule for service members and their dependents limits the Military Annual Percentage Rate (MAPR) on these loans to 36%. All fees and charges should be included in calculating the rate. The rule also prohibits contracts requiring the use of a check or access to a bank account, mandatory arbitration, or unreasonable legal notice. Any credit agreement subject to this regulation that fails to comply with the regulation is void and cannot be enforced. The rule further provides that a creditor or assignee who knowingly violates the regulation shall be subject to certain criminal penalties.

The Department of Defense strongly encourages service members and their families to choose alternatives that are specifically designed to help resolve financial crises, rebuild credit rating, and establish savings for emergencies. Payday loans, vehicle title loans, and tax refund loans can propel an already overextended borrower into a deeper spiral of debt.

Family and Morale, Welfare and Recreation Command Family Programs

Directorate, Army Community Service
4700 King St.
Alexandria, VA 22302
Phone: 703-681-5375
DSN: 761-5375

MyArmyLifeToo

www.myarmylifetoo.com

This portal is the single gateway to comprehensive information on the support available to Army personnel and families, including resources to strengthen home and family life, Army basic training, lifelong learning, finances, employment, and relevant news, along with links to other key resources.

U.S. Coast Guard

2100 Second St., SW, Room 6320
Washington, DC 20593
Phone: 202-267-6160
Toll free: 1-800-368-5647 (Safety)
Toll free: 1-877-669-8724 (Recruiting)
www.uscg.mil

The U.S. Coast Guard can provide key resources, including core publications, career information, and related news, as well as comprehensive background about its mission, community services, history, photos, and reports.

Military HOMEFRONT

www.militaryhomefront.dod.mil

Military HOMEFRONT is the official Department of Defense website for information to help improve the quality of life for troops and their families. Members of all branches of the military service and their families will find reliable, up-to-date details and advice on such topics as education, housing, legal matters, parenting, personal finances, pay and benefits, relocation, and health care. Military HOMEFRONT also makes it easier for leaders to locate official quality-of-life program information and resources for its troops and families. In addition, service providers can access desk guides, policies, forms, and other resources.

Military Sentinel

www.ftc.gov/sentinel/military

Military Sentinel is a gateway to consumer education materials covering a wide range of consumer protection issues, from auto leasing, to identity theft, to work-at-home scams. It allows members of the U.S. Armed Forces to enter consumer complaints directly into a database that is immediately accessible by over 500 law enforcement organizations throughout the United States, Canada, and Australia. These law enforcement agencies use this complaint data to target cases for prosecution and other enforcement measures. Members of the Judge Advocate General's staff and others in the Department of Defense can also use this information to help protect armed services members and their families from consumer protection–related problems.

60   www.USA.gov

To contact an organization, use the directory beginning on page 62.

HELP FROM THE CONSUMER FINANCIAL PROTECTION BUREAU

The Consumer Financial Protection Bureau (CFPB) offers resources specifically for servicemembers and their families. The Office of Servicemember Affairs is dedicated to helping military personnel plan for their financial futures, as well as protect themselves from frauds that are targeted at military communities. For more information visit, www.consumerfinance.gov/servicemembers.

Military OneSource

www.militaryonesource.com
Toll free: 1-800-342-9647
Military OneSource is an excellent hub of information and assistance for military personnel and their families. This 24/7 resource offers a variety of services and tools to meet the special needs and improve the lives of service men and women, both personally and professionally. In addition to in-person counseling and direct links to all of the armed services home sites, Military OneSource offers advice and whom-to-contact information on matters such as health, education, training, moving, shopping, legal issues, and finances. Podcasts, webinars, discussion boards, and news feeds cover special topics and provide answers to help resolve problems.

Commissaries and Exchanges

Consumers who shop at military commissaries and exchanges and who have a question or problem should contact the local manager before contacting the regional office. If your problem is not resolved at the local level, then write or call the regional office nearest you. Be sure to discuss the problem with the local and regional offices of a commissary or exchange before contacting the national headquarters.

Wounded Warrior Resource Center

www.woundedwarriorresourcecenter.com
The Wounded Warrior Resource Center website (WWRC) provides wounded service members, their families, and caregivers with information they need in the areas of military facilities, health care services, and benefits. It supports access to the Wounded Warrior Resource Call Center and trained specialists who are available 24 hours a day, 7 days a week by phone at 1-800-342-9647 or by e-mail at wwrc@militaryonesource.com. Information is also available on how to connect to other families for support and recreation.

National Resource Directory

www.nationalresourcedirectory.gov
The National Resource Directory provides wounded, ill, and injured service members, veterans, their families, and those who support them, with a web-based "yellow book." It has information on, and access to, the full range of medical and non-medical services and resources needed to achieve their personal and professional goals across the transitions from recovery to rehabilitation to community reintegration. The National Resource Directory, an online partnership of the departments of Defense, Labor, and Veterans Affairs, provides links to the services and resources of federal, state, and local government agencies; veterans' service, non-profit, community-based, and philanthropic organizations; professional associations; and academic institutions.

SOCAP INTERNATIONAL

Many of the companies listed in this *Handbook* are members of the Society of Consumer Affairs Professionals International (SOCAP). A professional organization established in 1973, the Society's goal is to improve the marketplace for consumers by improving customer care through education and networking. SOCAP members are identified in the automotive and corporate directories by the SOCAP logo (see Key at right). For more information, contact SOCAP (p. 111).

KEY:

✉   Email

◌   SOCAP International Member

◆   Provided financial support for the publication of the *2012 Consumer Action Handbook*.

TTY Numbers for people with hearing disabilities. For more information see the box on page 58.

62   www.USA.gov

To contact an organization, use the directory beginning on page 62.

Acura
Customer Relations Department
1919 Torrance Blvd.
Mail Stop 500-2N7E
Torrance, CA 90501-2746
310-783-2000
Toll free: 1-800-382-2238
www.acura.com

Alfa-Romeo
7454 Brokerage Dr.
Orlando, FL 32809
407-856-5000
www.alfaromeo.com

American Honda Motor Company, Inc.
Honda Automobile Customer Service
1919 Torrance Blvd.
Mail Stop 500 - 2N7D
Torrance, CA 90501-2746
310-783-2000
Toll free: 1-800-999-1009
www.honda.com

American Suzuki Motor Corporation
Customer Relations Department
PO Box 1100
Brea, CA 92822-1100
714-572-1490 (Motorcycle/ATV/ Marine)
Toll free: 1-800-934-0934 (Automotive)
www.suzuki.com

Aston Martin
Customer Relations Department
U.S. National Headquarters
One Premier Pl.
Irvine, CA 92618
949-341-5800
www.astonmartin.com

Audi of America, Inc.
Customer Relations
3800 W. Hamlin Rd.
Auburn Hills, MI 483226
Toll free: 1-800-822-2834
✉: auditalk@audi.com
www.audiusa.com

BMW
Customer Relations
300 Chestnut Ridge Rd.
Woodcliff Lake, NJ 07677-7731
201-307-4000
Toll free: 1-800-831-1117
www.bmwusa.com

Contacting Your Automotive Manufacturer

If you have a problem with a car purchased from a local dealer, first try to work it out with the dealer. If the problem is not resolved, contact the manufacturer's regional or national office. Ask for the Consumer Affairs Office.

If you are still unsuccessful, consider contacting the automotive dispute resolution resources listed at the end of this section. The method used to resolve your dispute may be mediation, arbitration, or conciliation. Decisions of arbitrators are usually binding and must be accepted by both the customer and the business. Ask for a copy of the rules of the program before you file your case. See page 55 for an overview of ispute resolution programs.

A local or state consumer agency (p. 112) could also be a useful resource in resolving problems with your vehicle. If you have a new vehicle, be sure to ask whether you have any protection under a state "lemon" law.

Buick
Customer Assistance Center
PO Box 33136
Detroit, MI 48232-5136
Toll free: 1-800-521-7300
TTY: 1-800-735-2900
www.buick.com

Cadillac
Customer Assistance Center
PO Box 33169
Detroit, MI 48232-5169
Toll free: 1-800-458-8006
TTY: 1-800-255-2683
www.cadillac.com

Chevrolet
Customer Assistance Center
PO Box 33170
Detroit, MI 48232-5170
Toll free: 1-800-222-1020
TTY: 1-800-833-2438
www.chevrolet.com

Chrysler
Chrysler Group, LLC
Customer Assistance Center
PO Box 21-8004
Auburn Hills, MI 48321-8004
Toll free: 1-800-992-1997
www.chrysler.com

Dodge
Toll free: 1-800-992-1997
www.dodge.com

Ferrari North America, Inc.
Corporate Office
250 Sylvan Ave.
Englewood Cliffs, NJ 07632
201-816-2600
www.ferrari.com

Ford Motor Company
Customer Relationship Center
PO Box 6248
Dearborn, MI 48126
Toll free: 1-800-392-3673
TTY: 1-800-232-5952
www.ford.com

GMC
PO Box 33172
Detroit, MI 48232-5172
Toll free: 1-800-462-8782
TTY: 1-800-462-8583
www.gmc.com

Hyundai Motor America
PO Box 20850
Fountain Valley, CA 92728-0850
714-965-3000
Toll free: 1-800-633-5151
✉: consumeraffairs@hmausa.com
www.hyundaiusa.com

Infiniti
See: Nissan North America, Inc.
Toll free: 1-800-662-6200
www.infiniti.com

Isuzu Motors America, Inc.
Owner Relations Department
1400 S. Douglass Rd., Suite 100
Anaheim, CA 92806
714-935-9300
Toll free: 1-800-255-6727
www.isuzu.com

Jaguar Cars
555 MacArthur Blvd.
Mahwah, NJ 07430-2327
Toll free: 1-800-452-4827
www.jaguarusa.com

Jeep
See: Chrysler
Toll free: 1-800-992-1997
www.jeep.com/en

Kia Motors America, Inc.
PO Box 52410
Irvine, CA 92619-2410
Toll free: 1-800-333-4542
www.kia.com

Land Rover
Customer Relationship Center
555 MacArthur Blvd.
Mahwah, NJ 07430
Toll free: 1-800-637-6837
www.landroverusa.com

Lexus
A Division of Toyota Motor Sales,
USA, Inc.
PO Box 2991
Mail Drop L201
Torrance, CA 90501-2732
Toll free: 1-800-255-3987
TTY: 711
www.lexus.com

Lincoln
See: Ford Motor Company
www.lincoln.com

**Mazda North American
Operations**
PO Box 19734
Irvine, CA 92623-9734
Toll free: 1-800-222-5500
www.mazdausa.com

Mercedes Benz USA, LLC
Customer Assistance Center
Three Mercedes Dr.
Montvale, NJ 07645
Toll free: 1-800-367-6372
www.mbusa.com

Mercury
See: Ford Motor Company
www.mercuryvehicles.com

**Mitsubishi Motors North
America, Inc.**
Customer Relations
PO Box 6400
Cypress, CA 90630-0014
Toll free: 1-888-648-7820
www.mitsubishicars.com

Nissan North America, Inc.
PO Box 685003
Franklin, TN 37068-5003
Toll free: 1-800-647-7261
www.nissanusa.com

Oldsmobile
Customer Assistance Center
PO Box 33171
Detroit, MI 48232-5171
Toll free: 1-800-442-6537
TTY: 1-800-833-9935
www.oldsmobile.com

**Peugeot Motors
of America, Inc.**
Overlook at Great Notch
150 Clove Rd.
Little Falls, NJ 07424
973-812-4444
www.peugeot.com

Pontiac
See: GMC
Toll free: 1-800-762-2737
TTY: 1-800-833-9935
www.pontiac.com

**Porsche Cars North
America, Inc.**
Owner Relations
980 Hammond Dr., Suite 1000
Atlanta, GA 30328
Toll free: 1-800-767-7243
www.porsche.com/usa

Saab Automobile USA
Customer Assistance Center
PO Box 33166
Detroit, MI 48232-5166
Toll free: 1-800-955-9007
www.saabusa.com

Saturn
See: GMC
Customer Assistance Center
Toll free: 1-800-553-6000
www.saturn.com

Smart USA
2555 Telegraph Rd.
Bloomfield Hills, MI 48302
Toll free: 1-800-762-7887
www.smartusa.com

Subaru of America, Inc.
Customer/Dealer Services
Subaru Plaza
PO Box 6000
Cherry Hill, NJ 08034-6000
Toll free: 1-800-782-2783
www.subaru.com

**Toyota Motor Sales
USA, Inc.**
Customer Experience Center
Department WC 11
19001 S. Western Ave.
Torrance, CA 90501
310-468-4000
Toll free: 1-800-331-4331
TTY: 1-800-443-4999
www.toyota.com

**Volkswagen Group of
America, Inc.**
Customer Care
2200 Ferdinand Porshe Dr.
Herndon, VA 20171
Toll free: 1-800-822-8987
www.vw.com or
volkswagengroupamerica.com

Volvo Cars of North America
Customer Care Center
One Volvo Dr.
PO Box 914
Rockleigh, NJ 07647
Toll free: 1-800-458-1552
www.volvocars.com

Yamaha Motor Corporation
Customer Relations
6555 Katella Ave.
Cypress, CA 90630
714-761-7435
Toll free: 1-800-962-7926
(Customer Relations)
Toll free: 1-800-252-5265 (Yamaha
Card)
www.yamaha-motor.com

**BBB Auto Line
Council of Better Business Bureaus, Inc.**
4200 Wilson Blvd., 8th Floor
Arlington, VA 22203-1838
703-276-0100
Toll free: 1-800-955-5100
TTY: 703-276-1862
✉: info@cbbb.bbb.org
www.bbb.org
Third-party dispute resolution program for automobile manufacturers.

DOT Auto Safety Hotline
1200 New Jersey Ave., SE
West Building
Washington, DC 20590
Toll free: 1-888-327-4236
TTY: 1-800-424-9153
www-odi.nhtsa.dot.gov/contact.cfm
Consumers can contact the DOT Auto Safety Hotline to report safety defects in vehicles, tires, and child safety seats. Information is available about air bags, child safety seats, seat belts, and general highway safety. Consumers who experience a safety defect in their vehicle are encouraged to report the defect to the Hotline in addition to the dealer or manufacturer.

International Association of Lemon Law Administrators
www.ialla.net
This organization supports and promotes government agencies that administer motor vehicle warranty and related laws, through consumer and industry education and other intergovernmental activities.

Contacting Automotive Dispute Resolution Programs

An automotive dispute resolution program is another resource to consult if you need to solve a problem with your car's manufacturer or dealership. If you have been unable to reach an agreement your manufacturer, consider contacting the automotive dispute resolution resources listed here. The method used to resolve your dispute may be mediation, arbitration, or conciliation. Decisions of arbitrators are usually binding and must be accepted by both the customer and the business. Ask for a copy of the rules of the program before you file your case.

Read the contract that you signed when you purchased your car. Manufacturers and dealers may have included a clause that requires you to agree to mandatory arbitration, waiving your right to sue or settle a disagreement in a court of law.

Motorist Assurance Program (MAP)
201 Park Washington Ct.
Falls Church, VA 22046
703-538-3557
✉: map@motorist.org
www.motorist.org
MAP accredits those auto repair shops that apply and follow industry developed standards for inspecting vehicles as well as meet other requirements. MAP handles inquiries/disputes between accredited shops and customers and offers information to consumers about how to locate a repair shop, how to talk to a technician, and how to work successfully with auto repair shops.

National Automobile Dealers Association (NADA)
8400 Westpark Dr.
McLean, VA 22102
Toll free: 1-800-252-6232
✉: nadainfo@nada.org
www.nada.org
NADA is a third-party dispute resolution organization. The national office makes referrals to state auto dealer associations.

RV Consumer Group
PO Box 520
Quilcene, WA 98376
www.rv.org
RV Consumer Group is a non-profit organization dedicated to the safety of recreational vehicles. This group is not aligned or affiliated with the RV industry. It offers books and memberships to help consumers select the best RV for them.

See page 55 for more information about dispute resolution programs.

Contacting Your Local Better Business Bureau

Better Business Bureaus (BBBs) are non-profit organizations that encourage honest advertising and selling practices and are supported primarily by local businesses. BBBs offer a variety of consumer services, including consumer education materials; business reports, particularly unanswered or unsettled complaints or other problems; mediation and arbitration services; and information about charities and other organizations that are seeking public donations. They also provide ratings (A, B, C, D, or F) of local companies to express the BBB's confidence that the company operates in a trustworthy manner and demonstrates a willingness to resolve customer concerns.

Complaints should be submitted in writing so that an accurate record exists of the dispute. The BBB will then present the complaint to the company involved. If the complaint is not resolved, the BBB may offer an alternative dispute settlement process. BBBs do not judge or rate individual products or brands, handle employer/employee wage disputes, or give legal advice.

If you need help with a consumer question or complaint, call your local BBB or visit its website.

BBB*OnLine* (**www.bbb.org/online**) provides Internet users an easy way to verify the legitimacy of online businesses. Companies carrying the BBB*OnLine* seal have been checked out by the BBB and agree to resolve customer concerns.

The Council of Better Business Bureaus, the umbrella organization for the BBBs, can assist with complaints about the truthfulness and accuracy of national advertising claims, including children's advertising; provide reports on national soliciting charities; and help to settle disputes with automobile manufacturers through the BBB Auto Line program (p. 65).

Council

Council of Better Business Bureaus, Inc.
4200 Wilson Blvd., 8th Floor
Arlington, VA 22203-1838
703-276-0100

Alabama

Birmingham
1210 S. 20th St.
Birmingham, AL 35205
Toll free: 1-800-824-5274 (AL)
205-558-2222

Cullman
202 1st Ave., SE, Suite I
Cullman, AL 35055
256-775-2917

Decatur
254 Moulton St. E, 3rd Floor
Decatur, AL 35601
256-355-2226

Dothan
1971 S. Brannon Stand Rd.
Suite 1
Dothan, AL 36305
334-794-0492

Huntsville
107 Lincoln St., SE
Huntsville, AL 35801
256-533-1640

Mobile
960 S. Schillinger Rd., Suite I
Mobile, AL 36695
251-433-5494

Montgomery
4750 Woodmere Blvd., Suite D
Montgomery, AL 36107
334-273-5530

Alaska

Anchorage
341 W. Tudor Rd., Suite 209
Anchorage, AK 99503
907-562-0704

Arizona

Phoenix
4428 N. 12th St.
Phoenix, AZ 85014-4585
602-264-1721

Prescott
1569 W. Gurley St.
Prescott, AZ 86305
928-772-3410

Siera Vista
2160 E. Fry Blvd.
Suite C5 PMB 172
Siera Vista, AZ 85635
520-888-5353

Tucson
434 S. Williams Blvd., Suite 102
Tucson, AZ 85711
520-888-5353

Arkansas

Little Rock
12521 Kanis Rd.
Little Rock, AR 72211
501-664-4888

California

Bakersfield
1601 H St., Suite 101
Bakersfield, CA 93301
661-322-2074

Culver City
6125 Washington Blvd., 3rd Floor
Culver City, CA 90232
310-945-3166

Fresno
4201 W. Shaw Ave., Suite 107
Fresno, CA 93722
559-222-8111

Long Beach
3363 Linden Ave., Suite A
Long Beach, CA 90807
562-216-9242

Los Angeles
315 N. La Cadena Dr.
Colton, CA 92324
909-825-7280

Oakland
1000 Broadway, Suite 625
Oakland, CA 94607
510-844-2000

Placentia
550 W. Orangethorpe Ave.
Placentia, CA 92870
714-985-8922

Sacramento
3075 Beacon Blvd.
West Sacramento, CA 95691
916-443-6843

San Diego
5050 Murphy Canyon Rd.
Suite 110
San Diego, CA 92123
858-496-2131

San Jose
1112 S. Bascom Ave.
San Jose, CA 95128
408-278-7400

Santa Barbara
PO Box 129
Santa Barbara, CA 93101
805-963-8657

Stockton
11 S. San Joaquin St., 8th Floor
Stockton, CA 95202
209-948-4880

Colorado

Colorado Springs
25 N. Wahsatch Ave.
Colorado Springs, CO 80903
719-636-1155

Denver
1020 Cherokee St.
Denver, CO 80204-4039
303-758-2100

Fort Collins
8020 S. County Rd. 5, Suite 100
Fort Collins, CO 80528
970-484-1348

Connecticut

Wallingford
94 S. Turnpike Rd.
Wallingford, CT 06492-4322
203-269-2700

Delaware

Wilmington
60 Reads Way
New Castle, DE 19720
302-221-5255

District of Columbia

Washington
1411 K St., NW, Suite 1000
Washington, DC 20005-3404
202-393-8000

Florida

Clearwater
2655 McCormick Dr.
Clearwater, FL 33759
727-535-5522

Jacksonville
4417 Beach Blvd., Suite 202
Jacksonville, FL 32207
904-721-2288

Longwood
1600 S. Grant St.
Longwood, FL 32750
407-621-3300

Miami Lakes
14750 N.W. 77 Ct., #317
Miami Lakes, FL 33016
561-842-1918

Pensacola
912 E. Gadsden St.
Pensacola, FL 32501
850-429-0002

Stuart
101 S.E. Ocean Blvd., Suite 202
Stuart, FL 34994
772-223-1492

West Palm Beach
4411 Beacon Circle, Suite 4
West Palm Beach, FL 33407
561-842-1918

Georgia

Atlanta
503 Oak Place, Suite 590
Atlanta, GA 30349
404-766-0875

Augusta
1227 Augusta West Parkway
Suite 15
Augusta, GA 30909
706-210-7676

Columbus
PO Box 2587
Columbus, GA 31902
706-324-0712

Macon
277 Martin Luther King, Jr. Blvd.
Suite 102
Macon, GA 31201-3495
478-742-7999

Savannah
6555 Abercorn St., Suite 120
Savannah, GA 31405-5817
912-354-7521

Hawaii

Honolulu
1132 Bishop St., Suite 615
Honolulu, HI 96813
808-536-6956

Idaho

Boise
1200 N. Curtis Rd.
Boise, ID 83706
208-342-4649

Idaho Falls
453 River Parkway
Idaho Falls, ID 83402
208-523-9754

Illinois

Chicago
330 N. Wabash Ave., Suite 2006
Chicago, IL 60611-7621
312-832-0500

Peoria
112 Harrison St.
Peoria, IL 61602
309-688-3741

Rockford
810 E. State St., 3rd Floor
Rockford, IL 61104-1001
815-963-2226

Indiana

Evansville
3101 N. Green River Rd., Suite 410
Evansville, IN 47715
812-473-0202

Fort Wayne
4011 Parnell Ave.
Fort Wayne, IN 46805
260-423-4433

Indianapolis
151 N. Delaware St., Suite 2020
Indianapolis, IN 46204-2599
317-488-2222

Merriville
7863 Broadway, Suite 124
Merriville, IN 46410
219-791-9550

Osceola
10775 McKinley Highway, Suite B
Osceola, IN 46561
574-675-9315

Iowa

Bettendorf
2435 Kimberly Rd., Suite 260 N
Bettendorf, IA 52722-4100
563-355-6344

Des Moines
505 5th Ave., Suite 950
Des Moines, IA 50309
515-243-8137

Kansas

Wichita
345 N. Riverview St., Suite 720
Wichita, KS 67203
Toll free: 1-800-856-2417

Kentucky

Lexington
1460 Newtown Pike
Lexington, KY 40511
859-259-1008

Louisville
844 S. Fourth St.
Louisville, KY 40203
502-583-6546

Louisiana

Alexandria
5220-C Rue Verdun
Alexandria, LA 71303
318-473-4494

Baton Rouge
748 Main St.
Baton Rouge, LA 70802
225-346-5222

Houma
801 Barrow St., Suite 400
Houma, LA 70360
985-868-3456

Lafayette
4007 W. Congress St., Suite B
Lafayette, LA 70506
337-981-3497

Lake Charles
2309 E. Prien Lake Rd.
Lake Charles, LA 70601
337-478-6253

Monroe
212 Walnut St., #210
Monroe, LA 71201
Toll free: 1-800-960-7756
318-387-4600

New Orleans
710 Baronne St., Suite C
New Orleans, LA 70113
504-581-6222

Shreveport
401 Edwards St., Suite 135
Shreveport, LA 71101
318-222-7575

Maryland

Baltimore
502 S. Sharp St., Suite 1200
Baltimore, MD 21201
410-347-3990

Massachusetts

Marlborough
290 Donald Lynch Blvd., Suite 102
Marlborough, MA 01752
508-652-4800

Worcester
340 Main St., Suite 802
Worcester, MA 01608
508-755-2548

Michigan

Grand Rapids
40 Pearl St., NW, Suite 354
Grand Rapids, MI 49503
616-774-8236

Detroit
26777 Central Park Blvd., Suite 100
Southfield, MI 48076-4163
248-223-9400

Minnesota

St. Paul
2706 Gannon Rd.
St. Paul, MN 55116-2600
651-699-1111

Mississippi

Ridgeland
601 Renaissance Way, Suite A
Ridgeland, MS 39157
601-707-0960

Missouri

Kansas City
8080 Ward Parkway, Suite 401
Kansas City, MO 64114
816-421-7800

Springfield
430 S. Glenstone Ave., Suite A
Springfield, MO 65802
417-862-4222

St. Louis
211 N. Broadway, Suite 2060
St. Louis, MO 63102
314-645-3300

Nebraska

Lincoln
3633 O St., Suite 1
Lincoln, NE 68510
402-436-2345

Omaha
11811 P St.
Omaha, NE 68137
402-391-7612

Nevada

Las Vegas
6040 S. Jones Blvd.
Las Vegas, NV 89118
702-320-4500

Sparks
4834 Sparks Blvd., Suite 102
Sparks, NV 89436
775-322-0657

New Hampshire

Concord
48 Pleasant St.
Concord, NH 03301
603-224-1991

New Jersey

Trenton
1700 Whitehorse-Hamilton
Square Rd., Suite D-5
Trenton, NJ 08690-3596
609-588-0808

New Mexico

Albuquerque
2625 Pennsylvania St., NE
Suite 2050
Albuquerque, NM 87110-3658
505-346-0110

Farmington
308 N. Locke Ave.
Farmington, NM 87401-5855
505-326-6501

New York

Amherst
100 Bryant Woods South
Amherst, NY 14228
716-881-5222

Farmingdale
399 Conklin St., Suite 300
Farmingdale, NY 11735
516-420-0500

New York
257 Park Ave. S, 4th Floor
New York, NY 10016
212-533-6200

Rochester
55 St. Paul St.
Rochester, NY 14604
716-881-5222

Tarrytown
150 White Plains Rd., Suite 107
Tarrytown, NY 10591-5521
914-333-0550

North Carolina

Asheville
112 Executive Park
Asheville, NC 28801
828-253-2392

Charlotte
13860 Ballantyne Corporate Place
Suite 225
Charlotte, NC 28277
704-927-8611

Greensboro
3608 W. Friendly Ave.
Greensboro, NC 27410-4895
336-852-4240

Raleigh
5540 Munford Rd., Suite 130
Raleigh, NC 27612-2655
919-277-4222

Winston-Salem
500 W. 5th St., Suite 202
Winston-Salem, NC 27101-2728
336-725-8348

Ohio

Akron
222 W. Market St.
Akron, OH 44303
330-253-4590

Canton
1434 Cleveland Ave., NW
Canton, OH 44703
330-454-9401

Cincinnati
Seven W. 7th St., Suite 1600
Cincinnati, OH 45202
513-421-3015

Cleveland
2800 Euclid Ave., 4th Floor
Cleveland, OH 44115
216-241-7678

Columbus
1169 Dublin Rd.
Columbus, OH 43215-1005
614-486-6336

Dayton
15 W. Fourth St., Suite 300
Dayton, OH 45402-1830
Toll free: 1-800-776-5301
937-222-5825

Lima
219 N. McDonel St.
Lima, OH 45801
419-223-7010

Toledo
Integrity Place
7668 King's Pointe Rd.
Toledo, OH 43617
419-531-3116

Youngstown
International Towers
25 Market St.
Youngstown, OH 44501
Toll free: 1-866-887-9222
330-744-3111

Oklahoma

Oklahoma City
17 S. Dewey St.
Oklahoma City, OK 73102-2400
405-239-6081

Tulsa
1722 S. Carson Ave., Suite 3200
Tulsa, OK 74119
918-492-1266

Oregon

Lake Oswego
4004 S.W. Kruse Way Pl., Suite 375
Lake Oswego, OR 97035
503-212-3022

Pennsylvania

Bethlehem
50 W. North St.
Bethlehem, PA 18018-3907
610-866-8780

Harrisburg
1337 N. Front St.
Harrisburg, PA 17102
717-364-3250

Scranton/Wilkes-Barre
4099 Birney Ave.
Moosic, PA 18507
570-342-5100

Philadelphia
1880 John F. Kennedy Blvd.
Suite 1330
Philadelphia, PA 19103
215-985-9313

Pittsburgh
400 Holiday Dr., Suite 220
Pittsburgh, PA 15220
412-456-2700

Puerto Rico

San Juan
530 Avenida De La Constitución,
#206
San Juan, PR 00901
787-289-8710

South Carolina

Columbia
1515 Burnette Dr.
Columbia, SC 29210
803-254-2525

Conway
1121 3rd Ave.
Conway, SC 29526
843-488-2227

Greenville
408 N. Church St., Suite C
Greenville, SC 29601-2164
864-242-5052

South Dakota

Sioux Falls
300 N. Phillips Ave., #202
Sioux Falls, SD 57104
605-271-2066

Tennessee

Chattanooga
1010 Market St., Suite 200
Chattanooga, TN 37402
423-266-6144

Clarksville
214 Main St.
Clarksville, TN 37040
931-503-2222

Columbia
502 N. Garden St., Suite 201
Columbia, TN 38401
931-388-9222

Cookeville
18 N. Jefferson St.
Cookeville, TN 38501
931-520-0008

Franklin
367 Riverside Dr., Suite 110
Franklin, TN 37064
615-250-7431

Knoxville
255 N. Peters Rd., Suite A
Knoxville, TN 37923
865-692-1600

Memphis
3693 Tyndale Dr.
Memphis, TN 38125
901-759-1300

Murfreesboro
530 Uptown Square
Murfreesboro, TN 37129
615-242-4222

Nashville
201 4th Ave. N., Suite 100
Nashville, TN 37219
615-242-4222

Texas

Abilene
3300 S. 14th St., Suite 307
Abilene, TX 79605-5052
325-691-1533

Amarillo
720 S. Tyler St., Suite B112
Amarillo, TX 79101
806-379-6222

Austin
1005 La Posada Dr.
Austin, TX 78752
512-445-2911

Beaumont
550 Fannin St., Suite 100
Beaumont, TX 77701-2011
409-835-5348

College Station
418 Tarrow St.
College Station, TX 77840-1822
979-260-2222

Corpus Christi
719 S. Shoreline, Suite 304
Corpus Christi, TX 78401
361-852-4949

Dallas
1601 Elm St., Suite 3838
Dallas, TX 75201-3093
214-220-2000

El Paso
720 Arizona Ave.
El Paso, TX 79902
915-577-0191

Fort Worth
101 Summit Ave., Suite 707
Fort Worth, TX 76102-5978
817-332-7585

Harker Heights
445 E. Central Texas Expressway
Suite 1
Harker Heights, TX 76548
254-699-0694

Houston
1333 W. Loop South, Suite 1200
Houston, TX 77027
713-868-9500

Longview
2401 Judson Rd., #102
Longview, TX 75605
903-758-3222

Lubbock
3333 66th St.
Lubbock, TX 79413-5711
806-763-0459

Midland
10100 Liberator Ln.
Midland, TX 79711
432-563-1880

San Angelo
3134 Executive Dr., Suite A
San Angelo, TX 76904
325-949-2989

San Antonio
1800 Northeast Loop 410
Suite 400
San Antonio, TX 78217-5296
210-828-9441

Tyler
3600 Old Bullard Rd.
Building 1, Suite 101
Tyler, TX 75701
903-581-5704

Weslaco
502 E. Expressway 83, Suite C
Weslaco, TX 78596
956-968-3678

Wichita Falls
4245 Kemp Blvd., Suite 900
Wichita Falls, TX 76308-2830
940-691-1172

Utah

Salt Lake City
5673 S. Redwood Rd., Suite 22
Salt Lake City, UT 84123-5322
801-892-6009

Virginia

Norfolk
586 Virginian Dr.
Norfolk, VA 23505
757-531-1300

Richmond
720 Moorefield Park Dr., Suite 300
Richmond, VA 23236
804-648-0016

Roanoke
31 W. Campbell Ave.
Roanoke, VA 24011
540-342-3455

Washington

DuPont
1000 Station Dr., Suite 222
DuPont, WA 98327
206-431-2222

Spokane
152 S. Jefferson, Suite 200
Spokane, WA 99201
509-455-4200

West Virginia

Charleston
1018 Kanawha Blvd. E, Suite 301
Charleston, WV 25301
304-345-7502

Wisconsin

Milwaukee
10101 W. Greeenfield Ave.
Suite 125
West Allis, WI 53214
414-847-6000

A

A&W Restaurants, Inc.
See: YUM! Brands, Inc.
Toll free: 1-866-456-2929
www.awrestaurants.com

AAMCO Transmissions, Inc.
Consumer Affairs
201 Gibraltar Rd.
Horsham, PA 19044
610-668-2900 ext. 224
Toll free: 1-800-523-0401
Toll free: 1-800-292-8500 ext. 224
www.aamco.com

Abbott Nutrition Products Division
Consumer Relations
625 Cleveland Ave.
Columbus, OH 43215-1754
Toll free: 1-800-227-5767
www.abbottnutrition.com

Abercrombie & Fitch
Customer Service
720 5th Ave., 8th Floor
New York, NY 10019
614-219-5380
✉: abercrombie@abercrombie.com
www.abercrombie.com

Accor North America
PO Box 326
Worthington, OH 43085
Toll free: 1-800-557-3435
www.accor-na.com

Adidas USA
Customer Service
5055 N. Greeley Ave.
Portland, OR 97217
Toll free: 1-800-448-1796
✉: consumer.relations@adidas.com
www.adidas.com

Adobe Systems, Inc.
345 Park Ave.
San Jose, CA 95110-2704
408-536-6000
Toll free: 1-800-833-6687
(Customer and Technical
Support)
www.adobe.com

Aetna, Inc.
151 Farmington Ave.
Hartford, CT 06156
860-273-0123
www.aetna.com

Contacting Corporate Consumer Affairs Departments

The following directory lists the addresses and phone numbers for hundreds of corporations. Many companies have a consumer affairs department that handles consumer questions and concerns. Consumer affairs offices are set up within companies because they want to hear from you. If you do not find the company you are looking for, try checking your public libraries for the following resources:

*   *The Standard & Poor's Register of Corporations, Directors and Executives*
*   *Trade Names Directory*
*   *Standard Directory of Advertisers*
*   *Dun & Bradstreet Directory*

To identify the name of a company that manufactures a specific product, check the product label and other documents given to you at the time of your purchase. *The Thomas Register of American Manufacturers*, another resource available at many public libraries, might also be helpful. It lists the manufacturers of thousands of products.

If you have a complaint about an item or service, it is usually best to go back to the seller BEFORE you contact the companies in this directory. Follow up with a letter, phone call, or e-mail message to the consumer affairs department of the company to let it know about your complaint and whether the seller was able to resolve your problem.

Aflac
1932 Wynnton Rd.
Columbus, GA 31999
Toll free: 1-800-992-3522
www.aflac.com

AirTran Airways
Customer Relations
1800 Phoenix Blvd., Suite 104
Atlanta, GA 30349
Toll free: 1-866-247-2428
Toll free: 1-800-965-2107 ext. 8900
(Baggage)
www.airtran.com

Alamo Rent A Car
Customer Service
600 Corporate Park Dr.
Saint Louis, MO 63105
Toll free: 1-800-445-5664
TTY: 1-800-522-9292
www.alamo.com

Alaska Airlines
Customer Care
PO Box 24948-SEAGT
Seattle, WA 98124-0948
Toll free: 1-800-654-5669
Toll free: 1-877-815-8253 (Baggage)
TTY: 1-800-682-2221
www.alaskaair.com

Alberto Culver Company
Consumer Relations
2525 Armitage Ave.
Melrose Park, IL 60160
708-450-3000
Toll free: 1-800-333-0005
✉: actesting@alberto.com
(Testing Hair Products)
www.alberto.com

Albertson's
Customer Service
157 S. Howard St.
Spokane, WA 99201
208-395-6200
Toll free: 1-877-932-7948 (Customer Service)
www.albertsons.com

Alcon Laboratories, Inc.
Technical Consumer Affairs
6201 South Freeway, TC-24
Fort Worth, TX 76134-2099
Toll free: 1-800-862-5266
✉: consumeraffairs.ft.worth@alconlabs.com
www.alconlabs.com

Allied Van Lines, Inc.
Customer Service
700 Oakmont Ln.
Westmont, IL 60559
Toll free: 1-800-470-2851
(Customer Service)
✉: custsvc@alliedvan.com
www.allied.com

Allstate Insurance Company
PO Box 12055
1819 Electric Rd., SW
Roanoke, IL 24018
847-402-5000
Toll free: 1-800-255-7828 (Claims)
www.allstate.com

Amana Appliances
Customer Service
553 Benson Rd.
Benton Harbor, MI 49022
Toll free: 1-866-616-2664
www.amana.com

Amazon.com, Inc.
Customer Service
PO Box 81226
Seattle, WA 98108-1226
Toll free: 1-800-201-7575
www.amazon.com

AMC Entertainment, Inc.
PO Box 725489
Atlanta, GA 31139-9923
✉: CustomerService@
MovieTickets.com
www.amctheatres.com

American Airlines, Inc.
Customer Relations
PO Box 619612 Mail Drop 2400
Dallas/Fort Worth Airport, TX
75261-9612
817-967-2000
Toll free: 1-800-535-5225 (Baggage)
www.aa.com

**American Automobile
Association (AAA)** ○
Member Relations
1000 A A A Dr., Mail Space 61
Heathrow, FL 32746
407-444-8402
www.aaa.com

American Eagle Outfitters
Customer Service
150 Thorn Hill Dr.
Warrendale, PA 15086
Toll free: 1-888-232-4535
✉: custserv@ae.com
www.ae.com

**American Express
Company** ○ ◆
Customer Service
PO Box 981540
El Paso, TX 79998-1540
Toll free: 1-800-528-4800
Toll free: 1-877-297-4438 (Gift
Cards)
TTY: 1-800-221-9950
www.americanexpress.com

American Girl ○
PO Box 620497
Middleton, WI 53562-0497
Toll free: 1-800-360-1861
✉: im_cs@americangirl.com
www.americangirl.com

**American Greetings
Corporation**
Consumer Relations
One American Rd.
Cleveland, OH 44144
Toll free: 1-800-777-4891
(Consumer Products)
✉: consumer.relations@
amgreetings.com
www.americangreetings.com

American Tourister
See: Samsonite Corporation
Toll free: 1-800-765-2247
Toll free: 1-800-262-8282 (Warranty
and Repair)
✉: Questions@
AmericanTourister.com
www.americantourister.com

America Online, Inc.
Member Services
22000 AOL Way
Dulles, VA 20166
Toll free: 1-800-827-6364
www.aol.com

Amtrak
Customer Relations
60 Massachusetts Ave., NE
Washington, DC 20002
Toll free: 1-800-872-7245
TTY: 1-800-523-6590
www.amtrak.com

Amway Corporation
Customer Service - North
American Business Region
7575 Fulton St., E
Ada, MI 49355-0001
616-787-6000
Toll free: 1-800-253-6500
Toll free: 1-800-529-8772
(Personalized Health)
TTY: 1-800-548-3878
www.amway.com

Andersen Corporation ○
Window Care Call Center
100 4th Ave., N
Bayport, MN 55003-1096
Toll free: 1-888-888-7020 (Service)
www.andersenwindows.com

Angie's List
1030 E. Washington St.
Indianapolis, AK 46202
Toll free: 1-888-888-5478
www.angieslist.com

Anheuser-Busch, Inc.
Customer Relationship Group
One Busch Pl.
St. Louis, MO 63118
Toll free: 1-800-342-5283
www.anheuser-busch.com

Anthem
2015 Staples Mills Rd.
Richmond, VA 23230
804-354-7000
www.anthem.com

Applebee's
11201 Renner Blvd.
Lenexa, KS 66219
Toll free: 1-888-592-7753
www.applebees.com

Apple Computer, Inc.
One Infinite Loop
Cupertino, CA 95014
408-996-1010
Toll free: 1-800-676-2775 (Customer
Service)
Toll free: 1-800-275-2273 (Technical
Support)
www.apple.com

Arby's Restaurant Group, Inc.
1155 Perimeter Center W
12th Floor
Atlanta, GA 30338
678-514-4100
www.arbys.com

◆ *Provided financial support for the publication of the Consumer Action Handbook.*

Atlas World Group, Inc.
Customer Service
1212 Saint George Rd.
Evansville, IN 47711-2364
Toll free: 1-800-638-9797
www.atlasvanlines.com

AT&T, Inc.
Customer Relations
175 E. Houston St.
San Antonio, TX 78205
210-821-4105
Toll free: 1-800-464-7928 (Wireless
Customer Service)
www.att.com

Avis RentACar System, LLC
Customer Service
Tulsa, OK
Toll free: 1-800-352-7900
TTY: 1-800-331-2323
✉: custserv@avis.com
www.avis.com

Avon Products, Inc.
Customer Service
1345 Avenue of the Americas
New York, NY 10105
212-282-7000
Toll free: 1-800-367-2866
Toll free: 1-800-445-2866 (Product
Information)
www.avon.com

B

Bacardi USA, Inc. ⏎
Consumer Affairs
890 Mountain Ave., Suite 105
New Providence, NJ 07974
Toll free: 1-800-222-2734
www.bacardi.com

Bally Total Fitness Corporation
Member Services
PO Box 1090
Norwalk, CA 90651-1090
Toll free: 1-866-402-2559
www.ballyfitness.com

Banana Republic
Customer Services
5900 N. Meadows Dr.
Grove City, OH 43123
Toll free: 1-888-277-8953
TTY: 1-888-906-1345
✉: custserv@bananarepublic.com
www.bananarepublic.com

Bank of America Corporation
Toll free: 1-800-432-1000
TTY: 1-800-288-4408
www.bankofamerica.com

Barnes & Noble
Toll free: 1-800-843-2665
www.bn.com

Baskin-Robbins
Toll free: 1-800-859-5339
✉: support@baskinrobbins.com
www.baskinrobbins.com

Bassett Baby Furniture
3525 Fairystone Park Highway
PO Box 626
Bassett, VA 24055
Toll free: 1-877-308-7485
www.bassettfurniture.com

Bayer HealthCare, LLC ⏎
Consumer Care
36 Columbia Rd.
PO Box 1910
Morristown, NJ 07962-1910
Toll free: 1-800-331-4536
www.consumercare.bayer.com

Becton, Dickinson and Company ⏎
Customer Service
One Becton Dr., Mail Code 376
Franklin Lakes, NJ 07417
201-847-6800
Toll free: 1-888-237-2762
www.bd.com

Beech-Nut Nutrition Corporation
Consumer Affairs
100 Hero Dr.
Amsterdam, NY 12010
314-436-7667
Toll free: 1-800-233-2468
✉: beech-nut@beech-nut.com
www.beechnut.com

Beiersdorf, Inc. ⏎
Consumer Relations
Wilton Corporate Center
187 Danbury Rd.
Wilton, CT 06897
Toll free: 1-800-227-4703
www.beiersdorf.us

Bellisio Foods, Inc.
Consumer Affairs
PO Box 16630
Duluth, MN 55816
✉: info@bellisiofoods.com
www.bellisiofoods.com

Ben & Jerrys Homemade, Inc.
Consumer Services
30 Community Dr.
South Burlington, VT 05403-6828
802-846-1500
www.benjerry.com

Benihana, Inc.
Customer Relations Manager
8685 N.W. 53rd Terrace
Miami, FL 33166
Toll free: 1-800-327-3369
✉: CustomerService@benihana.com
www.benihana.com

Best Buy Company, Inc.
Customer Care
7601 Penn Ave. S
Richfield, MN 55440
612-291-1000
Toll free: 1-888-237-8289
www.bestbuy.com

Best Western International, Inc.
Customer Service
PO Box 10203
Phoenix, AZ 85064
Toll free: 1-800-528-1238
TTY: 1-800-528-2222
✉: customerservice@bestwestern.com
www.bestwestern.com

BIC Corporation ⏎
Consumer Affairs
One BIC Way, Suite 1
Shelton, CT 06484-6299
Toll free: 1-800-546-1111
www.bicworld.com

Big Lot Stores, Inc.
Customer Service
300 Phillipi Rd.
Columbus, OH 43228-5311
Toll free: 1-800-877-1253
✉: talk2us@biglots.com
www.biglots.com

Birds Eye Foods, Inc.
See: Pinnacle Foods Group, LLC
www.birdseyefoods.com

Bissell Homecare, Inc. ⟲
Customer Service
PO Box 3606
Grand Rapids, MI 49501
Toll free: 1-800-237-7691
www.bissell.com

BJ's Wholesale Club, Inc.
Member Care
25 Research Dr.
Westborough, MA 01581
Toll free: 1-800-257-2582
www.bjs.com

Black & Decker, Inc. ⟲
Customer Service
101 Schilling Rd.
Hunt Valley, MD 21031
410-716-3900
Toll free: 1-800-544-6986
www.blackanddecker.com

Blockbuster Entertainment Corporation
Customer Care
3000 Redbud Blvd.
McKinney, TX 75270
Toll free: 1-866-692-2789
(Blockbuster Online)
Toll free: 1-800-406-6843 (In-Store)
✉: online.consumerrelations@
blockbuster.com
www.blockbuster.com

Bloomingdale's, Inc.
Customer Service
PO Box 8215
Mason, OH 45040
Toll free: 1-888-529-2254
www.bloomingdales.com

Bob Evans Farms, Inc.
Consumer Relations
3776 S. High St.
Columbus, OH 43207
Toll free: 1-800-939-2338
www.bobevans.com

Bojangles Restaurants, Inc.
Customer Relations
9432 Southern Pine Blvd.
Charlotte, NC 28273
Toll free: 1-888-300-4265
www.bojangles.com

BP Corporation
Consumer Relations
28301 Ferry Rd.
Warrenville, IL 60555
Toll free: 1-800-333-3991
✉: bpconsum@bp.com
www.bp.com

The Breathe Right Company
Toll free: 1-800-858-6673
www.breatheright.com

Bridgestone Retail Operations, LLC ⟲ ◆
Consumer Affairs
PO Box 6397
Bloomingdale, IL 60108
Toll free: 1-800-367-3872
**www.
firestonecompleteautocare.com**

Brinker International
6820 LBJ Freeway
Dallas, TX 75240
972-980-9917
www.brinker.com

Brio Tuscan Grill
Guest Feedback
777 Goodale Blvd.
Suite 100
Columbus, OH 43212
Toll free: 1-888-452-7286
www.brioitalian.com

Bristol-Myers Squibb Company
Customer Relations
345 Park Ave.
New York, NY 10154
Toll free: 1-800-321-1335
✉: drug.information@bms.com
www.bms.com

British Airways
Customer Relations
PO Box 300686
Jamaica, NY 11430-0686
Toll free: 1-800-247-9297
Toll free: 1-800-828-8144 (Baggage Claims)
Toll free: 1-800-403-0882 (Online Support)
TTY: 1-866-393-0961
www.britishairways.com

Brown-Forman Beverages Worldwide
Consumer Support
3310 West End Ave., Suite 600
Nashville, TN 37203
502-585-1100
Toll free: 1-800-753-4567
www.brown-forman.com

Brown Shoe Company, Inc.
Consumer Care
8300 Maryland Ave.
St. Louis, MO 63105
314-854-4000
Toll free: 1-800-766-6465
✉: info@brownshoe.com
www.brownshoe.com

Buca di Beppo
1300 Nicollet Mall, Suite 5003
Minneapolis, MN 55403
Toll free: 1-866-328-2822
✉: famiglia@bucainc.com
www.bucadibeppo.com

Budget Rent A Car System, Inc.
Customer Service
Six Sylvan Way
Parsippany, NJ 07054
Toll free: 1-800-214-6094
TTY: 1-800-826-5510
www.budget.com

Bulova Corporation
Customer Relations
One Bulova Ave.
Woodside, NY 11377
Toll free: 1-800-228-5682
✉: service@bulova.com
www.bulova.com

Burger King Corporation
Consumer Relations Department
5505 Blue Lagoon Dr.
Miami, FL 33126
305-378-3535 (Consumer Relations)
www.bk.com

Burlington Coat Factory Direct Corporation
1830 Route 130 N
Burlington, NJ 08016
609-387-7800
Toll free: 1-888-223-2628
www.burlingtoncoatfactory.com

Bush Brothers Company 🌀
Consumer Relations
PO Box 52330
Knoxville, TN 37950-2330
Toll free: 1-800-590-3797
✉: letters@bushbros.com
www.bushbeans.com

C

Calvin Klein
See: Phillips-Van Heusen
Corporation
212-719-2600
Toll free: 1-866-214-6694
www.calvinklein.com

Campbell Soup Company 🌀
Consumer Affairs
One Campbell Pl.
Camden, NJ 08103-1701
Toll free: 1-800-257-8443
www.campbellsoup.com

Canon USA, Inc.
One Canon Plaza
Lake Success, NY 11042-1198
Toll free: 1-800-652-2666
TTY: 1-866-251-3752
www.usa.canon.com

Capital One
General Correspondence
PO Box 30285
Salt Lake City, UT 84130-0285
1-800-955-7070
TTY: 1-800-206-7986
✉: webinfo@capitalone.com
www.capitalone.com

Captain D's Seafood
1717 Elm Hill Pike, Suite A-1
Nashville, TN 37210
Toll free: 1-800-314-4819
www.captainds.com

Carfax, Inc.
Consumer Affairs
5860 Trinity Parkway, Suite 600
Centerville, VA 20120
703-218-0340
✉: carfaxwebsupport@carfax.com
www.carfax.com/help

Carnival Cruise Lines 🌀
Guest Relations
3655 N.W. 87th Ave.
Miami, FL 33178-2428
Toll free: 1-888-227-6482
✉: guestcare@carnival.com
www.carnival.com

Carrier Air Conditioning Company
Customer Relations
PO Box 4808,
Carrier Parkway
Syracuse, NY 13221-4808
Toll free: 1-800-227-7437
www.residential.carrier.com

Carvel Corporation
Retail Stores/Food Service
301 Congress Ave., Suite 1100
Austin, TX 78701
Toll free: 1-800-322-4848
www.carvel.com

Casio, Inc.
570 Mt. Pleasant Ave.
Dover, NJ 07801
973-361-5400
Toll free: 1-800-706-2534 (Repairs)
Toll free: 1-800-435-7732
(Technical Support)
✉: memberservices@casio.com
www.casio.com

Casual Male Retail Group
Customer Service
555 Turnpike St.
Canton, MA 02021
Toll free: 1-800-767-0319
✉: info@casualmale.com
www.cmrginc.com

Chanel, Inc.
Consumer Relations
Nine W. 57th St., 44th Floor
New York, NY 10019
212-688-5055
Toll free: 1-800-550-0005
✉: consumerrelations@
chanelusa.com
www.chanel.com

Chase Bank (J.P. Morgan Chase Bank)
PO Box 36520
Louisville, KY 40233-6520
212-270-6000 (Corporate)
Toll free: 1-800-935-9935
(Checking and Savings)
TTY: 1-800-242-7383
www.chase.com

Chattem, Inc. 🌀
Consumer Affairs
PO Box 22219
Chattanooga, TN 37409
Toll free: 1-888-442-4464
www.chattem.com

Check 'n Go
7755 Montgomery Rd., Suite 400
Cincinnati, OH 45236
Toll free: 1-888-372-9329
✉: comments@checkngo.com
www.checkngo.com

The Cheesecake Factory 🌀
26901 Malibu Hills Rd.
Calabasas Hills, CA 91301
818-871-3000
www.thecheesecakefactory.com

Chevron Corporation
Consumer Connection Center
PO Box 4000
Bellaire, TX 77402-4000
www.chevron.com

Chick-fil-A, Inc.
Customer Feedback
PO Box 500367
Atlanta, GA 31150
404-765-8000
Toll free: 1-866-232-2040
www.chick-fil-a.com

Children's Place 🌀
Customer Service
500 Plaza Dr.
Secaucus, NJ 07094
Toll free: 1-877-752-2387
www.childrensplace.com

Chili's Grill and Bar
See: Brinker International
Toll free: 1-800-983-4637 (Guest Relations)
www.chilis.com

Chipotle Mexican Grill, Inc.
1401 Wynkoop St., Suite 500
Denver, CO 80202
303-595-4000
www.chipotle.com

Choice Hotels 🌀
Guest Relations
6811 E. Mayo Blvd., Suite 100
Phoenix, AZ 85054
Toll free: 1-800-300-8800
www.choicehotels.com

Church & Dwight Company, Inc. 🌀
Consumer and Professional Relations
469 North Harrison St.
Princeton, NJ 08543-5297
609-683-5900
Toll free: 1-800-524-1328
www.churchdwight.com

Citigroup, Inc.
Client Services
100 Citibank Dr.
San Antonio, TX 78245-9004
Toll free: 1-800-627-3999 (Banking)
Toll free: 1-800-950-5114 (Credit
cards)
TTY: 1-800-788-0002
www.citibank.com

The Clorox Company ⟲
Consumer Services
Mail Stop 2334
1221 Broadway
Oakland, CA 94612-1888
510-271-7000
Toll free: 1-800-835-4523 (GLAD)
Toll free: 1-800-227-1860
(Household Cleaners)
Toll free: 1-800-292-2200 (Laundry
Brands)
Toll free: 1-800-426-6228
(Insecticides)
www.thecloroxcompany.com

The Coca-Cola Company ⟲
Industry and Consumer Affairs
PO Box 1734
Atlanta, GA 30301
404-676-2121
Toll free: 1-800-438-2653
www.thecocacolacompany.com

**Coldwell Banker Real Estate
Corporation**
Customer Service
One Campus Dr.
Parsippany, NJ 07054
Toll free: 1-877-373-3829
www.coldwellbanker.com

**The Colgate-Palmolive
Company** ⟲ ◆
Consumer Affairs
300 Park Ave.
New York, NY 10022
Toll free: 1-800-468-6502
✉: colgate-palmolive_consumer_
affairs@colpal.com
www.colgate.com

Colonial Penn Life Insurance
Customer Service
399 Market St.
Philadelphia, PA 19181
Toll free: 1-877-877-8052
www.colonialpenn.com

Combe, Inc. ⟲
Consumer Resources
1101 Westchester Ave.
White Plains, NY 10604-3597
Toll free: 1-800-431-2610
www.combe.com

Comcast Corporation
One Comcast Center
Philadelphia, PA 19103
Toll free: 1-800-266-2278
www.comcast.com

ConAgra Foods ⟲
Consumer Affairs
One ConAgra Dr.
Omaha, NE 68102
Toll free: 1-800-722-1344
✉: consumeraffairs@
conagrafoods.com
www.conagrafoods.com

Conair Cuisinart Corporation
Consumer Affairs
150 Milford Rd.
East Windsor, NJ 08520
203-351-9000
Toll free: 1-800-326-6247 (Personal
Care)
Toll free: 1-800-334-4031 (Oral Care)
Toll free: 1-800-726-0190
✉: feedback@conair.com
www.conair.com

Continental Airlines, Inc.
Customer Care -NH CCR
900 Grand Plaza Dr.
Houston, TX 77067-4323
Toll free: 1-800-932-2732
Toll free: 1-800-335-2247 (Baggage)
TTY: 1-800-343-9195
✉: custo@coair.com
www.continental.com

Costco Wholesale Corporation
Member Service
PO Box 34331
Seattle, WA 98124
Toll free: 1-800-774-2678
Toll free: 1-800-955-2292 (Online
Members)
www.costco.com

Coty Inc. ⟲
Consumer Affairs
118 American Rd.
Morris Plains, NJ 07950
Toll free: 1-800-715-4023
Toll free: 1-800-953-5080 (Sally
Hansen, N.Y.C., and LaCross
brands)
Toll free: 1-800-954-5080 (Borghese
brand)
www.coty.com

Cox Communications
1550 W. Deer Valley Rd.
Phoenix, AZ 85027
www.cox.com

craigslist, Inc.
989 Market St.,
Suite 200
San Francisco, CA 94103
415-278-0404
✉: info@craigslistfoundation.org
www.craigslist.org

Crayola, LLC ⟲
Consumer Affairs
PO Box 431
Easton, PA 18044-0431
Toll free: 1-800-272-9652
www.crayola.com

Cricket Wireless
10307 Pacific Center
San Diego, CA 92121
Toll free: 1-800-274-2538
www.mycricket.com

Crowne Plaza
See: InterContinental Hotels
Group PLC
Toll free: 1-800-465-2680
www.crowneplaza.com

Curves International
100 Ritchie Rd.
Waco, TX 76712
Toll free: 1-800-848-1096
www.curves.com

CVS Caremark Corporation
Customer Relations Department
One CVS Dr.
Woonsocket, RI 02895
401-765-1500
Toll free: 1-800-746-7287
✉: customercare@cvs.com
www.cvs.com

◆ *Provided financial support for the publication of the Consumer Action Handbook.*

D

Dairy Queen Corporation
Customer Relations
7505 Metro Blvd.
Minneapolis, MN 55439
952-830-0200
www.dairyqueen.com

The Dannon Company, Inc.
Consumer Response Center
PO Box 90296
Allentown, PA 18109-0296
Toll free: 1-877-326-6668
www.dannon.com

Darden Restaurants
PO Box 695011
Orlando, FL 32859-5011
407-245-4000
✉: dardeninfo@darden.com
www.darden.com

Days Inns Worldwide, Inc.
See: Wyndham Hotel Group
Toll free: 1-800-441-1618
www.daysinn.com

Dean DeLuca
Customer Care
4115 E. Harry St.
Wichita, KS 67218
316-821-3200
Toll free: 1-800-221-7714
✉: customercare@deandeluca.com
www.deandeluca.com

Dell, Inc.
Customer Service
One Dell Way
Round Rock, TX 78682
Toll free: 1-800-624-9897
(Customer Service)
Toll free: 1-866-243-9297
(Technical Support)
TTY: 1-877-335-5889
www.dell.com

Del Laboratories, Inc.
Consumer Relations
410 American Rd.
Morris Plains, NJ 07950
Toll free: 1-800-953-5080
www.dellabs.com

Del Monte Foods Company
Consumer Affairs
PO Box 80
Pittsburgh, PA 15230-0080
415-247-3000
Toll free: 1-800-543-3090
www.delmonte.com

Delta Air Lines, Inc.
Customer Care
PO Box 20980
Department 980
Atlanta, GA 30320-2980
404-773-0305
Toll free: 1-800-325-8224
(Baggage)
www.delta.com

Delta Faucets Company
55 E. 111th St.
Indianapolis, IN 46280
317-848-1812
Toll free: 1-800-345-3358
✉: customerservice@
deltafaucet.com
www.deltafaucet.com

Denny's Corporation
Call Center
203 E. Main St. P-8-6
Spartanburg, SC 29319
Toll free: 1-800-733-6697
(Customer Service)
www.dennys.com

The Dial Corporation
19001 N. Scottsdale Rd.
Scottsdale, AZ 85254-1619
480-754-3425
Toll free: 1-800-258-3425
www.dialsoap.com

Diamond Foods, Inc.
Consumer Affairs
1050 S. Diamond St.
Stockton, CA 95205-7087
209-467-6000
www.diamondfoods.com

Dick's Sporting Goods
345 Court St.
Caraopolis, PA 15108
Toll free: 1-877-846-9997
✉: customersupport@
dickssportinggoods.com
www.dickssportinggoods.com

Dillard's, Inc.
Customer Service Department
PO Box 486
Little Rock, AR 72203
501-376-5200
Toll free: 1-800-345-5273
TTY: 1-800-444-1732
✉: questions@dillards.com
www.dillards.com

Diners Club International
Customer Service
PO Box 6500
Sioux Falls, SD 57117
702-797-5532
Toll free: 1-800-234-6377
www.dinersclubus.com

DIRECTV Enterprises, Inc.
PO Box 6550
Greenwood Village, CO 80155-6550
Toll free: 1-800-531-5000
TTY: 1-800-779-4388
www.directv.com

Discover Financial Services, Inc.
Card Customer Service
PO Box 30943
Salt Lake City, UT 84130-0943
224-405-0900 (Headquarters)
801-902-3100
Toll free: 1-800-347-2683
TTY: 1-800-347-7449
www.discoverfinancial.com

Dish Network
Toll free: 1-888-333-3474
✉: feedback@customermail.
dishnetwork.com
www.dishnetwork.com

Dole Food Company, Inc.
Consumer Center
PO Box 5700
Thousand Oaks, CA 91359-5700
Toll free: 1-800-356-3111
✉: Dole.Consumer.Center@dole.
com
www.dole.com

Dollar Rent A Car, Inc.
Customer Service 2W2
PO Box 33167
Tulsa, OK 74153-1167
918-669-3000
Toll free: 1-800-800-5252
(Customer Service)
✉: rhelpdesk@dollar.com
www.dollar.com

Domino's Pizza, Inc.
Customer Service
30 Frank Lloyd Wright Dr.
PO Box 997
Ann Arbor, MI 48106
734-930-3030
Toll free: 1-888-366-4667
www.dominos.com

DoubleTree
See: Hilton Hospitality, Inc.
Toll free: 1-800-222-8733
www.doubletree.com

Dr. Pepper/Snapple Group, Inc.
Consumer Relations
PO Box 869077
Plano, TX 75086-9077
972-673-7000
Toll free: 1-800-696-5891
www.drpeppersnapplegroup.com

DSW
Customer Service
810 DSW Dr.
Columbus, OH 43219
Toll free: 1-866-379-7463
www.dsw.com

Dunkin Donuts
Consumer Care
130 Royall St.
Canton, MA 02021
Toll free: 1-800-859-5339
www.dunkindonuts.com

DuPont Company
Corporate Information Center
Chestnut Run Plaza 705/GS38
PO Box 80705
Wilmington, DE 19880-0705
Toll free: 1-800-441-7515
✉: info@dupont.com
www.dupont.com

Duracell North America
Consumer Relations
Berkshire Corporate Park
Bethel, OH 06801
Toll free: 1-800-551-2355
www.duracell.com

E

E. & J. Gallo Winery
Consumer Relations
3840 Kilroy Airport Way
Long Beach, CA 90806
Toll free: 1-877-687-9463
✉: consumerrelations@ejgallo.com
www.gallo.com

Eagle Family Foods
Consumer Response
One Strawberry Ln.
Orrville, OH 44667
Toll free: 1-888-656-3245
www.eaglebrand.com

Eastman Kodak Company
Kodak Information Center/
Consumer Contact Center
343 State St.
Rochester, NY 14650
Toll free: 1-800-235-6325 (Digital Cameras, Printer Docks, Photo Printers)
Toll free: 1-800-242-2424
www.kodak.com

e-Bay, Inc.
2065 Hamilton Ave.
San Jose, CA 95125
Toll free: 1-800-322-9266
www.eBay.com

Eddie Bauer, Inc.
Customer Satisfaction Center
PO Box 7001
Groveport, OH 43125
Toll free: 1-800-426-8020
TTY: 1-800-462-6757
✉: CustomerCare@csc.eddiebauer.com
www.eddiebauer.com

eHarmony
Customer Care
PO Box 3640
Pasadena, CA 90408
www.eharmony.com

The Electrolux Group
Consumer Assistance Center
250 Bobby Jones Expressway
Martinez, GA 30907
Toll free: 1-877-435-3287
www.electrolux.com

Eli Lilly Company
Consumer Communications
Lilly Corporate Center
Indianapolis, IN 46285
317-276-2000
Toll free: 1-800-545-5979
www.lilly.com

Elizabeth Arden, Inc.
Consumer Affairs
309 South St.
New Providence, NJ 07974
Toll free: 1-800-217-2927
✉: consumer@elizabetharden.com
www.elizabetharden.com

Embassy Suites
See: Hilton Hospitality, Inc.
Toll free: 1-800-362-2779
www.embassysuites.com

Enterprise Rent-A-Car
600 Corporate Park Dr.
Saint Louis, MO 63105-4211
Toll free: 1-800-264-6350
✉: customerservice@enterprise.com
www.enterprise.com

Equifax
Office of Consumer Affairs
PO Box 740241
Atlanta, GA 30374
Toll free: 1-800-685-1111
www.equifax.com

The Estee Lauder Companies, Inc.
Consumer Communications
767 5th Ave.
New York, NY 10153
212-572-4200
Toll free: 1-888-311-3883
✉: asampogn@estee.com
www.elcompanies.com

Ethan Allen, Inc.
PO Box 1966
Danbury, CT 06813
Toll free: 1-888-324-3571
✉: orders@ethanallen.com
www.ethanallen.com

The Eureka Company
Consumer Service Department
PO Box 3900
Peoria, IL 61701
Toll free: 1-800-282-2886
www.eureka.com

Expedia, Inc.
Customer Support
333 108th Ave., NE
Bellevue, WA 98004
Toll free: 1-800-397-3342
✉: travel@customercare.expedia.com
www.expedia.com

Experian
National Consumer Assistance Center
PO Box 2104
Allen, TX 75013
Toll free: 1-888-397-3742
www.experian.com

ExxonMobil
Customer Relations
PO Box 1049
Buffalo, NY 14240-1049
Toll free: 1-800-243-9966
www.exxonmobil.com

◆ *Provided financial support for the publication of the Consumer Action Handbook.*

F

Facebook, Inc.
1601 S. California Ave.
Palo Alto, CA 94304
650-543-4800
✉: info@facebook.com
www.facebook.com

Fairfield Inn
See: Marriott International, Inc.
Toll free: 1-800-721-7033
www.fairfieldinn.com

Farmers Insurance
4680 Wilshire Blvd.
Los Angeles, CA 90010
Toll free: 1-800-435-7764
TTY: 1-888-891-1660
www.farmers.com

FedEx Corporation
Customer Relations
3875 Airways Blvd.
Module H3 Department 4634
Memphis, TN 38116
Toll free: 1-800-463-3339
www.fedex.com

**Fingerhut Direct
Marketing, Inc.**
Customer Service
6250 Ridgewood Rd.
St. Cloud, MN 56303
Toll free: 1-800-208-2500
✉: customerservice@fingerhut.
com
www.fingerhut.com

Fisher-Price
Consumer Affairs
636 Girard Ave.
East Aurora, NY 14052
716-687-3000
Toll free: 1-800-432-5437
TTY: 1-800-382-7470
✉: fpconaff@fisher-price.com
www.fisher-price.com

Florsheim, Inc.
Customer Service
333 W. Estabrook Blvd.
Glendale, WI 53212
Toll free: 1-866-454-0449
✉: us.consumers@florsheim.com
www.florsheim.com

Flowers Foods, Inc.
1919 Flowers Circle
Thomasville, GA 31757
229-226-9110
www.flowersfoods.com

Food Lion, Inc.
Customer Relations
PO Box 1330
Salisbury, NC 28145-1330
Toll free: 1-800-210-9569
www.FoodLion.com

Forever 21, Inc.
Customer Service
2001 S. Alameda St.
Los Angeles, CA 90058
213-741-5100
Toll free: 1-888-494-3837
www.forever21.com

Fortune Brands
Corporate Affairs Department
520 Lake Cook Rd.
Deerfield, IL 60015
847-484-4400
✉: mail@fortunebrands.com
www.fortunebrands.com

Frigidaire Home Products
PO Box 212378
Martinez, GA 30917
Toll free: 1-800-374-4432
www.frigidaire.com

Frito-Lay
Consumer Affairs
PO Box 660634
Dallas, TX 75266-6234
972-334-7000
Toll free: 1-800-352-4477
www.fritolay.com

Frontier Airlines, Inc.
Customer Relations
7001 Tower Rd.
Denver, CO 80249-7312
Toll free: 1-800-432-1359
www.frontierairlines.com

FTD, Inc.
Customer Service
3113 Woodcreek Dr.
Downers Grove, IL 60515
630-719-7756
Toll free: 1-800-736-3383
www.ftd.com

Fuji Photo Film USA, Inc.
Consumer Information Service
Center
1100 King George Post
Edison, NJ 08837
Toll free: 1-800-800-3854
www.fujifilm.com

G

Gap, Inc.
Customer Relations
100 Gap Online Dr.
Grove City, OH 43123-8605
Toll free: 1-800-427-7895
TTY: 1-888-906-1104
✉: custserv@gap.com
www.gap.com

Gateway, Inc.
Customer Service
PO Box 6137
Temple, TX 76503
www.gateway.com

GEICO
One GEICO Plaza
Washington, DC 20076
Toll free: 1-877-418-1312 (Car)
Toll free: 1-888-395-1200 (Home)
Toll free: 1-888-532-5433 (Life)
TTY: 1-800-833-8255
www.geico.com

General Electric Company
3135 Easton Turnpike
Fairfield, CT 06828
203-373-2211
Toll free: 1-800-626-2005
www.ge.com

General Mills, Inc.
Consumer Services
PO Box 9452
Minneapolis, MN 55440
Toll free: 1-800-248-7310
www.generalmills.com

Georgia-Pacific Corporation
Consumer Affairs
133 Peachtree St. NE
Atlanta, GA 30303
Toll free: 1-800-283-5547
(Consumer Products)
www.gp.com

Gerber Products Company
Consumer Affairs
445 State St.
Fremont, MI 49413-0001
Toll free: 1-800-284-9488
www.gerber.com

Giant Food, Inc.
8301 Professional Pl., Suite 115
Landover, MD 20785
Toll free: 1-888-469-4426
www.giantfood.com

GlaxoSmithKline Consumer Healthcare
Consumer Information
PO Box 13398
Five Moore Dr.
Research Triangle Park, NC 27709
412-200-4000
Toll free: 1-888-825-5249 (Customer Response Center)
✉: consumer.communications@gsk.com
www.gsk.com

The Golden Grain Company
PO Box 049003
Chicago, IL 60604-9003
Toll free: 1-800-421-2444
www.ricearoni.com

Gold's Gym International
Customer Care Department
125 E. John Carpenter Freeway
Suite 1300
Irving, TX 75062
214-574-4653
Toll free: 1-866-465-3775
www.goldsgym.com

Goodrich Corporation
Consumer Relations Department
PO Box 19001
Greenville, SC 29602-9001
Toll free: 1-877-788-8899
www.bfgoodrichtires.com

The Goodyear Tire & Rubber Company
Department 728
1144 E. Market St.
Akron, OH 44316-0001
330-769-2121
Toll free: 1-800-321-2136
✉: consumer_relations@goodyear.com
www.goodyear.com

Google.com
1600 Amphitheatre Parkway
Mountain View, CA 94043
650-253-0000
www.google.com

Graco Children's Products, Inc.
Consumer Services
150 Oaklands Blvd.
Exton, PA 19341
Toll free: 1-800-345-4109
www.gracobaby.com

Greyhound Lines, Inc.
PO Box 660362
Dallas, TX 75266-0362
214-849-8000
214-849-6246 (Baggage)
Toll free: 1-800-231-2222 (Fares/Schedules)
TTY: 1-800-345-3109
www.greyhound.com

Guess? Inc.
Customer Service
1444 S. Alameda St.
Los Angeles, CA 90021
213-765-3100
Toll free: 1-877-444-8377
www.guess.com

Guinness Company
801 Main Ave.
Norwalk, CT 06851
203-229-2100
Toll free: 1-800-521-1591
✉: guinness@consumer-care.net
www.guinness.com

H

H & R Block, Inc.
Customer Support
One H & R Block Way
Kansas City, MO 64105
www.hrblock.com

Hallmark Cards, Inc.
Consumer Affairs
PO Box 419034
Mail Drop #216
Kansas City, MO 64141
Toll free: 1-800-425-5627
www.hallmark.com

Hampton Inn &Suites
See: Hilton Hospitality, Inc.
Toll free: 1-800-426-7866
www.hamptoninn.com

Hanes Hosiery
Consumer Relations
PO Box 3013
Winston-Salem, NC 27102
Toll free: 1-800-225-4872
www.haneshosiery.com

Harry & David
Customer Service
2500 South Pacific Highway
Medford, OR 97501-2675
541-864-2121
Toll free: 1-877-322-1200
✉: service@harryanddavid.com
www.harryanddavid.com

Hartz Mountain Corporation
Consumer Affairs
400 Plaza Dr.
Secaucus, NJ 07094
Toll free: 1-800-275-1414
www.hartz.com

Hasbro, Inc.
Consumer Affairs
PO Box 200
Dept. C-847
Pawtucket, RI 02862-0200
401-727-6899
Toll free: 1-800-255-5516
✉: customersupport@hasbro.com
www.hasbro.com

Heinz North America
Consumer Resource Center/Consumer Affairs
PO Box 57
Pittsburgh, PA 15230
Toll free: 1-800-255-5750
www.heinz.com

Hershey Food Corporation
Consumer Relations
100 Crystal A Dr.
Hershey, PA 17033
Toll free: 1-800-468-1714
www.hersheys.com

Hertz Corporation
Customer Relations
PO Box 26120
Oklahoma City, OK 73126
Toll free: 1-800-654-4173
TTY: 1-800-654-2280
www.hertz.com

Hewlett-Packard Company
3000 Hanover St.
Bldg. 6A Mail Stop 1247
Palo Alto, CA 94304
650-857-1501
Toll free: 1-800-474-6836
www.hp.com

Hilton Garden Inn
See: Hilton Hospitality, Inc.
Toll free: 1-877-782-9444
www.hiltongardeninn.com

◆ *Provided financial support for the publication of the Consumer Action Handbook.*

Hilton Hospitality, Inc.
Guest Assistance
755 Crossover Ln.
Memphis, TN 38117
901-374-6476
Toll free: 1-800-445-8667
www.hilton.com

Holiday Inn/Holiday Inn Express
See: InterContinental Hotels
Group PLC
Toll free: 1-800-465-4329
www.holiday-inn.com

Home Depot USA, Inc.
Customer Care
2455 Paces Ferry Rd.
Atlanta, GA 30339-4024
770-433-8211
Toll free: 1-800-466-3337
Toll free: 1-800-430-3376 (Website Questions)
✉: customercare@homedepot.com
www.homedepot.com

HomeGoods
See: TJX Companies, Inc.
Toll free: 1-800-888-0776
www.homegoods.com

Home Shopping Network
Customer Service
PO Box 9090
Clearwater, FL 33758
Toll free: 1-800-284-3900 (Phone Orders)
Toll free: 1-800-933-2887 (Online Orders)
TTY: 1-800-753-5353
www.hsn.com

Homewood Suites
See: Hilton Hospitality, Inc.
Toll free: 1-800-225-5466
www.homewoodsuites.com

Hoover Company
TTI Floor Care North America
7005 Cochran Rd.
Glenwillow, OH 44139
Toll free: 1-800-944-9200
www.hoover.com

Hormel Foods Company ⌕
Consumer Affairs
One Hormel Pl.
Austin, MN 55912
Toll free: 1-800-523-4635
www.hormel.com

Howard Johnson, Inc.
1910 8th Ave., NE
Aberdeen, SD 57402-4090
Toll free: 1-800-544-9881
www.hojo.com

Humana, Inc.
PO Box 14601
Lexington, KY 40512-4601
502-580-1000
Toll free: 1-800-448-6262
www.humana.com

Hyatt Hotels & Resorts ⌕
Consumer Affairs
9805 Q St.
Omaha, NE 68127
402-592-6465
Toll free: 1-800-323-7249
www.hyatt.com

I

IBM Corporation
One New Orchard Rd.
Armonk, NY 10504-1722
914-499-1900
Toll free: 1-800-426-4968
(Customer Service)
TTY: 1-800-426-3383
✉: askibm@vnet.ibm.com
www.ibm.com

Ikea
Customer Relations
420 Alan Wood Rd.
Conshohocken, PA 19428
Toll free: 1-800-434-4532
www.ikea.com

Intel
Consumer Relations
2200 Mission College Blvd.
Santa Clara, CA 95054
916-377-7000
916-356-8080 (Headquarters)
www.intel.com

InterContinental Hotels Group PLC
Guest Relations
PO Box 30321
Salt Lake City, UT 84130-321
Toll free: 1-800 621-0555
www.ihgplc.com

J

Jack in the Box, Inc.
Guest Relations
9330 Balboa Ave.
San Diego, CA 92123-1516
858-571-2121
Toll free: 1-800-955-5225
www.jackinthebox.com

Jackson Hewitt Tax Service, Inc.
Three Sylvan Way, Suite 301
Parsippany, NJ 07054
Toll free: 1-800-234-1040
www.jacksonhewitt.com

JanSport, Inc.
2011 Farallon Dr.
San Leandro, CA 94577
501-614-4000
Toll free: 1-800-558-3600
✉: consumer_relations@vfc.com
www.jansport.com

Janssen Pharmaceuticals, Inc.
PO Box 200
Titusville, NJ 08560
Toll free: 1-800-526-7736
www.janssenpharmaceuticalsinc.com

Jarden Consumer Solutions, Inc. ⌕
Consumer Affairs
2381 Executive Center Dr.
Boca Raton, FL 34331
Toll free: 1-800-458-8407
www.sunbeam.com

JCPenney Company, Inc.
Corporate Customer Relations
PO Box 10001
Dallas, TX 75301-7311
972-431-1000
Toll free: 1-800-222-6161
www.jcpenney.com

J. Crew
Customer Relations
One Ivy Crescent
Lynchburg, VA 24513-1001
Toll free: 1-800-562-0258
✉: contactus@jcrew.com
www.jcrew.com

Jenny Craig, Inc.
Customer Care
5770 Fleet St.
Carlsbad, CA 92008
Toll free: 1-800-597-5366
✉: WebCustomerService@
jennycraig.com
www.jennycraig.com

JetBlue Airways Corporation
Customer Relations
PO Box 17435
Salt Lake City, UT 84117-7435
Toll free: 1-800-538-2583
TTY: 1-800-336-5530
✉: promise@jetblue.com
www.jetblue.com

Jiffy Lube International, Inc.
Customer Service
PO Box 4427
Houston, TX 77210-4458
713-546-4100
Toll free: 1-800-344-6933
www.jiffylube.com

**John Hancock Financial
Services, Inc.**
601 Congress Street
Boston, MA 02210-2805
617-572-6000
Toll free: 1-800-732-5543
TTY: 1-800-832-5282
www.johnhancock.com

**Johnson & Johnson Consumer
Products, Inc.** ⟳
PO Box 726
Langhorne, PA 19047-0726
732-524-0400
Toll free: 1-800-526-3967
www.jnj.com

Just Born, Inc ⟳
Consumer Relations
1300 Stefko Blvd.
Bethlehem, PA 18017
610-867-7568
Toll free: 1-888-645-3453
(Consumer Relations)
✉: consumerrelations@justborn.
com
www.justborn.com

JVC Company of America ⟳
Customer Care
3600 Formosa Ave.
Building N
McAllen, TX 78503
973-317-5000
Toll free: 1-800-252-5722
✉: customerrelations@jvc.com
www.jvcservice.com

K

Kao Brands Company
Consumer Relations Dept.
2535 Spring Grove Ave.
Cincinnati, OH 45214
www.kaobrands.com

**Kawasaki Motor Corporation,
USA**
Consumer Services
PO Box 25252
Santa Ana, CA 92799-5252
949-460-5688
www.kawasaki.com

Kayak
55 N. Water St., Suite 1
Norwalk, CT 06854
www.kayak.com

Kellogg Company ⟳ ◆
Consumer Affairs
PO Box CAMB
Battle Creek, MI 49016
269-961-2000 (Corporate)
Toll free: 1-800-962-1413
www.kelloggcompany.com

KFC
PO Box 725489
Atlanta, GA 31139
Toll free: 1-800-225-5532
www.kfc.com

Kimberly-Clark Corporation ⟳
Consumer Services
Dept. INT
PO Box 2020
Neenah, WI 54957-2020
Toll free: 1-888-525-8388
www.kimberly-clark.com

The Kirby Company
Customer Relations
1920 W. 114th St.
Cleveland, OH 44102
Toll free: 1-800-494-8586
✉: consumer@kirbywhq.com
www.kirby.com

KitchenAid
Customer Satisfaction Center
553 Benson Rd.
Benton Harbor, MI 49022
269-923-5000
Toll free: 1-800-422-1230 (Large
Appliances)
Toll free: 1-800-541-6390 (Small
Appliances)
www.kitchenaid.com

Kmart Corporation
Customer Service
847-286-2500
Toll free: 1-866-562-7848
✉: help@customerservice.kmart.com
www.kmart.com

Kohler Company
444 Highland Dr.
Kohler, WI 53044
Toll free: 1-800-456-4537
www.kohler.com

Kohl's Corporation ⟳
Customer Service
N56 W 17000 Ridgewood Dr.
Menomonee Falls, WI 53051
262-703-7000
Toll free: 1-866-887-8884
Toll free: 1-800-564-5740 (Credit)
✉: customer.service@kohls.com
www.kohls.com

Kona Grill, Inc.
7150 E. Camelback Rd., #220
Scottsdale, AZ 85251
480-922-8100
www.konagrill.com

Kraft Foods, Inc. ⟳
Consumer Relations
One Kraft Court
Glenview, IL 60025
Toll free: 1-800-535-5666
www.kraftfoods.com

Kroger Company
1014 Vine St.
Cincinnati, OH 45202-1100
Toll free: 1-800-576-4377
www.kroger.com

L

LA Fitness International, LLC
Member Services
PO Box 54170
Irvine, CA 92619-1300
949-255-7200
www.lafitness.com

Land O'Lakes, Inc. ⟳
Consumer Affairs
PO Box 64050
St. Paul, MN 55164-9784
Toll free: 1-800-328-4155
(Consumer Affairs)
www.landolakes.com

◆ *Provided financial support for the publication of the Consumer Action Handbook.*

Lands End, Inc.
Customer Service
1 Lands End Ln.
Dodgeville, WI 53595
Toll free: 1-800-963-4816
TTY: 1-800-541-3459
www.landsend.com

Lane Bryant
777 S. State Rd. 7
Margate, FL 33068
Toll free: 1-866-886-4731
www.lanebryant.com

Lane Furniture
Consumer Services
PO Box 1627
Highway 145 South
Tupelo, MS 38802
Toll free: 1-877-405-3745
✉: service@lanefurniture.com
www.lanefurniture.com

La-Z-Boy, Inc.
Consumer Services
1284 N. Telegraph Rd.
Monroe, MI 48162-3309
Toll free: 1-800-375-6890
✉: cservice@la-z-boy.com
www.la-z-boy.com

LeapFrog Enterprises, Inc.
Customer Support
6401 Hollis St., Suite 100
Emeryville, CA 94608-1071
Toll free: 1-800-701-5327
✉: support@leapfrog.com
www.leapfrog.com

Leap Wireless International, Inc.
Cricket Communications, LLC
5887 Copley Dr.
San Diego, CA 92111
858-882-6000
Toll free: 1-800-274-2538
www.leapwireless.com

Lee Jeans
Consumer Services
9001 W. 67th St.
Merriam, KS 66202
Toll free: 1-800-453-3348
www.lee.com

L'eggs Products
Consumer Relations
1000 E. Hanes Mill Rd.
Winston-Salem, NC 27105
Toll free: 1-800-925-3447
www.leggs.com

LEGO Systems, Inc
Consumer Affairs
555 Taylor Rd.
PO Box 1138
Enfield, CT 06083-1138
Toll free: 1-800-838-9647
Toll free: 1-877-518-5346((Shop at Home)
www.lego.com

Lennox Industries, Inc. ⟳
Consumer Affairs
PO Box 799900
Dallas, TX 75379
Toll free: 1-800-953-6669
www.lennox.com

LensCrafters
4000 Luxottica Pl.
Mason, OH 45040
513-765-6000
Toll free: 1-877-753-6727
www.lenscrafters.com

Levi Strauss & Company ⟳
1155 Battery St.
San Francisco, CA 94111
415-501-6000
Toll free: 1-866-860-8907
✉: customerservice@levisstore.com
www.levi.com

Lexmark International, Inc.
740 W. New Circle Rd.
Lexington, KY 40550
Toll free: 1-800-539-6275
www.lexmark.com

LG Electronics, Inc ⟳
Customer Service
PO Box 240007
201 James Record Rd.
Huntsville, AL 35813
256-772-8860
Toll free: 1-800-243-0000 (Appliances)
Toll free: 1-800-793-8896 (Phones)
www.lge.com

Liberty Mutual Insurance Group ⟳
Customer Service
100 Liberty Way
Dover, NH 03820
Toll free: 1-800-398-8924
✉: Liberty.Service@libertymutual.com
www.libertymutual.com

Lillian Vernon Corporation
Customer Service
100 Lillian Vernon Dr.
Virginia Beach, VA 23479-0002
Toll free: 1-800-901-9291
TTY: 303-682-7999
✉: custservice@lillianvernon.com
www.lillianvernon.com

Limited Brands, Inc.
Customer Service
Three Limited Parkway
Columbus, OH 43230
614-415-7000
Toll free: 1-800-945-5088
www.limitedbrands.com

LinkedIn Corporation
2029 Stierlin Ct.
Mountain View, CA 94043
www.linkedin.com

Little Tikes Company
Consumer Services
2180 Barlow Rd.
Hudson, OH 44236
Toll free: 1-800-321-0183
✉: littletikes.cares@littletikescare.com
www.littletikes.com

L.L. Bean, Inc.
15 Casco St.
Freeport, ME 04033-0001
207-552-3028
Toll free: 1-800-441-5713
TTY: 1-800-545-0090
www.llbean.com

Loehmann's
Customer Service
2500 Halsey St.
Bronx, NY 10461
1-800-366-5634
www.loehmanns.com

Longhorn Steakhouse
See: Darden Restaurants
407-245-4000
www.longhornsteakhouse.com

Long John Silver's Restaurants, Inc.
1900 Colonel Sanders Ln.
Louisville, KY 40213
www.ljsilvers.com

L'Oreal USA
575 Fifth Ave.
New York, NY 10017
212-818-1500 (Headquarters)
Toll free: 1-800-322-2036
www.lorealusa.com

Lowe's Companies, Inc.
Customer Care
PO Box 1111
North Wilkesboro, NC 28656
Toll free: 1-800-445-6937
✉: customercare@lowes.com
www.lowes.com

M

MAACO Franchising, Inc.
610 Freedom Business Center
Suite 200
King of Prussia, PA 19406
610-265-6606
Toll free: 1-800-523-1180
www.maaco.com

Macy's
Customer Service
PO Box 8113
Mason, OH 45040
Toll free: 1-800-526-1202 (Customer Service)
Toll free: 1-877-493-9207 (Credit)
www.macys.com

Magic Chef
Customer Service
777 Mark St.
Wood Dale, IL 49022
Toll free: 1-888-775-0202
www.magicchef.com

Magnavox
See: Philips Consumer Electronics
North America
Toll free: 1-800-705-2000
www.magnavox.com

Marriott International, Inc.
Guest Relations
1818 N. 90th St.
Omaha, NE 68114-1315
Toll free: 1-800-535-4028
✉: customer.care@marriott.com
www.marriott.com

Mars Chocolate North America
800 High St.
Hackettstown, NJ 07840
908-852-1000
✉: askus@masterfoodsusa.com
www.masterfoods.com

Marshalls, Inc.
See: TJX Companies, Inc.
Toll free: 1-888-627-7425
www.marshallsonline.com

Massachusetts Mutual Insurance Company (Mass Mutual)
Customer Relations
1295 State St.
Springfield, MA 01111-0001
Toll free: 1-800-272-2216 (Life Insurance)
Toll free: 1-800-505-8952 (Long Term Insurance)
www.massmutual.com

MasterCard Worldwide
Consumer Inquiries
(Contact your issuing bank first)
2000 Purchase St.
Purchase, NY 10577
Toll free: 1-800-307-7309
✉: Consumer_Inquiries@mastercard.com
www.mastercard.com

Match.com, LLC
PO Box 25472
Dallas, TX 75225
www.match.com

Mattel, Inc.
Worldwide Consumer Affairs
333 Continental Blvd.
El Segundo, CA 90245-5012
310-252-2000
Toll free: 1-800-524-8697
TTY: 1-800-382-7470
www.mattel.com

Maybelline, Inc.
Consumer Affairs
PO Box 1010
Clark, NJ 07066
Toll free: 1-800-944-0730
www.maybelline.com

Mayflower Transit, LLC
One Mayflower Dr.
St. Louis, MO 63026
636-305-4000
Toll free: 1-800-241-1321
Toll free: 1-800-325-9970 (Claims)
www.mayflower.com

Maytag
Customer Service
553 Benson Rd.
Benton Harbor, MI 49022
Toll free: 1-800-344-1274
www.maytag.com

McCormick & Schmicks Seafood Restaurants
720 S.W. Washington St., Suite 550
Portland, OR 97205
503-226-3440
www.mccormickandschmicks.com

McCormick & Company, Inc.
Consumer Affairs
211 Schilling Circle
Hunt Valley, MD 21031
410-527-6000
Toll free: 1-800-632-5847
www.mccormick.com

McDonalds Corporation
Customer Satisfaction Department
2111 McDonalds Dr
Oak Brook, IL 60523
Toll free: 1-800-244-6227
www.mcdonalds.com

McKee Foods Corporation
PO Box 750
Collegedale, TN 37315
Toll free: 1-800-522-4499
www.mckeefoods.com

Medco Health Solutions, Inc.
Public Affairs
100 Parsons Pond Dr.
Franklin Lakes, NJ 07417
201-269-3400
Toll free: 1-800-631-7780
www.medco.com

Meineke Car Care Centers, Inc.
Customer Relations Department
PO Box 32401
128 S. Tryon St., Suite 900
Charlotte, NC 28232-2401
704-377-3070
Toll free: 1-800-447-3070
www.meineke.com

Mellon Financial Corporation
BNY Mellon Center
Pittsburgh, PA 15258
412-234-5000
www.mellon.com

The Mentholatum Company, Inc.
Consumer Affairs
707 Sterling Dr.
Orchard Park, NY 14127
716-677-2500
Toll free: 1-800-688-9046
www.mentholatum.com

◆ *Provided financial support for the publication of the Consumer Action Handbook.*

Merck & Co., Inc.
Consumer Relations
One Merck Dr.
Whitehouse Station, NJ 08889
www.merck.com

Merrill Lynch Company, Inc.
(Contact local branch manager first)
250 Vesey St.
New York, NY 10080
212-449-1000
Toll free: 1-800-637-7455
TTY: 1-800-657-3323
www.merrilllynch.com

MetLife, Inc.
200 Park Ave.
New York, NY 10166
Toll free: 1-800-638-5433
www.metlife.com

Michelinas
See: Bellisio Foods, Inc.
218-723-5555
✉: michelinas@bellisiofoods.com
www.michelinas.com

Michelin North America, Inc.
Consumer Relations Department
PO Box 19001
Greenville, SC 29650
Toll free: 1-866-866-6605
www.michelin-us.com

Microsoft Corporation
Customer Service
1 Microsoft Way
Redmond, WA 98052-6399
425-882-8080
Toll free: 1-800-642-7676
TTY: 1-800-892-5234
www.microsoft.com

Midas, Inc.
Consumer Relations
1300 Arlington Heights Rd.
Itasca, IL 60143
Toll free: 1-800-621-8545
www.midas.com

MillerCoors
Consumer Affairs
3939 W. Highland Blvd.
Milwaukee, WI 53208
Toll free: 1-800-645-5376
✉: contact@millercoors.com
www.millercoors.com

Milton Bradley
See: Hasbro, Inc.
Toll free: 1-888-836-7025
✉: customersupport@hasbro.com
www.hasbro.com/miltonbradley

Mitsubishi Digital Electronics America, Inc.
Consumer Relations Department
9351 Jeronimo Rd.
Irvine, CA 92618
Toll free: 1-800-332-2119
✉: mdeaservice@mdea.com
www.mitsubishi-tv.com

Money Management International
14141 Southwest Freeway
Suite 1000
Sugar Land, TX 77478-3494
Toll free: 1-866-889-9347
www.moneymanagement.org

Morgan Stanley
Client Advocate
1585 Broadway
New York, NY 10036
212-761-4000
Toll free: 1-800-869-3326
✉: clientadvocate@morganstanley.com
www.morganstanley.com

Motel 6
Guest Relations
PO Box 326
Worthington, OH 43085
614-601-4089
Toll free: 1-800-557-3435
www.motel6.com

Motorola Mobility, Inc.
Corporate Communications
600 N. U.S. Highway 45
Libertyville, IL 60048
847-523-5000
Toll free: 1-800-331-6456
TTY: 847-538-7116
www.motorola.com

Motts, Inc.
Consumer Relations
PO Box 869077
Plano, TX 75086-9077
Toll free: 1-800-426-4891
www.motts.com

Mozilla Firefox ◆
650 Castro St., Suite 300
Mountain View, CA 94041-2021
www.mozilla.org

Movado Group, Inc.
650 From Rd., Suite 375
Paramus, NJ 07652-3556
201-267-8000
Toll free: 1-800-810-2311
www.movadogroupinc.com

Mutual of Omaha Insurance Company
Customer Service
Mutual of Omaha Plaza
Omaha, NE 68175
402-342-7600
Toll free: 1-800-228-7104
Toll free: 1-800-775-1000 (Claims)
✉: individualclaims@mutualofomaha.com
www.mutualofomaha.com

Myspace, LLC
8391 Beverly Blvd., #349
Los Angeles, CA 90048
310-969-7400
✉: info@myspace.com
www.myspace.com

N

Nabisco Foods Group
See: Kraft Foods, Inc.
Toll free: 1-800-622-4726
www.nabiscoworld.com

National Amusements, Inc.
PO Box 9126
Dedham, MA 02027-9126
781-461-1600
✉: customer_service@national-amusements.com
www.national-amusements.com

National Car Rental System, Inc.
Customer Services
8420 St. John Industrial Dr.
St. Louis, MO 63114
Toll free: 1-800-468-3334
TTY: 1-800-328-6323
www.nationalcar.com

Nationwide Mutual Insurance Company
Customer Relations
One Nationwide Plaza
Columbus, OH 43215?220
Toll free: 1-877-669-6877 (Auto and Property Insurance)
Toll free: 1-800-882-2822 (General Inquiries)
Toll free: 1-800.848-6331 (Investments)
www.nationwide.com

NaturaLawn of America
One E. Church St.
Fredrick, MD 21701
301-694-5440
Toll free: 1-800-989-5444
✉: natural@nl-amer.com
www.nl-amer.com

Nautica Enterprises, Inc.
Consumer Relations
40 West 57th St.
New York, NY 10019
Toll free: 1-866-376-4184
www.nautica.com

The Neiman-Marcus Group, Inc. ↻
Customer Relations
PO Box 650589
Dallas, TX 75265-0589
214-761-2660
Toll free: 1-888-888-4757
www.neimanmarcus.com

Nestlé Purina PetCare Company ↻
Office of Consumer Affairs
Checkerboard Square
St. Louis, MO 63164
314-982-1000
Toll free: 1-800-778-7462
www.purina.com

Nestlé USA ↻
Consumer Services Center
800 N. Brand Blvd.
Glendale, CA 91203
Toll free: 1-800-225-2270
www.nestle.com

Nestlé Waters North America, Inc.
900 Long Ridge Rd.
Building 2
Stamford, CT 06902-1138
203-531-4100
Toll free: 1-866-676-1672
www.nestle-watersna.com

Netflix Inc. ↻
Customer Service
100 Winchester Circle
Los Gatos, CA 95032
Toll free: 1-866-716-0414
www.netflix.com

Neutrogena Corporation
Consumer Affairs
199 Grandview Rd.
Skillman, NJ 08558
Toll free: 1-800-582-4048
✉: ntgweb@neuus.jnj.com
www.neutrogena.com

New England Financial
See: MetLife, Inc.
Toll free: 1-800-388-4000
www.nefn.com

Newport News
5100 City Line Rd.
Hampton, VA 23630-5100
Toll free: 1-800-759-3950
✉: customercare@newport-news.com
www.newport-news.com

Newsweek, Inc.
555 W. 18th St.
New York, NY 10011
Toll free: 1-800-631-1040
✉: newsweek@emailcustomerservice.com
www.newsweek.com

New York and Company
Customer Service
450 W. 33rd St.
Fifth Floor
New York, NY 10001
Toll free: 1-800-723-5333
www.nyandcompany.com

New York Life Insurance Company
Corporate Compliance
Department
One Rockwood Rd.
Sleepy Hollow, NY 10591
Toll free: 1-800-710-7945
www.newyorklife.com

Nexxus Products Company
Toll free: 1-800-444-6399
www.nexxus.com

Nickelodeon
1515 Broadway
New York, NY 10036
212-846-2543
www.nick.com

Nike, Inc. ↻
Consumer Services
PO Box 4027
One Bowerman Dr.
Beaverton, OR 97005
503-671-6453
Toll free: 1-800-344-6453
www.nike.com

Nikon, Inc.
Consumer Affairs
1300 Walt Whitman Rd.
Melville, NY 11747-3064
631-547-4200
310-414-8107 (Parts)
Toll free: 1-800-645-6687 (Technical and Service Repair)
www.nikonusa.com

Nine West Group, Inc.
Customer Relations
9 West Plaza
1129 Westchester Ave.
White Plains, NY 10604
914-640-6400
Toll free: 1-800-999-1877
www.ninewest.com

Nintendo
4820 150th Ave., NE
Redmond, WA 98052
Toll free: 1-800-255-3700
www.nintendo.com

Nokia USA
Customer Contact Center
6021 Connection Dr.
Irving, TX 75039
Toll free: 1-888-665-4228
TTY: 1-800-246-6542
✉: customercare@nokia.com
www.nokia.com

Nordstrom, Inc.
Customer Service
1700 7th Ave., Suite 300
Seattle, WA 98101
Toll free: 1-888-282-6060
www.nordstrom.com

Norelco Consumer Products Company
See: Philips Consumer Electronics
North America
Toll free: 1-800-243-3050
www.usa.philips.com

North American Van Lines
Claims Department
PO Box 988
Ft. Wayne, IN 46801-0988
Toll free: 1-800-348-2111
www.navl.com

◆ *Provided financial support for the publication of the Consumer Action Handbook.*

The North Face, Inc.
Customer Service
2013 Farallon Dr.
San Leandro, CA 94577
Toll free: 1-888-863-1968
Toll free: 1-855-500-8639
(Warranties)
✉: tnfsupport@vfc.com
www.thenorthface.com

**Northwestern Mutual Life
Insurance Company**
Corporate Relations
720 E. Wisconsin Ave.
Milwaukee, WI 53202-4797
414-271-1444
www.northwesternmutual.com

Norwegian Cruise Lines
Guest Relations
7665 Corporate Center Dr.
Miami, FL 33126
Toll free: 1-866-625-1164
Toll free: 1-866-584-9756 (Special Needs)
www.ncl.com

Novartis Pharmaceuticals Corporation ⟳
Customer Interaction Center
One Health Plaza
East Hanover, NJ 07936-1080
862-778-8300
Toll free: 1-888-669-6682
www.pharma.us.novartis.com

The NutraSweet Company
Customer Service
10 S. Wacker Dr.
Chicago, IL 60606
Toll free: 1-800-323-5321
www.nutrasweet.com

NutriSystem, Inc.
Customer Service
600 Office Center Dr.
Fort Washington, PA 19034
215-706-5300
Toll free: 1-800-585-5483
✉: feedback@nutrisystem.com.
www.nutrisystem.com

O

**Ocean Spray
Cranberries, Inc.** ⟳
Consumer Affairs Department
One Ocean Spray Dr.
Lakeville-Middleboro, MA 02349
Toll free: 1-800-662-3263
www.oceanspray.com

Office Depot, Inc.
PO Box 5009
Boca Raton, FL 33431-0809
Toll free: 1-800-463-3768
www.officedepot.com

OfficeMax, Inc.
Customer Service
263 Shuman Blvd.
Naperville, IL 60563
630-438-7800
Toll free: 1-800-283-7674
✉: online@officemax.com
www.officemax.com

Old Navy
Customer Relations
200 Old Navy Ln.
Grove City, OH 43123-8605
Toll free: 1-800-653-6289
TTY: 1-800-449-4253
✉: custserv@oldnavy.com
www.oldnavy.com

Olive Garden
See: Darden Restaurants
PO Box 695017
Orlando, FL 32869
Toll free: 1-800-331-2729
www.olivegarden.com

Olympus America
3500 Corporate Parkway
PO Box 610
Center Valley, PA 18034-0610
Toll free: 1-800-622-6372
Toll free: 1-888-553-4448 (Digital Cameras)
www.olympusamerica.com

Omni Hotels
Guest Relations
420 Decker Dr.
Irving, TX 75062
Toll free: 1-800-809-6664
www.omnihotels.com

1-800-FLOWERS
Customer Satisfaction Department
One Old Country Rd., Suite 500
Carle Place, NY 11514
Toll free: 1-800-356-9377
Toll free: 1-800-716-4851
(Customer Service)
www.1800flowers.com

On the Border
See: Brinker International
Toll free: 1-800-682-6882
www.ontheborder.com

Orbitz, Inc. ⟳
Customer Service
500 W. Madison St.
Chicago, IL 60661
Toll free: 1-888-656-4546
www.orbitz.com

Orkin
Customer Care Center
2170 Piedmont Rd., NE
Atlanta, GA 30324
Toll free: 1-888-675-4662
www.orkin.com

Oster
See: Jarden Consumer Solutions, Inc.
Toll free: 1-800-334-0759
www.oster.com

Outback Steakhouse
2202 N. West Shore Blvd.
Suite 500
Tampa, FL 33607-5761
813-282-1225
✉: newsoutback@outback.com
www.outback.com

Overstock.com, Inc.
Customer Service
6350 S. 3000 E
Salt Lake City, UT 84121
Toll free: 1-800-843-2446
www.overstock.com

Owens Corning
Consumer Relations
One Owens Corning Parkway
Toledo, OH 43659
Toll free: 1-800-438-7465
✉: answers@answers.owenscorning.com
www.owenscorning.com

P

Palm, Inc.
Customer Service
950 W. Maude Ave.
Sunnyvale, CA 94085
408-617-7000
Toll free: 1-877-426-3777
www.palm.com

Panasonic Company
Consumer Affairs
Panazip 2F-3
One Panasonic Way
Secaucus, NJ 07094
201-348-7000
Toll free: 1-800-211-7262
www.panasonic.com

Papa Johns International, Inc.
PO Box 99900
Louisville, KY 40269-9990
502-261-4987
Toll free: 1-877-547-7272
www.papajohns.com

Pathmark Stores, Inc.
Customer Relations
Two Paragon Dr.
Montvale, NJ 07645
Toll free: 1-866-443-7374
✉: customers@pathmark.com
www.pathmark.com

Payless ShoeSource, Inc.
Customer Service
3231 S.E. Sixth Ave.
Topeka, KS 66607
Toll free: 1-877-474-6379
✉: CustomerService@csr.
payless.com
www.payless.com

PayPal.com
2211 N. First St.
San Jose, CA 95131
402-935-2050
www.paypal.com

PearleVision
Customer Service
4000 Luxottica Pl.
Mason, OH 45040
Toll free: 1-800-937-3937
www.pearlevision.com

Pennzoil
See: Shell Oil Company
713-546-4000
Toll free: 1-800-237-8045
www.pennzoil.com

Pep Boys Auto
3111 W. Allegheny Ave.
Philadelphia, PA 19132
Toll free: 1-800-737-2697
✉: custserv@pepboys.com
www.pepboys.com

Pepperidge Farm, Inc.
Consumer Affairs
595 Westport Ave.
Norwalk, CT 06851
Toll free: 1-888-737-7374
www.pepperidgefarm.com

Pepsi-Cola Company
Public Affairs
700 Anderson Hill Rd.
Purchase, NY 10577
914-253-2000
Toll free: 1-800-433-2652
www.pepsico.com

Perdue Farms, Inc.
Consumer Relations
PO Box 1656
Horsham, PA 19044-6656
Toll free: 1-800-473-7383
www.perdue.com

Petco
Toll free: 1-877-738-6742
www.petco.com

PetSmart, Inc.
Customer Service
1435 International Dr.
Eau Claire, WI 54701
Toll free: 1-888-839-9638
✉: CustomerCare@petsmart.com
www.petsmart.com

P.F. Chang's China Bistro, Inc.
7676 E. Pinnacle Peak Rd.
Scottsdale, AZ 85255
Toll free: 1-866-732-4264
www.pfchangs.com

Pfizer, Inc.
Consumer Affairs
PO Box 2219
Chattanooga, TN 37409-0219
212-733-2323
Toll free: 1-800-879-3477
(Customer Response)
Toll free: 1-800-438-1985 (Medical
Questions)
www.pfizer.com

Pharmavite Corporation
Consumer Affairs
PO Box 9606
Mission Hills, CA 91346-9606
818-221-6200
Toll free: 1-800-276-2878 (Nature
Made)
Toll free: 1-888-676-9569 (Soy Joy)
www.pharmavite.com

Philip Morris USA
Quality Department
PO Box 18583
Pittsburgh, PA 15236
804-274-2000
Toll free: 1-800-343-0975
www.philipmorrisusa.com

**Philips Consumer Electronics
North America**
Customer Service
3000 Minuteman Rd., Mail Stop 109
Andover, MA 01810
Toll free: 1-888-744-5477
www.philips.com

**Phillips-Van Heusen
Corporation**
Customer Services
1001 Frontier Rd., Mail Stop 44
Bridgewater, NJ 08807
Toll free: 1-800-388-9122 (Van
Heusen)
Toll free: 1-800-950-2277 (Bass)
Toll free: 1-800-866-7292 (Izod)
Toll free: 1-866-214-6694 (Calvin
Klein)
www.pvh.com

Pinnacle Foods Group, LLC
PO Box 3900
Peoria, IL 61612
www.pinnaclefoodscorp.com

**Pioneer Electronics Service,
Inc.**
Customer Service
Toll free: 1-800-228-7221(Parts)
Toll free: 1-800-421-1404 (General
Service)
www.pioneerelectronics.com

Pirelli Tire Corporation
100 Pirelli Dr.
Rome, GA 30161
Toll free: 1-800-747-3554
www.us.pirelli.com

Pizza Hut
See: YUM! Brands, Inc.
14841 Dallas Parkway
Plano, TX 75054
972-338-7700
Toll free: 1-800-948-8488
www.pizzahut.com

Playskool
See: Hasbro, Inc.
Toll free: 1-800-752-9755
✉: customersupport@hasbro.com
www.hasbro.com/playskool

PlayStation
See: Sony Corporation of America
Toll free: 1-800-345-7669
www.us.playstation.com

Playtex Products, Inc.
Consumer Affairs
PO Box 537
Neenah, WI 54957
Toll free: 1-888-310-4290
www.playtexproductsinc.com

Polaroid Corporation
Customer Care Center
4400 Baker Ave.
Minnetonka, MN 55343
Toll free: 1-800-765-2764 (Product Support)
Toll free: 1-888-312-2615 (Order Support)
✉: info@polaroid.com
www.polaroid.com

Polo/Ralph Lauren Corporation
Consumer Relations
625 Madison Ave., 11th Floor
New York, NY 10022
Toll free: 1-888-475-7674
✉: customerassistance@ralphlauren.com
www.polo.com

Popeyes Louisiana Kitchen
AFC Enterprises, Inc.
Customer Relations
5555 Glenridge Connector, NE
Suite 300
Atlanta, GA 30342
404-459-4450
Toll free: 1-877-767-3937
✉: popeyescommunications@popeyes.com
www.popeyes.com

Prestige Brands
Office of Consumer Affairs
90 N. Broadway
Irvington, NY 10533
Toll free: 1-800-443-4908
www.prestigebrandsinc.com

Price Chopper Supermarkets
Consumer Services
461 Nott St.
Schenectady, NY 12308
518-355-5000
Toll free: 1-800-666-7667
www.pricechopper.com

Priceline.com, Inc.
800 Connecticut Ave.
Norwalk, CT 06854
Toll free: 1-800-774-2354
www.priceline.com

Princess Cruise Lines
24844 Avenue Rockefeller
Santa Clarita, CA 91355
Toll free: 1-800-774-6237
✉: customerrelations@princesscruises.com
www.princess.com

The Procter & Gamble Company ◆
Consumer Relations
PO Box 599
Cincinnati, OH 45201
513-983-1100
Toll free: (Toll free numbers appear on all labels)
www.pg.com

The Progressive Corporation
Customer Service
6300 Wilson Mills Rd.
Mayfield Village, OH 44143
440-461-5000 (Corporate)
Toll free: 1-800-776-4737
www.progressive.com

Prudential Financial, Inc.
Policyowner Relations Dept.
One Corporate Drive
Shelton, CT 06484
Toll free: 1-800-778-2255 (Insurance)
Toll free: 1-888-778-2888 (Annuities)
Toll free: 1-800-732-0416 (Long-Term Care)
TTY: 1-800-526-8061
www.prudential.com

Publishers Clearing House
Consumer Affairs
382 Channel Dr.
Port Washington, NY 11050
516-883-5432
Toll free: 1-800-459-4724
www.pch.com

Publix
Consumer Relations
PO Box 407
Lakeland, FL 33802-0407
1-800-242-1227
Toll free: 1-800-242-1227
www.publix.com

Q

Qdoba Mexican Grill
4865 Ward Rd., Suite 500
Wheat Ridge, CO 80033-1902
720-898-2300
Toll free: 1-888-497-3622
✉: info@qdoba.com
www.qdoba.com

The Quaker Oats Company
Consumer Response/QTG
PO Box 049003
Chicago, IL 60604-9003
312-821-1000
Toll free: 1-800-367-6287
www.quakeroats.com

QuikTrip Corporation
PO Box 3475
Tulsa, OK 74101
918-615-7700
Toll free: 1-800-848-1966
www.quiktrip.com

Quiznos
1001 17th St., Suite 200
Denver, CO 80202
720-359-3300 (Headquarters)
Toll free: 1-866-486-2783 (Customer Comments)
www.quiznos.com

QVC, Inc.
Customer Service
1200 Wilson Drive at Studio Park
West Chester, PA 19380
Toll free: 1-800-367-9444
TTY: 1-800-544-3316
✉: QVCcares@QVC.com
www.qvc.com

R

Radio Shack Corporation
Customer Care
Riverfront Campus, Mail Stop #CF4-216
300 Radio Shack Circle
Fort Worth, TX 76102-1964
817-415-3011
Toll free: 1-800-843-7422
✉: RadioShack.Customer.Care@RadioShack.com
www.radioshack.com

Radisson Hotels Resorts
11340 Blondo St., Suite 100
Omaha, NE 68164
Toll free: 1-800-615-7253
www.radisson.com

Ramada Inn
See: Wyndham Hotel Group
Toll free: 1-800-828-6644
www.ramada.com

Reckitt Benckiser, Inc.
Consumer Relations
PO Box 224
Parsippany, NJ 07054-0224
Toll free: 1-800-228-4722
✉: corpcomms@reckittbenckiser.com
www.reckittbenckiser.com

Red Lobster
Guest Relations
1000 Darden Center Dr.
Orlando, FL 32837
407-245-4000
Toll free: 1-800-562-7837
www.redlobster.com

Regal Ware, Inc.
Consumer Service
1675 Reigle Dr.
Kewaskum, WI 53040
262-626-2121
✉: info@regalware.com
www.regalware.com

Remington Products Company
Consumer Services
PO Box 1
DeForest, WI 53532
Toll free: 1-800-392-6544
✉: ContactUs@remingtonproducts.com
www.remington-products.com

Rent-A-Center
Customer Service
5501 Headquarters Dr.
Plano, TX 75024
Toll free: 1-800-422-8186
www.rentacenter.com

Residence Inn
See: Marriott International, Inc.
Toll free: 1-800-228-2800
www.residenceinn.com

Rich Products
Consumer Relations
PO Box 20670
127 Airport Rd.
St. Simons Island, GA 31522
912-638-5000
Toll free: 1-888-732-7251
✉: rsp-consumer.relations@rich.com
www.rich.com

Rite Aid Corporation
Customer Support
PO Box 3165
Harrisburg, PA 17105
717-761-2633
Toll free: 1-800-748-3243
Toll free: 1-888-213-9920 (Rebates)
TTY: 1-800-821-1833
www.riteaid.com

Rolex Watch USA, Inc.
665 5th Ave., 5th Floor
New York, NY 10022
212-758-7700
www.rolex.com

Roto-Rooter Corporation
225 E. 5th Street
Cincinnati, OH 45202
513-762-6690
Toll free: 1-800-438-7686
www.rotorooter.com

Royal Caribbean International
Corporate Guest Relations
1050 Caribbean Way
Miami, FL 33132
Toll free: 1-800-256-6649
Toll free: 1-800-398-9819 (Website)
www.royalcaribbean.com

Rubbermaid
Consumer Services
3320 W. Market St.
Fairlawn, OH 44333
Toll free: 1-888-895-2110
www.rubbermaid.com

Ruth's Chris Steakhouse
Ruth's Hospitality Group, Inc.
400 International Parkway, #325
Heathrow, FL 32746-5500
407-333-7440
www.ruthschris.com

S

Safeway, Inc.
Customer Service Center
MS 10501
PO Box 29093
Phoenix, AZ 85038-9093
Toll free: 1-877-723-3929
www.safeway.com

Saks Fifth Avenue
Customer Relations
PO Box 10327
Jackson, MS 39289
212-940-5027
Toll free: 1-877-551-7257
✉: service@saks.com
www.saks.com

Sam's Club
Member Service
608 S.E. Simple Savings Dr.
Bentonville, AR 72716-0745
Toll free: 1-888-746-7726
www.samsclub.com

Samsonite Corporation
Customer Service
575 West St., Suite 110
Mansfield, MA 02048
Toll free: 1-800-765-2247
Toll free: 1-800-262-8282 (Warranty)
✉: questions@samsonite.com
www.samsonite.com

Samsung Electronics America
Customer Service and Technical Support
85 Challenger Rd.
Ridgefield Park, NJ 07660
Toll free: 1-800-726-7864
Toll free: 1-888-987-4357 (Mobile Phones)
TTY: 1-888-899-7608
www.samsung.com

Sanofi-Aventis U.S., LLC
55 Corporate Dr.
Bridgewater, NJ 08807-2854
Toll free: 1-800-981-2491
www.sanofi.us

Sara Lee Foods
Consumer Affairs
PO Box 756
Neenah, WI 54957-0756
Toll free: 1-800-323-7117 (Bakery)
Toll free: 1-800-925-3326 (Meats)
Toll free: 1-800-392-7733 (Body Care)
www.saraleefoods.com

Sargento Foods Inc.
Consumer Affairs
One Persnickety Pl.
Plymouth, WI 53073
920-893-8484 (Corporate)
Toll free: 1-800-243-3737
www.sargento.com

Schering-Plough HealthCare Products, Inc.
See: Merck & Co., Inc.
www.merck.com

◆ Provided financial support for the publication of the Consumer Action Handbook.

Schering-Plough HealthCare Products, Inc.
Consumer Relations
One Merck Dr.
Whitehouse Station, NJ 08889
908-298-4000
Toll free: 1-800-317-2165
www.schering-plough.com

SC Johnson and Son, Inc.
1525 Howe St.
Racine, WI 53403
Toll free: 1-800-494-4855
www.scjohnsonwax.com

The Scotts Company
Help Center
14111 Scottslawn Rd.
Marysville, OH 43041
Toll free: 1-888-270-3714
www.scotts.com

Seabourn Cruise Line
Guest Relations
300 Elliott Ave., W
Seattle, WA 98119
206-626-9179
Toll free: 1-866-755-5619
✉: guestrelations@seabourn.com
www.seabourn.com

Sealy Corporation
Consumer Support
One Office Parkway at Sealy Dr.
Trinity, NC 27370
Toll free: 1-800-697-3259
www.sealy.com

Sears, Roebuck and Company
Sears National Customer Relations
3333 Beverly Rd.
Hoffman Estates, IL 60179
847-286-2500
Toll free: 1-800-549-4505 (Retail)
Toll free: 1-800-697-3277 (Online)
TTY: 1-800-659-7017
www.sears.com

Seneca Foods Corporation
Consumer Affairs
3736 S. Main St.
Marion, NY 14505
315-926-8100
Toll free: 1-800-872-1110
www.senecafoods.com

Serta, Inc.
Customer Service
Three Golf Center #392
Hoffman Estates, IL 60169
847-645-0200
Toll free: 1-888-557-3782
✉: customer.service@serta.com
www.serta.com

7-Eleven, Inc.
Customer Relations
Location 231
PO Box 711
Dallas, TX 75221-0711
Toll free: 1-800-255-0711
www.7-eleven.com

Sharp Electronics Corporation
Customer Service
Sharp Plaza
Mahwah, NJ 07495
Toll free: 1-800-237-4277
www.sharpusa.com

Shell Oil Company
Customer Care
PO Box 2463
Houston, TX 77252
713-241-6161 (Headquarters)
Toll free: 1-888-467-4355
Toll free: 1-800-331-3703 (Shell Card)
✉: ShellCustomerCare@shell.com
www.shellus.com

Sheraton Hotels
See: Starwood Hotels & Resorts Worldwide, Inc.
www.sheraton.com

Sherwin-Williams Company
Midland Building
101 Prospect Ave., NW
PO Box 647
Cleveland, OH 44115
216-515-4825
Toll free: 1-800-474-3794
www.sherwin-williams.com

Simmons Bedding Company
Consumer Service
One Concourse Parkway
Suite 800
Atlanta, GA 30328-6188
Toll free: 1-877-399-9397
www.simmons.com

Slim-Fast Foods Company
Consumer Services Department
920 Sylvan Ave.
Second Floor
Englewood Cliffs, NJ 07632
Toll free: 1-800-754-6327
✉: support@slimfast.com
www.slimfast.com

Sonesta International Hotels Corporation
116 Huntington Ave.
Boston, MA 02116
617-421-5447
Toll free: 1-800-766-3782
✉: info@sonesta.com
www.sonesta.com

Sony Corporation of America
Customer Service
Consumer Information Service Center
12451 Gateway Blvd.
Fort Myers, FL 33913
239-768-7547
Toll free: 1-866-456-7669
Toll free: 1-800-345-7669 (PlayStation)
www.sony.com

Southwest Airlines
Customer Relations Department
PO Box 36647-1CR
Dallas, TX 75235
214-932-0333
Toll free: 1-800-435-9792
TTY: 1-800-533-1305
www.southwest.com

Spiegel Brands, Inc.
Customer Satisfaction
One Spiegel Ave.
Hampton, VA 23630-5367
Toll free: 1-800-222-5680
✉: clientservices@spiegel.com
www.spiegel.com

Spirit Airlines
2800 Executive Way
Miramar, FL 33025
Toll free: 1-800-772-7117
✉: customer@spirit.com
www.spiritair.com

Springs Global, Inc.
Public Relations Department of Corporate Communication
PO Box 70
Fort Mill, SC 29716
Toll free: 1-888-926-7888
Toll free: 1-800-221-6352 (Window Products)
www.springs.com

Sprint Nextel
KSOPHT0101-Z4300
6391 Sprint Parkway
Overland Park, KS 66251-4300
Toll free: 1-888-211-4727 (Sprint Phones)
Toll free: 1-800-639-6111 (Nextel Phones)
Toll free: 1-800-877-4646 (Wireline Service)
www.sprint.com/consumerinfo

Stanley Hardware
Customer Service
480 Myrtle St.
New Britain, CT 06053
Toll free: 1-800-622-4393
www.stanleyhardware.com

Staples, Inc.
Consumer Affairs
500 Staples Dr.
Framingham, MA 01702
Toll free: 1-800-378-2753
www.staples.com

Starbucks
Customer Relations
PO Box 3717
Seattle, WA 98124-3717
Toll free: 1-800-782-7282
www.starbucks.com

Starwood Hotels & Resorts Worldwide, Inc.
Customer Service
PO Box 6020
Lancaster, CA 93539
914-640-8100 (Headquarters)
Toll free: 1-800-625-5144
✉: customercare@ starwoodhotels.com
www.starwoodhotels.com

State Farm
Executive Customer Service
One State Farm Plaza
Bloomington, IL 61710
309-766-6393
✉: info@statefarm.com
www.statefarm.com

Stein Mart
1200 Riverplace Blvd.
Jacksonville, FL 32207
904-346-1500
Toll free: 1-888-783-4662
✉: e-customerservice@ steinmart.com
www.steinmart.com

Stop & Shop Supermarket Company
Customer Service Department
1385 Hancock St.
Quincy, MA 02169
Toll free: 1-800-767-7772
www.stopandshop.com

Subway Restaurants, Inc.
325 Bic Dr.
Milford, CT 06461
Toll free: 1-800-888-4848
www.subway.com

Suntrust Banks, Inc.
PO Box 4418 GA-Atlanta-0795
Atlanta, GA 30302-4418
Toll free: 1-800-786-8787
TTY: 1-800-854-8965
www.suntrust.com

Symantec Corporation
Customer Service
350 Ellis St.
Mountain View, CA 94043
Toll free: 1-800-721-3934
www.symantec.com

T

Taco Bell
Customer Relations
1 Glen Bell Way
Irvine, CA 92618
Toll free: 1-800-822-6235
www.tacobell.com

Talbots
Customer Service Department
One Talbots Dr.
Hingham, MA 02043
781-741-4028
Toll free: 1-800-992-9010
TTY: 1-800-624-9179
✉: customerservice@talbots.com
www.talbots.com

Target Stores
Guest Relations and Quality Assurance
PO Box 9350
Minneapolis, MN 55440
Toll free: 1-800-440-0680
✉: guest.relations@target.com
www.target.com

TEAC America, Inc.
Customer Service
7733 Telegraph Rd.
Montebello, CA 90640
323-727-7627 (Service)
✉: custser@teac.com
www.teac.com

Teleflora
PO Box 60910
Los Angeles, CA 90060-0910
Toll free: 1-800-835-3356
✉: service@teleflora.com
www.teleflora.com

Terminix
Customer Service
860 Ridge Lake Rd.
Memphis, TN 38120
Toll free: 1-800-837-6464
✉: customercare@terminix.com
www.terminix.com

Texas Instruments, Inc.
Consumer Relations
PO Box 660199
Dallas, TX 75266-0199
972-995-2011
Toll free: 1-800-842-2737
www.ti.com

T.G.I. Fridays
Guest Relations
4201 Marsh Ln.
Carrollton, TX 75007
Toll free: 1-800-374-4297 (Option 1)
www.tgifridays.com

3M
Customer Relations
3M Center
St. Paul, MN 55144-1000
651-737-6501
Toll free: 1-800-364-3577
www.3m.com

Thrifty Car Rental
PO Box 35250
Tulsa, OK 74153
918-669-2168
Toll free: 1-800-847-4389
TTY: 1-888-332-3677
✉: customercare@thrifty.com
www.thrifty.com

Time, Inc.
Consumer Affairs
3000 University Center Dr.
Tampa, FL 33612-6408
813-979-6625
Toll free: 1-866-550-6934
✉: subsvcs@time.customersvc.com
www.time.com

◆ *Provided financial support for the publication of the Consumer Action Handbook.*

Time Warner, Inc.
One Time Warner Center
New York, NY 10019
212-484-8000
www.timewarner.com

Timex Corporation
Customer Service
1302 Pike Ave.
North Little Rock, AR 72114
501-372-1111
Toll free: 1-800-448-4639
✉: custserv@timex.com
www.timex.com

T.J. Maxx
See: TJX Companies, Inc.
Toll free: 1-800-926-6299
www.tjmaxx.com

TJX Companies, Inc.
770 Cochituate Rd.
Framingham, MA 01701
508-390-1000
Toll free: 1-800-926-6299 (TJ Maxx)
Toll free: 1-800-888-0776 (Home Goods)
Toll free: 1-888-627-7425 (Marshalls)
www.tjx.com

T-Mobile
Customer Relations
PO Box 37380
Albuquerque, NM 87176-7380
Toll free: 1-877-453-1304 (Customer Care)
Toll free: 1-800-866-2453 (Product Questions)
TTY: 1-877-296-1018
www.tmobile.com

The Top-Flite Golf Company
Consumer Department
2180 Rutherford Rd.
Carlsbad, CA 92008
760-931-1771
Toll free: 1-866-834-6532
www.topflite.com

The Toro Company ↻
Consumer Customer Care
8111 Lyndale Ave., South
Bloomington, MN 55420
Toll free: 1-888-384-9939
✉: consumer.service@toro.com
www.toro.com

Toshiba America
Toll free: 1-800-631-3811
✉: customer_support@tacp.com
www.tacp.toshiba.com

Totes Isotoner Corporation
Customer Service
9655 International Blvd.
Cincinnati, OH 45246-5658
513-682-8200 (Warranties)
Toll free: 1-800-762-8712
✉: customerservice@totes.com
www.totes.com

Toys "R" Us, Inc.
Guest Relations
1 Geoffrey Way
Wayne, NJ 07470
973-617-3500
Toll free: 1-800-869-7787
✉: contactus@toysrus.com
www.toysrus.com

Trader Joe's
PO Box 5049
Monrovia, CA 91016
626-599-3700 ext. 3035
www.traderjoes.com

TransUnion LLC
Consumer Solutions
PO Box 2000
Chester, PA 19022
610-546-4600
Toll free: 1-800-888-4213 (Obtain a Report)
Toll free: 1-800-916-8800 (Disputes)
Toll free: 1-800-680-7289 (Frauds)
✉: fvad@transunion.com
www.transunion.com

Travelers Companies, Inc.
Consumer Affairs
One Tower Square 8MS
Hartford, CT 06183
Toll free: 1-866-336-2077 (Customer Advocacy)
Toll free: 1-800-252-4633 (Claim Inquiry)
www.travelers.com

Travelocity.com LP
Customer Service
3150 Sabre Dr.
Southlake, TX 76092
Toll free: 1-888-872-8356
TTY: 1-800-555-7585
✉: travelocity@travelocity.com
www.travelocity.com

Travelodge
See: Wyndham Hotel Group
Toll free: 1-800-835-2424
www.travelodge.com

True Value Company
Customer Service
8600 W. Bryn Mawr Ave.
Chicago, IL 60631-3505
773-695-5000
www.truevalue.com

TruGreen Lawn Care
Service Master Company
860 Ridge Lake Blvd.
Memphis, TN 38120
Toll free: 1-877-905-5147
✉: customercare@trugreenmail.com
www.trugreen.com

Turtle Wax, Inc.
Consumer Affairs
PO Box 247
Willowbrook, IL 60559-0247
Toll free: 1-800-887-8539
www.turtlewax.com

TV Guide
Customer Relations
11 W. 42nd St.
Sixteenth Floor
New York, NY 10036
Toll free: 1-800-866-1400
✉: feedback@tvguide.com
www.tvguide.com

Twitter, Inc.
795 Folsom St.
Suite 600
San Francisco, CA 94107
415-896-2008
www.twitter.com

Tyson Foods
Consumer Relations CP631
2200 Don Tyson Parkway
Springdale, AR 72762
Toll free: 1-800-643-3410
www.tyson.com

U

U-Haul International, Inc.
Customer Service
2727 North Central Ave.
Phoenix, AZ 85004
602-263-6771
Toll free: 1-800-789-3638
www.uhaul.com

Uniden America Corporation
Customer Service
4700 Amon Carter Blvd.
Fort Worth, TX 76155
817-858-3300
Toll free: 1-800-297-1023
TTY: 1-800-874-9314
✉: cservice@uniden.com
www.uniden.com

Unilever
Consumer Services
920 Sylvan Ave., 2nd Floor
Englewood Cliffs, NJ 07632
Toll free: 1-800-298-5018
✉: comments@unilever.com
www.unilever.com

Uniroyal Tires
Consumer Care Department
PO Box 19001
Greenville, SC 29602-9001
Toll free: 1-877-458-5878
www.uniroyal.com

United Airlines
Customer Relations
PO Box 66100
Chicago, IL 60666
Toll free: 1-800-864-8331
Toll free: 1-800-221-6903 (Baggage)
TTY: 1-800-323-0170
✉: customervoice9@united.com
www.united.com

United Healthcare
Customer Service
PO Box 740815
Atlanta, GA 30374-0815
Toll free: 1-888-545-5205
www.uhc.com

United Parcel Service (UPS)
Customer Service
55 Glenlake Parkway, NE
Atlanta, GA 30328
Toll free: 1-800-742-5877
TTY: 1-800-833-0056
www.ups.com

United Van Lines LLC
Claim Department
One United Dr.
St. Louis, MO 63026
Toll free: 1-800-948-4885
www.unitedvanlines.com

Uno Restaurant Holdings Corporation
100 Charles Park Rd.
Boston, MA 02132
617-323-9200
Toll free: 1-866-600-8667
✉: mail@unos.com
www.unos.com

US Airways
Customer Relations
4000 E. Sky Harbor Blvd.
Phoenix, AZ 85034
480-693-0800
Toll free: 1-800-428-4322
TTY: 1-800-245-2966
www.usairways.com

U.S. Bancorp
U.S. Bancorp Center
800 Nicollet Mall
Minneapolis, MN 55402
TTY: 1-800-872-2657
www.usbank.com

V

The Valvoline Company
Customer Service
PO Box 14000
Lexington, KY 40512
Toll free: 1-800-832-682
www.valvoline.com

Verizon Communications, Inc.
(Contact the Verizon office in your geographic area)
Toll free: 1-800-837-4966
TTY: 1-800-974-6006
www.verizon.com

Victoria's Secret Stores
Customer Service
North American Office
PO Box 16589
Columbus, OH 43216-6589
Toll free: 1-800-411-5116
TTY: 1-800-695-1788
✉: customercare@
victoriassecret.com
www.victoriassecret.com

Virgin Atlantic Airways Ltd.
PO Box 570
Canton, MA 02021
Toll free: 1-800-821-5438
TTY: 1 800 847 4641
✉: customer.relations.us@fly.
virgin.com
www.virgin-atlantic.com

Virgin Mobile USA, L.P.
Customer Resolutions
10 Independence Blvd.
Warren, NJ 07059
Toll free: 1-888-322-1122
✉: ourteam@virginmobileusa.com
www.virginmobileusa.com

Visa USA, Inc.
(Contact your issuing bank first)
PO Box 194607
San Francisco, CA 94119-4607
Toll free: 1-800-847-2911
✉: askvisausa@visa.com
www.visa.com

Vonage
Customer Care
23 Main St.
Holmdel, NJ 07733
Toll free: 1-866-243-4357
www.vonage.com

The Vons Companies, Inc.
See: Safeway, Inc.
Toll free: 1-877-723-3929
www.vons.com

W

W Hotels
See: Starwood Hotels & Resorts Worldwide, Inc.
www.whotels.com

Walgreen Company
Consumer Relations
200 Wilmot Rd.
Deerfield, IL 60015
Toll free: 1-800-925-4733 (In-store)
Toll free: 1-877-250-5823 (Online)
www.walgreens.com

Wal-Mart Stores, Inc.
Customer Relations
702 S.W. 8th St.
Bentonville, AR 72716-0117
479-273-4000
Toll free: 1-800-925-6278
Toll free: 1-800-966-6546 (Website Questions)
www.wal-mart.com

Walter Drake, Inc.
Customer Service
PO Box 3680
Oshkosh, WI 54903-3680
Toll free: 1-855-202-7393
TTY: 920-231-5506
www.wdrake.com

Wegmans Food Markets
Consumer Affairs
1500 Brooks Ave.
PO Box 30844
Rochester, NY 14603-0844
Toll free: 1-800-934-6267
www.wegmans.com

Weight Watchers International
Corporate Affairs
11 Madison Ave., 17th Floor
New York, NY 10010
Toll free: 1-800-651-6000
✉: customerservice@
weightwatchers.com
www.weightwatchers.com

Wells Fargo Company
Customer Service F4008-080
800 Walnut St.
Des Moines, IA 50309
Toll free: 1-800-869-3557 (General)
TTY: 1-800-877-4833
www.wellsfargo.com

Wendy's International, Inc.
One Dave Thomas Blvd.
Dublin, OH 43017
614-764-3100 ext. 2032
Toll free: 1-800-443-7266
www.wendys.com

Western Union Financial Services, Inc.
Customer Service
PO Box 4430
Bridgeton, MO 63044
720-332-1000
Toll free: 1-800-325-6000
Toll free: 1-800-448-1492 (Fraud)
www.westernunion.com

Westin
See: Starwood Hotels & Resorts
Worldwide, Inc.
914-640-8100
Toll free: 1-800-937-8461
www.westin.com

Whirlpool Corporation
Customer Service
553 Benson Rd.
Benton Harbor, MI 49022
Toll free: 1-800-688-2002
Toll free: 1-800-344-1274 (Maytag)
Toll free: 1-800-422-1230
(KitchenAid)
✉: whirlpool_
customerexperience@whirlpool.
com
www.whirlpoolcorp.com

Whole Foods Markets, Inc.
550 Bowie St.
Austin, TX 78703
512-542-0878
✉: customer.questions@
wholefoods.com
www.wholefoods.com

Williams-Sonoma, Inc.
10000 Covington Cross Dr.
Las Vegas, NV 89144
702-360-7000
Toll free: 1-877-812-6235
✉: CustomerService@williams-
sonoma.com
www.williams-sonoma.com

Winn-Dixie Stores, Inc.
Customer Service
5050 Edgewood Ct.
Jacksonville, FL 32254
Toll free: 1-866-946-6349
✉: Svc_WDCustResp@winn-
dixie.com
www.winn-dixie.com

Wrangler
Consumer Relations
PO Box 21488
Greensboro, NC 27420-1488
Toll free: 1-888-784-8571
✉: wranglerweb@vfc.com
www.wrangler.com

Wyndham Hotel Group
Customer Service
1910 8th Ave., NE
Aberdeen, SD 57401
Toll free: 1-800-347-7559
www.wyndhamworldwide.com

X

Xbox
See: Microsoft Corporation
Toll free: 1-800-469-9269
TTY: 1-866-740-9269
www.xbox.com

Xerox Corporation
Customer Relations
PO Box 4505
45 Glover Ave.
Norwalk, CT 06856
Toll free: 1-877-979-8498
✉: webmaster@xerox.com
www.xerox.com

Y

Yahoo! Inc.
Customer Care
701 First Ave.
Sunnyvale, CA 94089
Toll free: 1-866-562-7219 (Customer
Care)
✉: cc-advoc@yahoo-inc.com
www.yahoo.com

YUM! Brands, Inc.
Customer Relations
1441 Gardiner Ln.
Louisville, KY 40213
Toll free: 1-800-544-5774
www.yum.com

Z

Zappos.com, Inc.
Customer Loyalty
2280 Corporate Circle, Suite 100
Henderson, NV 89074
Toll free: 1-800-927-7671
✉: cs@zappos.com
www.zappos.com

Zenith Electronics LLC
Customer Service
2000 Millbrook Dr.
Lincolnshire, IL 60069
Toll free: 1-877-993-6484
www.zenithservice.com

CORPORATE CONSUMER CONTACTS

Contacting Federal Agencies

Many federal agencies have enforcement and/or complaint-handling duties for products and services used by the general public. Others act for the benefit of the public, but do not resolve individual consumer problems. Agencies also create fact sheets, booklets, and websites that may be helpful when making purchase decisions or dealing with consumer problems. Some agencies provide timely information to citizens through profile pages on social media outlets, blogs, text messages, and news feeds. If you need help in deciding which federal agency to contact, check the index at the end of this book or call the Federal Citizen Information Center (FCIC) toll free at 1-800-FED-INFO (333-4636).

Commission on Civil Rights

624 9th St., NW
Washington, DC 20425
202-376-8128 (Publications)
Toll free: 1-800-552-6843 (Complaint Referrals)
TTY: 202-376-8116 (Nationwide Complaint Referral)
✉: referrals@usccr.gov
www.usccr.gov
The U.S. Commission on Civil Rights is an independent, bipartisan agency charged with monitoring federal civil rights enforcement.

Consumer Financial Protection Bureau (CFPB)

1500 Pennsylvania Ave., NW
Washington, DC 20220
202-435-7000
Toll free: 1-855-411-2372
TTY: 1-855-729-2372
✉: info@consumerfinance.gov
www.consumerfinance.gov
The CFPB ensures that financial products and services work for consumers. The Bureau helps consumers by providing educational materials and accepts complaints. They also supervise banks, credit unions, and other financial companies. CFPB also works to make credit card, mortgage, and other loan disclosures clearer so consumers can understand their rights and responsibilities.

Consumer Product Safety Commission (CPSC) ◆

4330 East West Highway
Bethesda, MD 20814
Toll free: 1-800-638-2772 (CPSC Hotline; 8:00 am - 5:30 pm, ET)
TTY: 1-800-638-8270
✉: info@cpsc.gov
www.cpsc.gov
www.recalls.gov (Government Recalls)
www.saferproducts.gov (Report product safety incidents, injuries or concerns)

The CPSC protects the public from unreasonable risks of serious injury or death from thousands of types of consumer products under its jurisdiction, including products that pose a fire, electrical, chemical, or mechanical hazard or can injure children.

Department of Agriculture (USDA)

Center for Nutrition Policy and Promotion (CNPP)

3101 Park Center Dr., 10th Floor
Alexandria, VA 22302-1594
703-305-7600
www.cnpp.usda.gov
www.choosemyplate.gov
The CNPP works to improve the health and well-being of Americans by developing and promoting dietary guidance that links scientific research to the nutrition needs of consumers.

Food and Nutrition Service (FNS)

3101 Park Center Dr.
Alexandria, VA 22302
703-305-2281
www.fns.usda.gov
FNS provides children and low-income people access to food, a healthful diet, and nutrition education.

General Information Line

1400 Independence Ave., SW
Washington, DC 20250
202-720-2791
www.usda.gov
This automated information line provides answers regarding USDA programs and activities.

Meat and Poultry Hotline

Food Safety and Inspection Service
Toll free: 1-888-674-6854 (10:00 am - 4:00 pm, ET, English and Spanish)
TTY: 1-800-256-7072
✉: mphotline.fsis@usda.gov
www.fsis.usda.gov
This toll free service helps prevent foodborne illness by answering questions about the safe storage, handling, and preparation of meat, poultry, and egg products.

National Institute of Food and Agriculture

1400 Independence Ave., SW
Mail Stop 2215
Washington, DC 20250-2215
202-720-7947
www.nifa.usda.gov
www.extension.org
NIFA responds to issues that are critical to daily life (health, nutrition, parenting, personal finances) by sharing, relevant research-based information through a network of county extension offices. The educators in extension offices conduct workshops, create, and distribute publications. To find your local Cooperative Extension office, consult the county government listings in your local telephone directory.

◆ *Provided financial support for the publication of the Consumer Action Handbook.*

Department of Commerce (DOC)

Bureau of the Census
4600 Silver Hill Rd.
Washington, DC 20233
301-763-4636
Toll free: 1-800-923-8282
TTY: 1-800-877-8339
www.census.gov

Seafood Inspection Program
National Oceanic and Atmospheric Administration
(NOAA)
1315 East West Highway, F/SI - Room 10837
Silver Spring, MD 20910
301-713-2355
Toll free: 1-800-422-2750
✉: NMFS.Seafood.Services@noaa.gov
www.seafood.nmfs.noaa.gov
NOAA oversees fisheries management in the United
States and provides a voluntary inspection service to
the industry. The Seafood Inspection Program offers
product quality evaluation, grading, and
certification services. NOAA provides official marks
to eligible products, such as U.S. Grade A, Processed
Under Federal Inspection (PUFI) and Lot Inspection.

**United States Patent and Trademark Office
(USPTO)**
PO Box 1450
Arlington, VA 22313-1450
Toll free: 1-800-786-9199
TTY: 571-272-9950
✉: usptoinfo@uspto.gov
www.uspto.gov
The USPTO grants patents for intellectual property
and trademarks for brand names and symbols,
protecting the rights of inventors and designers.

Weights & Measures Division (WMD)
National Institute of Standards and Technology
100 Bureau Dr., Stop 2600
Gaithersburg, MD 20899-2600
301-975-4004
✉: owm@nist.gov
www.nist.gov/owm
The WMD promotes uniformity in U.S. weights and
measures laws, regulations, and standards to achieve
equity between buyers and sellers in the marketplace.

Department of Education (ED)

The Education Publications Center (EDPUBS)
PO Box 22207
Alexandria, VA 22304
Toll free: 1-877-433-7827 (in English and Spanish)
TTY: 1-877-576-7734
✉: edpubs@edpubs.ed.gov
www.edpubs.gov
This office helps consumers identify and order free
publications and resources from the U.S. Department
of Education.

Federal Student Aid Information Center
PO Box 84
Washington, DC 20044-0084
319-337-5665
Toll free: 1-800-433-3243
TTY: 1-800-730-8913 (in English and Spanish)
✉: FederalStudentAidCustomerService@ed.gov
www.studentaid.ed.gov
Federal Student Aid provides over $150 billion in
grants, work-study, and federal loans for students
attending career and trade schools, community
colleges, and four-year colleges or universities. Visit
the website to learn about planning and paying for
your postsecondary education and to apply for federal
student aid. Also, the website provides federal
student loan information such as descriptions of
repayment plans and actions to take if you are having
trouble making loan payments.

Office for Civil Rights (OCR)
400 Maryland Ave., SW
Washington, DC 20202-1100
202-245-6700
Toll free: 1-800-421-3481
TTY: 1-877-521-2172
✉: ocr@ed.gov
www.ed.gov/ocr
This office works to ensure equal access to education
and resolve complaints of discrimination.

Office of the Inspector General (OIG)
400 Maryland Ave., SW
Washington, DC 20202-1500
Toll free: 1-800-647-8733
www2.ed.gov/about/offices/list/oig/hotline.html
The OIG Hotline is available for anyone suspecting
fraud, waste, or abuse involving U.S. Department of
Education funds or programs.

Office of Postsecondary Education (OPE)
1990 K St., NW
Washington, DC 20006
202-502-7750
www2.ed.gov/about/offices/list/ope/index.html
www.ope.ed.gov/accreditation (Searchable
Accreditation Database)
OPE develops programs to increase access to
postsecondary education. This office works with
state accreditation agencies to recognize institutions
of higher learning that provide quality education.

Office of Special Education and Rehabilitative Services (OSERS)
400 Maryland Ave., SW
Washington, DC 20202-2800
202-245-7468
Toll free: 1-800-872-5327
TTY: 202-205-4208
www.ed.gov/about/offices/list/osers/index.html
www.ed.gov/about/offices/list/osers/osep/
index.html (Office of Special Education Programs)
www.ed.gov/about/offices/list/osers/rsa/index.
html, (Rehabilitation Services Administration)
www.ed.gov/about/offices/list/osers/nidrr/
index.html (National Institute of
Disability & Rehabilitation Research)
OSERS provides a wide array of support to parents and individuals, school districts and states in three main areas: special education, vocational rehabilitation and research.

Office of Vocational and Adult Education (OVAE)
400 Maryland Ave., SW
Washington, DC 20202-7100
202-245-7700
✉: ovae@ed.gov
www2.ed.gov/about/offices/list/ovae/index.
html
OVAE administers and coordinates programs that are related to adult education and literacy, career and technical education, and community colleges.

Department of Energy (DOE)

Public Affairs
1000 Independence Ave., SW
Washington, DC 20585
202-586-5575
Toll free: 1-800-342-5363
www.doe.gov
www.energy.gov/forconsumers.htm

Energy Efficiency and Renewable Energy (EERE)
Department of Energy, Mail Stop EE-1
Washington, DC 20585
202-586-9220
202-586-0303
Toll free: 1-877-337-3463
✉: eereic@ee.doe.gov
www.energysavers.gov
The EERE Information Center answers questions about EERE's products, services, and technology programs, and refers callers to the most appropriate EERE resources.

Department of Health and Human Services (HHS)

AIDS.gov
200 Independence Ave., SW
Room 443
Washington, DC 20201
Toll free: 1-800-458-5231
✉: info@cdcnpin.org
www.aids.gov
AIDS.gov works to increase HIV testing and care among people at-risk for living with HIV and AIDS.

HHS-TIPS Fraud Hotline
Office of Inspector General (OIG)
Attn: Hotline
PO Box 23489
Washington, DC 20026
Toll free: 1-800-447-8477
TTY: 1-800-377-4950
www.oig.hhs.gov
The mission of the Office of Inspector General (OIG) is to protect the integrity of HHS programs, as well as the health and welfare of the beneficiaries of those programs.

National Health Information Center (NHIC)
PO Box 1133
Washington, DC 20013-1133
301-565-4167
Toll free: 1-800-336-4797
✉: info@nhic.org
www.health.gov/nhic
www.healthfinder.gov
www.healthfinder.gov/espanol (in Spanish)
NHIC is a health information referral service that links consumers and health professionals with organizations best able to provide answers to their health-related questions.

Office for Civil Rights (OCR)
200 Independence Ave., SW
Room 509F, HHH Building
Washington, DC 20201
Toll free: 1-800-368-1019
TTY: 1-800-537-7697
✉: OCRMail@hhs.gov
www.dhhs.gov/ocr
OCR protects you from discrimination in healthcare and social service programs. They educate communities about civil and health information privacy rights, and investigate violations of these rights.

Administration for Children & Families (ACF)

370 L'Enfant Promenade, SW
Washington, DC 20447
Toll free: 1-888-289-8442 (Fraud Alert Hotline)
www.acf.hhs.gov
The ACF funds state, territory, local, and tribal organizations to provide family assistance (welfare), child support, child care, Head Start, child welfare, and other programs relating to children and families.

◆ *Provided financial support for the publication of the Consumer Action Handbook.*

Child Welfare Information Gateway

Administration for Children & Families (ACF)
1250 Mayland Ave., SW, 8th Floor
Washington, DC 20024
Toll free: 1-800-394-3366 (8:30 am - 5:30 pm, ET)
✉: info@childwelfare.gov
www.childwelfare.gov
Child Welfare Information Gateway connects child welfare and related professionals to comprehensive information and resources to help protect children and strengthen families.

National Runaway Switchboard (NRS)

Administration for Children & Families (ACF)
3080 N. Lincoln Ave.
Chicago, IL 60657
773-880-9860
Toll free: 1-800-786-2929 (24 hrs./7 days a week)
✉: info@1800RUNAWAY.org
www.1800runaway.org
www.facebook.com/1800RUNAWAY.org
(Information for youth and teens)
NRS helps keep America's runaway and at-risk youth safe and off the streets. The organization serves as the federally designated national communication system for runaway and homeless youth.

Office of Child Support Enforcement (OCSE)

Administration for Children & Families (ACF)
370 L'Enfant Promenade, SW
Washington, DC 20447
202-401-9373
www.acf.hhs.gov/programs/cse
The OCSE assures that assistance in obtaining support (both financial and medical) is available to children through locating parents, establishing paternity and support obligations, and enforcing those obligations.

Administration on Aging (AoA)

One Massachusetts Ave., NW
Washington, DC 20001
202-619-0724
✉: aoainfo@aoa.hhs.gov
www.aoa.gov
AoA is the Federal focal point and advocate agency for older persons and their concerns. In this role, AoA works to heighten awareness among other Federal agencies, organizations, groups, and the public about the valuable contributions that older Americans make to the nation. AoA also alerts others to the needs of vulnerable older people. Through information, referral and outreach efforts at the community level, AoA seeks to educate older people and their caregivers about the benefits and services available to help them.

Eldercare Locator

Administration on Aging (AoA)
Toll free: 1-800-677-1116 (M-F, 9:00 am-8:00 pm, ET)
TTY: 1-800-677-1116
✉: eldercarelocator@n4a.org
www.eldercare.gov
The Eldercare Locator is the first step to finding resources for older adults in any U.S. community. It is a free national service of the Administration on Aging that provides an instant connection to resources that enable older persons to live independently in their communities and offers support for caregivers. The Eldercare Locator is administered by The National Association of Area Agencies on Aging.

Centers for Disease Control and Prevention (CDC)

1600 Clifton Rd.
Atlanta, GA 30333
Toll free: 1-800-232-4636 (24 hrs./7 days a week)
TTY: 1-888-232-6348
✉: cdcinfo@cdc.gov
www.cdc.gov
www.cdc.gov/spanish (in Spanish)
CDC collaborates to create the expertise, information, and tools that people and communities need to protect their health through health promotion, prevention of disease, injury and disability, and preparedness for new health threats.

CDC National STD Hotline

Centers for Disease Control and Prevention (CDC)
Toll free: 1-800-232-4636 (24 hrs./7 days a week, in English and Spanish)
TTY: 1-888-232-6348 (in English and Spanish)
✉: cdcinfo@cdc.gov
www.cdc.gov/std
www.cdc.gov/std/Spanish (in Spanish)

HIV/AIDS Prevention

Centers for Disease Control and Prevention (CDC)
Toll free: 1-800-232-4636 (24 hrs./7 days a week, in English and Spanish)
TTY: 1-888-232-6348
✉: cdcinfo@cdc.gov
www.cdc.gov/hiv
www.cdc.gov/hiv/spanish (in Spanish)
The Division of HIV/AIDS Prevention provides national leadership and support for HIV prevention research and the development, implementation, and evaluation of evidence-based HIV prevention programs serving persons affected by, or at risk for, HIV infection.

Centers for Medicare & Medicaid Services (CMS)

Office of External Affairs
7500 Security Blvd.
Baltimore, MD 21244-1850
Toll free: 1-800-447-8477 (Medicare Fraud Hotline)
TTY: 1-877-486-2048
www.cms.gov
www.medicare.gov
The Medicare Service Center answers your questions about Medicare topics, manages your orders of Medicare publications, provides detailed information about the Medicare managed care plans in your area, shares Medicare health plan quality and customer satisfaction information. Contact the Center to obtain the phone number to your state Medicaid office.

Food and Drug Administration (FDA)

10903 New Hampshire Ave.
Silver Spring, MD 20993
Toll free: 1-888-463-6332
www.fda.gov
The FDA is responsible for protecting the public health by assuring the safety, efficacy, and security of human and veterinary drugs, biological products, medical devices, our nation's food supply, cosmetics, and products that emit radiation. The FDA also provides accurate, science-based health information to the public.

Center for Food Safety and Applied Nutrition Information Line (CFSAN)
Food and Drug Administration (FDA)
Outreach and Information Center
5100 Paint Branch Parkway, HFS-009
College Park, MD 20740
Toll free: 1-888-723-3366 (M-F, 10:00 am-4:00 pm, ET)
www.fda.gov/Food
The CFSAN Information Line is a general information line for questions pertaining to food safety and applied nutrition.

National Institutes of Health (NIH)

9000 Rockville Pike
Bethesda, MD 20892
301-496-4000
TTY: 301-402-9612
✉: NIHinfo@od.nih.gov
www.nih.gov
www.salud.nih.gov (in Spanish)
The National Institutes of Health (NIH) is the primary federal agency for conducting and supporting medical research.

AIDSinfo
National Institutes of Health (NIH)
PO Box 6303
Rockville, MD 20849-6303
301-315-2816
Toll free: 1-800-448-0440 (12:00 pm - 5:00 pm, ET, in English and Spanish)
TTY: 1-888-480-3739
✉: ContactUs@aidsinfo.nih.gov
www.aidsinfo.nih.gov
www.aidsinfo.nih.gov/infoSIDA (in Spanish)
www.aidsinfo.nih.gov/LiveHelp/default.aspx
(Real time, online assistance M-F, 12:00 pm - 4:00 pm ET. Spanish-speaking agents available)
AIDSinfo offers the latest federally approved information on HIV/AIDS clinical research, treatment and prevention, and medical practice guidelines for people living with HIV/AIDS, their families and friends, health care providers, scientists, and researchers.

National Cancer Institute (NCI)
National Institutes of Health (NIH)
NCI Office of Communications and Education
6116 Executive Blvd., Suite 300
Bethesda, MD 20892-8322
Toll free: 1-800-422-6237 (M-F, 8 :00am - 8:00 pm ET, English and Spanish)
✉: cancergovstaff@mail.nih.gov
www.cancer.gov
www.cancer.gov/espanol (in Spanish)
cissecure.nci.nih/livehelp/welcome.asp (Live help online chat, M-F, 8:00 am - 11:00 pm)
NCI coordinates the National Cancer Program, which conducts and supports research, training, health information dissemination, and other programs with respect to the cause, diagnosis, prevention, and treatment of cancer, rehabilitation from cancer, and the continuing care of cancer patients and the families of cancer patients.

National Institute of Allergy and Infectious Diseases (NIAID)
6610 Rockledge Dr.
MSC 6612
Bethesda, MD 20892-6612
301-496-5717
Toll free: 1-866-284-4107
TTY: 1-800-877-8339
✉: ocpostoffice@niaid.nih.gov
www.niaid.nih.gov

NIAID provides health information on allergic, infectious, and immunologic diseases. Diseases include food allergy, sinusitis, and genital herpes. Consumers can call or write to the institute with questions and can order publications over the phone or on the website.

◆ *Provided financial support for the publication of the Consumer Action Handbook.*

National Institute of Mental Health (NIMH)
National Institutes of Health (NIH)
6001 Executive Blvd.
Room 8184, MSC 9663
Bethesda, MD 20892-9663
301-443-4513
Toll free: 1-866-615-6464
TTY: 301-443-8431, 1-866-415-8051
✉: nimhinfo@nih.gov
www.nimh.nih.gov
NIMH is the federal agency that conducts and supports research that seeks to understand, treat, and prevent mental illness. Contact NIMH for information on the symptoms, diagnosis and treatment of mental disorders, clinical trials and research. A publications ordering system is available on the NIMH website. Some publications are available in Spanish.

Department of Homeland Security (DHS)

202-282-8000
www.dhs.gov

Transportation Security Administration (TSA)
601 S. 12th St.
Arlington, VA 20598-6002
Toll free: 1-866-289-9673
✉: TSA-ContactCenter@dhs.gov
www.tsa.gov
The TSA can assist you with questions or concerns about travel tips, permitted and prohibited items, and information on filing a claim for items that were damaged or lost during a TSA screening.

U.S. Citizenship and Immigration Services (USCIS)
Information and Customer Service Division
111 Massachusetts Ave., NW
MS 2260
Washington, DC 20529-2260
Toll free: 1-800-375-5283 (National Customer Service Center, M-F, 8:00 am - 8:00 pm, ET)
TTY: 1-800-767-1833
www.uscis.gov
www.uscis.gov/portal/site/uscis-es (in Spanish)
The USCIS is responsible for processing immigration and naturalization applications and establishing policies regarding immigration services.

U.S. Customs and Border Protection
1300 Pennsylvania Ave., NW
Washington, DC 20229
703-526-4200
Toll free: 1-877-227-5511
TTY: 1-866-880-6582
www.cbp.gov
CBP prevents individuals from entering the country illegally or bringing harmful and illegal substances into the U.S. They also protect agricultural products from pests and American businesses from theft of their intellectual property.

Federal Emergency Management Agency (FEMA)
500 C St., SW
Washington, DC 20472
Toll free: 1-800-621-3362
TTY: 1-800-462-7585
www.fema.gov
www.fema.gov/esp (in Spanish)
www.ready.gov (Disaster Preparedness)
www.listo.gov (Disaster Preparedness, in Spanish)
www.disasterassistance.gov (Disaster Assistance)
FEMA supports citizens and emergency personnel to build, sustain, and improve the nation's capability to prepare for, protect against, respond to, recover from, and mitigate all hazards.

FEMA Disaster Assistance
PO Box 10055
Hyattsville, MD 20782-8055
Toll free: 1-800-621-3362
TTY: 1-800-462-7585
www.fema.gov/assistance
www.disasterassistance.gov
FEMA Disaster Assistance provides information about how you can get help before, during, or after a disaster and apply for assistance from the federal government. This office also provides information to help you prepare for, respond to, and recover from disasters.

National Flood Insurance Program (NFIP)
Federal Emergency Management Agency
500 C St., SW
Washington, DC 20472
Toll free: 1-888-379-9531
TTY: 1-800-427-5593
✉: FloodSmart@dhs.gov
www.floodsmart.gov
NFIP provides a means for property owners to financially protect themselves. The NFIP offers flood insurance to homeowners, renters, and business owners if their community participates in the NFIP.

Department of Housing and Urban Development (HUD)

Office of Fair Housing and Equal Opportunity (FHEO)
451 7th St., SW, Room 5204
Washington, DC 20410-2000
202-708-4252
Toll free: 1-800-669-9777 (Complaints Hotline)
TTY: 1-800-927-9275
www.hud.gov/complaints/housediscrim.cfm
www.hud.gov/offices/fheo
FHEO enforces federal laws and establishes policies that make sure all Americans have equal access to the housing of their choice. If you believe that you have been the victim of housing discrimination, file a complaint with this office.

Department of Housing

451 7th St., SW
Washington, DC 20410
**portal.hud.gov/portal/page/portal/HUD/
program_offices/housing**
The Department of Housing provides public services
through its nationally administered programs.
It oversees the Federal Housing Administration
mortgage inusrance program and regulates the
housing industry business.

Federal Housing Administration (FHA)

451 7th St., SW
Washington, DC 20410
Toll free: 1-800-225-5342
TTY: 1-877-833-2483
✉: info@fhaoutreach.com
portal.hud.gov
FHA provides mortgage insurance on single-family,
multifamily, manufactured home, and hospital loans
made by FHA-approved lenders throughout the
United States and its territories.

Office of Interstate Land Sales

451 7th St., SW, Room 9146
Washington, DC 20410
202-708-0502
Toll free: 1-800-225-5342
TTY: (202) 708-1455
✉: hsg-respa@hud.gov
www.hud.gov/complaints/landsales.cfm
The Interstate Land Sales program protects
consumers from fraud and abuse when buying or
selling land from developers.

Office of Manufactured Housing Programs

451 7th St., SW, Room 9164
Washington, DC 20410-8000
202-708-6423
Toll free: 1-800-927-2891
TTY: 202-708-1455
✉: mhs@hud.gov
**www.hud.gov/offices/hsg/sfh/mhs/mhshome.
cfm**
The Manufactured Housing Program is a consumer
protection program that regulates the construction of
certain factory-built housing units called
"manufactured homes". HUD works with 37 states to
respond to consumer complaints.

Department of the Interior (DOI)

Fish and Wildlife Service

1849 C St., NW
Washington, DC 20240
202-208-5634 (Public Affairs routes all calls from here)
Toll free: 1-800-344-9453
www.fws.gov
The Fish and Wildlife Service works to conserve,
protect and enhance fish, wildlife and plants and their
habitats.

National Park Service (NPS)

1849 C St., NW
Room 7012
Washington, DC 20240
202-208-6843 (Public Affairs routes all calls from here)
www.nps.gov
www.recreation.gov (Federal recreational activities
and reservations)
NPS preserves the nation's national parks and
historic landmarks so that individuals may enjoy
the natural environment for years to come. You
can explore federal parks, forests, museums and
other recreation sites, and make reservations for an
upcoming visit.

Department of Justice (DOJ)

Americans with Disabilities Act (ADA) Information Line

950 Pennsylvania Ave., NW
Disability Rights Section–NYAV
Washington, DC 20530
Toll free: 1-800-514-0301 (M-W, F 9:00 am-5:30 pm, ET,
T 12:30 pm-5:30 pm, ET)
TTY: 1-800-514-0383
www.ada.gov
This service permits businesses, state and local
governments, or others to call and ask questions
about general or specific ADA requirements
including questions about the ADA Standards for
Accessible Design.

U.S. Trustee Program

Executive Offices for U.S. Trustees
20 Massachusetts Ave., NW
Suite 8000
Washington, DC 20530
202-307-1399
✉: ustrustee.program@usdoj.gov
www.justice.gov/ust
**www.justice.gov/ust/eo/bapcpa/ccde/cc_
approved.htm**
The Trustee Program protects the integrity of the
federal bankruptcy system. The Program monitors
the conduct of bankruptcy parties and private estate
trustees. It also identifies and helps investigate
bankruptcy fraud and abuse.

◆ Provided financial support for the publication of the Consumer Action Handbook.

Department of Labor (DOL)

Employee Benefits Security Administration (EBSA)
Department of Labor
200 Constitution Ave., NW
Office of Participant Assistance, Room N5623
Washington, DC 20210
Toll free: 1-866-444-3272
TTY: 1-877-889-5627
www.dol.gov/ebsa
www.askebsa.dol.gov
The EBSA provides information and assistance on private sector, employer-sponsored retirement benefit and health benefit plans. The agency educates plan participants, beneficiaries, and sponsors to insure that they have access to documents related to their benefit plan.

Job Corps
200 Constitution Ave., NW
Suite N4463
Washington, DC 20210
202-693-3000
Toll free: 1-800-733-5627
✉: national_office@jobcorps.gov
www.jobcorps.gov
Job Corps is a no-cost education and vocational training program that helps young people (ages 16 to 24) improve the quality of their lives through vocational and academic training.

National Contact Center
Department of Labor
Toll free: 1-866-487-2365
TTY: 1-877-889-5627
www.dol.gov

Occupational Safety and Health Administration (OSHA)
Department of Labor
200 Constitution Ave., NW
Washington, DC 20210
Toll free: 1-800-321-6742
TTY: 1-877-889-5627
www.osha.gov

OSHA ensures safe and healthful working conditions for working men and women by setting and enforcing standards and by providing training, outreach, education and assistance.

Office of Disability Employment Policy (ODEP)
Department of Labor
200 Constitution Ave., NW, Room S1303
Washington, DC 20210
202-693-7880
Toll free: 1-866-633-7365
TTY: 202-693-7881 or 1-877-889-5627
www.dol.gov/odep
www.disability.gov
ODEP works to create policies to ensure that people with disabilities are fully integrated in the workforce.

Veteran's Employment and Training Service (VETS)
Department of Labor
200 Constitution Ave., NW, Room S1325
Washington, DC 20210
Toll free: 1-866-487-2365
TTY: 1-877-889-5627
www.dol.gov/vets
VETS provides resources to prepare and assist veterans obtain meaningful careers and maximize their employment opportunities.

Department of State (DOS)

American Citizens Services and Crisis Management
Department of State
2201 C St., NW
Washington, DC 20520
202-501-4444
Toll free: 1-888-407-4747 (within U.S.)
www.travel.state.gov/travel

Contact the State Department for help with emergencies and non-emergencies affecting private Americans abroad.

National Passport Information Center (NPIC)
Toll free: 1-877-487-2778
TTY: 1-888-874-7793
www.travel.state.gov/passport
Contact the NPIC for information on U.S. passports, including the status of pending applications, as well as the locations of the over 4,500 passport acceptance facilities.

Visa Services
Washington, DC 20520
202-663-1225 (M-F, 8:30 am - 5:00 pm, ET)
Emergency after hours: 202-647-1512
✉: nvcinquiry@state.gov
www.travel.state.gov/visa
Contact Visa Services for information on U.S. visas for foreigners.

Department of Transportation (DOT)

Aviation Consumer Protection Division (ACPD)
Office of Aviation Enforcement and Proceedings
1200 New Jersey Ave., SE
Washington, DC 20590
202-366-2220 (Airline Service Complaints)
Toll free: 1-800-778-4838 (Air travelers with disabilities hotline)
TTY: 202-366-0511; Toll free: 1-800-455-9880
✉: airconsumer@dot.gov
airconsumer.ost.dot.gov/problems.htm
airconsumer.ost.dot.gov/spanish (in Spanish)
The ACPD receives complaints from members of the public regarding air travel consumer issues. It verifies compliance with the Department's aviation consumer protection requirements and provides guidance to the industry and members of the public on consumer protection matters.

Federal Aviation Administration (FAA)
800 Independence Ave., SW
Washington, DC 20591
202-366-4000
Toll free: 1-866-835-5322
www.faa.gov
The FAA works to ensure that all air travel is safe.

Federal Motor Carrier Safety Administration (FMCSA)
1200 New Jersey Ave., SE
Suite W60-300
Washington, DC 20590
202-366-2519
Toll free: 1-800-832-5660 (FMCSA Information Line)
TTY: 1-800-877-8339
www.fmcsa.dot.gov
www.protectyourmove.gov (Interstate moving information)
The FMCSA provides information about your rights when moving across state lines (interstate moves). Consumers should submit household goods commercial complaints or dangerous safety violations involving a commercial truck or bus (including charter buses) to this agency.

National Highway Traffic Safety Administration (NHTSA)
1200 New Jersey Ave., SE
West Building
Washington, DC 20590
Toll free: 1-888-327-4236 (Vehicle Safety Hotline)
TTY: 1-800-424-9153
www.nhtsa.dot.gov
NHTSA wants to hear from consumers regarding potential defects in their cars. NHTSA's hotline has information on safety recalls, crash test ratings, child safety seats; bicycles; air bags; and impaired and distracted driving prevention.

Department of the Treasury

Bureau of the Public Debt
Treasury Direct
PO Box 7015
Parkersburg, WV 26106-7015
Toll free: 1-800-722-2678
www.publicdebt.treas.gov
www.treasurydirect.gov
This agency borrows moneys to make sure that the federal government continues to operate. You can contact them to purchase bonds or to check on the maturity of bonds you have already purchased.

Internal Revenue Service (IRS)
Toll free: 1-800-829-1040 (Help for individuals)
Toll free: 1-800-829-4933 (Help for businesses)
TTY: 1-800-829-4059
www.irs.gov
Free tax help is available from the Internal Revenue Service at www.IRS.gov 24 hours a day, seven days a week. Numerous on-line applications, resources and taxpayer assistance services are available. Learn about electronic filing options, look up the status of your refund, print tax forms and instructions, look for preparers who can electronically file tax returns and find ways to connect with the IRS through New Media. If your personal tax questions require face-to-face assistance you may visit the Taxpayer Assistance Centers closest to you. Locations are listed on www.irs.gov.

Office of the Comptroller of the Currency (OCC)
Customer Assistance Group
1301 McKinney St., Suite 3450
Houston, TX 77010
Toll free: 1-800-613-6743 (M-F, 7:00 am-7:00 pm CST)
TTY: 713-658-0340
www.helpwithmybank.gov
The Office of the Comptroller of the Currency charters, regulates, and supervises all national banks. The OCC also supervises federal savings associations (thrifts) and the federal branches and agencies of foreign banks.

United States Mint
Customer Service Center
2799 Reeves Rd.
Plainfield, IN 46168
202-756-6468
TTY: 1-888-321-6468 (M-F, 8:30 am - 5:00 pm, ET)
www.usmint.gov
The Mint produces the the coins that circulate throughout the US. They also produce special edition coinage that can be purchased for coin collections.

Department of Veterans Affairs (VA) ◆

1722 I St., NW
Washington , DC 20421
Toll free: 1-800-827-1000
TTY: 1-800-829-4833
www.va.gov
The VA oversees and administers benefits for veterans and their families. Some programs include home loans, life insurance policies, financing education through the GI bill, job training, and health resources. For more information about VA medical care or benefits, write, call or visit your nearest VA facility.

◆ *Provided financial support for the publication of the Consumer Action Handbook.*

National Cemetery Administration (NCA)
810 Vermont Ave., NW
Washington, DC 20420
202-461-6240
TTY: 1-800-829-4833
www.cem.va.gov
Contact the NCA for information about burials, headstones or markers, the State Cemetery Grants Program, and presidential memorial certificates for veterans.

Veterans Benefits Administration (VBA)
810 Vermont Ave., NW
Washington, DC 20420
202-461-9763 (Publications only)
Toll free: 1-800-827-1000
TTY: 1-800-829-4833
www.vba.va.gov/VBA
The VBA helps veterans receive benefits, such as educational and financial resources.

Veterans Health Administration (VHA)
810 Vermont Ave., NW
Washington, DC 20420
Toll free: 1-877-222-8387
www.va.gov/health (Veteran health resources)
VHA serves the needs of America's veterans by providing primary care, specialized care, and related medical and social support services.

Environmental Protection Agency (EPA)

Energy Star Program
1200 Pennsylvania Ave., NW
Room 6202J
Washington, DC 20460
703-412-3086
Toll free: 1-888-782-7937
✉: hotline@energystar.gov
www.energystar.gov
The ENERGY STAR label is awarded to products for the home and office that are highly energy-efficient. The program encourages the use of energy-efficient products that both protect the environment and save consumers money.

Indoor Environments Division
1200 Pennsylvania Ave., NW
Mail Code 6609J
Washington, DC 20460
202-343-9370
Toll free: 1-800-438-4318
✉: IAQINFO@aol.com
www.epa.gov/iaq/iaqxline.html
This agency is a central source of information on indoor air quality. It is responsible for implementing the Indoor Environments Program, a voluntary (non-regulatory) program to address indoor air pollution.

National Pesticide Information Center
Toll free: 1-800-858-7378 (6:30 am - 4:30 pm, PT)
✉: npic@ace.orst.edu
www.npic.orst.edu
A service that provides objective, science-based information about a wide variety of pesticide-related subjects, including pesticide products, pesticide poisonings, toxicology, and environmental chemistry.

National Service Center for Environmental Publications (NSCEP)
PO Box 42419
Cincinnati, OH 45242-0419
Toll free: 1-800-490-9198
✉: nscep@bps-lmit.com
www.epa.gov/nscep
NSCEP distributes EPA's publications to the public. Consumers can order copies by phone and mail or download digital versions of the publications.

Safe Drinking Water Hotline
1200 Pennsylvania Ave., NW, 4606M
Washington, DC 20460
703-412-3330
Toll free: 1-800-426-4791 (10:00 am - 4:00 pm, ET, in English and Spanish)
www.epa.gov/safewater/hotline
The Office of Ground Water and Drinking Water helps protect public health by ensuring safe drinking water and protecting ground water.

Equal Employment Opportunity Commission (EEOC)

131 M St., NE
Washington, DC 20507
202-663-4900
Toll free: 1-800-669-4000
TTY: 202-663-4494
✉: info@eeoc.gov
www.eeoc.gov
The EEOC enforces laws that make discrimination illegal in the workplace. The commission oversees all types of work situations including hiring, firing, promotions, harassment, training, wages, and benefits.

Federal Communications Commission (FCC)

Consumer Center
445 12th St., SW
Washington, DC 20554
Toll free: 1-888-225-5322
TTY: 1-888-835-5322
✉: fccinfo@fcc.gov
www.fcc.gov/cgb
FCC accepts public inquiries, informal complaints, and questions regarding cable, radio, satellite, telephone, television and wireless services.

Wireless Telecommunications Bureau (WTB)
445 12th St., SW
Washington, DC 20554
Toll free: 1-877-480-3201
TTY: 717-338-2824
wireless.fcc.gov
The WTB handles the majority of FCC's wireless telecommunication programs. They provide guidance for consumers about selecting wireless communication providers and products.

Federal Deposit Insurance Corporation (FDIC) ◆

Division of Depositor and Consumer Protection
Consumer Response Center
1100 Walnut St., Box #11
Kansas City, MO 64106
Toll free: 1-877-275-3342
TTY: 1-800-925-4618
www.fdic.gov
www2.fdic.gov/STARSMAIL/index.asp (Online Consumer Assistance Form)
FDIC responds to questions about federal deposit insurance coverage and handles complaints and inquiries about FDIC-insured state banks which are not members of the Federal Reserve System.

Federal Maritime Commission (FMC)

800 N. Capitol St., NW
Washington, DC 20573
202-523-5807
✉: Complaints@fmc.gov
www.fmc.gov
FMC assists consumers engaged in disputes with transporting carriers, ocean transportation intermediaries and cruise operators.

Federal Reserve System

Federal Reserve Consumer Help
PO Box 1200
Minneapolis, MN 55480
Toll free: 1-888-851-1920 (8:00 am - 6:00 pm, CT)
TTY: 1-877-766-8533 (8:00 am - 6:00 pm, CT)
✉: consumerhelp@federalreserve.gov
www.federalreserveconsumerhelp.gov
This division receives and tracks consumer complaints and questions regarding practices by banks and other financial institutions supervised by the Board of Governors of the Federal Reserve System.

Federal Trade Commission (FTC) ◆

Bureau of Consumer Protection ◆
Consumer Response Center
600 Pennsylvania Ave., NW
Washington, DC 20580
Toll free: 1-877-382-4357
TTY: 1-866-653-4261
www.ftc.gov
www.OnGuardOnline.gov (Online security tips)
www.Admongo.gov (Advertising literacy for kids)
The FTC works for the consumer to prevent fraudulent, deceptive, and unfair business practices in the marketplace and to provide information to help consumers spot, stop, and avoid them. To file a complaint or to get free information on consumer issues, visit the website or call the toll free number above. The FTC records consumer complaints (Internet, telemarketing, identity theft, and other fraud-related complaints) into the Consumer Sentinel Network, a secure, online database and investigative tool available to hundreds of civil and criminal law enforcement agencies.

General Services Administration (GSA) ◆

Federal Citizen Information Center (FCIC) ◆
1275 1st St., NE
11th Floor
Washington, DC 20417
To order the *Consumer Information Catalog* send your name and address to: Catalog, Pueblo, CO 81009
202-501-1794
Toll free: 1-800-333-4636
www.USA.gov (the U.S. government's official web portal)
www.GobiernoUSA.gov (USA.gov in Spanish)
www.Publications.USA.gov
www.kids.gov (government websites for kids)
FCIC publishes the free, quarterly *Consumer Information Catalog*, which lists nearly 200 free and low-cost Federal booklets on a wide variety of consumer topics, and maintains a family of websites to help provide free, timely and useful information to citizens. Consumers can get the information they need in three ways: through printed publications at www. Publications.USA.gov, by calling toll free 1-800-FED-INFO (333-4636), or by visiting www.USA.gov, the U.S. government's official web portal. You can also follow FCIC on social media on Facebook: www.facebook.com/USAgov and on Twitter: @USAgov.

Surplus Federal Property Sales
✉: gsaauctionshelp@gsa.gov
Toll free: 1-800-333-7472
www.gsaauctions.gov
GSA helps federal agencies dispose of unneeded property by selling directly to the public. It sells personal property, real estate, and vehicles to the public through online auctions.

◆ *Provided financial support for the publication of the Consumer Action Handbook.*

National Council on Disability (NCD)

1331 F St., NW
Suite 850
Washington, DC 20004
202-272-2004
TTY: 202-272-2074
✉: ncd@ncd.gov
www.ncd.gov
The NCD is an independent federal agency making recommendations to the President and Congress on policies affecting Americans with disabilities. NCD works to empower individuals with disabilities and to promote equal opportunity.

National Credit Union Administration (NCUA)

1775 Duke St.
Alexandria, VA 22314-3428
703-518-6300
Toll free: 1-800-827-9650 (Fraud Hotline)
✉: consumerassistance@ncua.gov
www.ncua.gov
NCUA is the federal agency that charters and supervises federal credit unions and insures savings in federal and most state-chartered credit unions across the country through the National Credit Union Share Insurance Fund.

Office of Personnel Management (OPM)

1900 E St., NW
Washington, DC 20415
202-606-1800
TTY: 202-606-2532
✉: general@opm.gov
www.opm.gov
www.usajobs.gov (Federal employment opportunities)
OPM manages the civil service of the federal government, coordinates recruiting of new government employees, and manages their health insurance and retirement benefits programs. OPM also provides resources for locating student jobs, summer jobs, scholarships, and internships.

Pension Benefit Guaranty Corporation (PBGC)

Customer Contact Center
PO Box 151750
Alexandria, VA 22315-1750
Toll free: 1-800-400-7242
TTY: 1-800-877-8339
✉: mypension@pbgc.gov
www.pbgc.gov
The PBGC protects the retirement incomes of workers in private sector defined pension benefit plans. When you call, it helps to have your social security number and your plan's name or number.

Securities and Exchange Commission (SEC) ◆

Office of Investor Education and Advocacy (OIEA)
100 F St., NE
Washington, DC 20549-0213
Toll free: 1-800-732-0330
✉: help@sec.gov
www.investor.gov (Investor information)
www.sec.gov/complaint.shtml (Complaint form)
The SEC's Office of Investor Education and Advocacy serves individual investors and is ready to assist you in resolving your complaints and answering questions. OIEA's website, www.investor.gov, is an online resource to help you invest wisely and avoid fraud.

Small Business Administration (SBA)

409 3rd St., SW, Suite 7600
Washington, DC 20416
202-205-6740
Toll free: 1-800-827-5722 (Information)
TTY: 704-344-6640
✉: answerdesk@sba.gov
www.sba.gov
The SBA helps Americans start, build and grow businesses. Through an extensive network of field offices and partnerships the SBA aids, counsels, assists and protects the interests of small business concerns.

Social Security Administration (SSA)

Office of Public Inquiries
6401 Security Blvd.
Baltimore, MD 21235
Toll free: 1-800-772-1213
TTY: 1-800-325-0778 (M-F, 7:00 am - 7:00 pm, ET)
www.socialsecurity.gov
www.socialsecurity.gov/espanol (in Spanish)
The Social Security Administration provides retirement, survivors and disability benefits, as well as administers Supplemental Security Income (SSI) payments.

U.S. Commodity Futures Trading Commission (CFTC)

Office of External Affairs
Three Lafayette Center
1155 21st St., NW
Washington, DC 20581
202-418-5000
TTY: 202-418-5514
✉: questions@cftc.gov
www.cftc.gov
CFTC protects market users and the public from fraud, manipulation, and abusive practices related to the sale of commodity and financial futures and options, and to foster open, competitive, and financially sound futures and option markets. In pursuit of its mission, the CFTC investigates and prosecutes commodities fraud, including foreign currency schemes, energy manipulation and hedge fund fraud, and works with other federal and state agencies to bring criminal and other actions.
The CFTC also engages in public education and outreach by participating in consumer groups and issuing Consumer Advisories and other educational materials.

U.S. Postal Service (USPS)

Toll free: 1-800-275-8777
usps.com
The USPS is the federal agency responsible for the delivery of mail across the nation. You can visit your local post office to ship packages, purchase money orders, and apply for a passport (at select locations. The USPS has also made many of their services available online, such as purchasing and printing postage, tracking packages, and changing your address.

United States Postal Inspection Service
Attn: Mail Fraud
222 S. Riverside Plaza, Suite 1250
Chicago, IL 60606-6100
Toll free: 1-877-876-2455
postalinspectors.uspis.gov
If you believe you have been the victim of a crime involving the U.S. mail or need assistance with postal-related problems of a law enforcement nature, you should contact your nearest Postal Inspection Service office. Addresses and telephone numbers can be found in the government pages of your telephone book or by visiting the Postal Inspection Service website.

◆ *Provided financial support for the publication of the Consumer Action Handbook.*

AARP
601 E. St., NW
Washington, DC 20049
Toll free: 1-888-687-2277
Toll free: 1-800-646-2283 (Fraud Fighter Hotline)
TTY: 1-877-434-7589
✉: member@aarp.org
www.aarp.org
AARP is committed to addressing the consumer problems and issues that affect the financial security of people 50 years and older. Through advocacy at the federal and state levels, AARP works to make the marketplace safer for all consumers. AARP also employs a variety of strategies to help AARP members protect themselves from fraud and deceptive practices.

American Council on Consumer Interests (ACCI)
5100 E. Vogel Rd., Suite 202
Evansville, IN 47715
812-470-1985
✉: information@consumerinterests.org
www.consumerinterests.org
ACCI is a consumer policy research and education organization consisting of a world-wide community of researchers, educators, and related professionals.

American Council on Science and Health (ACSH)
1995 Broadway, Suite 202
New York, NY 10023-5860
212-362-7044
✉: acsh@acsh.org
www.acsh.org
A nonprofit public education group, ACSH provides consumers with up-to-date, scientifically sound information on the relationship among human health and chemicals, foods, lifestyles, and the environment. Booklets and special reports on a variety of topics are available.

Contacting National Consumer Organizations
National Consumer Organizations are committed to assisting consumers and protecting their rights via advocacy, research, and outreach efforts. Some organizations assist individuals with problems, while others collect consumer complaints and statistics to better understand consumer trends and direct their advocacy efforts.

Center for Auto Safety (CAS)
1825 Connecticut Ave., NW
Suite 330
Washington, DC 20009-5708
202-328-7700
www.autosafety.org
CAS advocates on behalf of consumers in auto safety and quality, fuel-efficiency, emissions, and related issues. For advice on specific problems, CAS requests that consumers write a brief statement of the problem or question, including the year, make, and model of the vehicle. Mail it with a stamped, self-addressed envelope to the address above.

Center for Science in the Public Interest (CSPI)
1220 L St., NW, Suite 300
Washington, DC 20005
202-332-9110
✉: cspi@cspinet.org
www.cspinet.org
A non-profit, membership organization, CSPI conducts research, education, and advocacy on nutrition, health, food safety, and related issues. It also provides consumers with current information about their health and well-being via its monthly *Nutrition Action Healthletter*.

Center for the Study of Services (CSS)
1625 K St., NW, 8th Floor
Washington, DC 20006
202-347-7283
Toll free: 1-800-213-7283
✉: questions@cssresearch.org
www.checkbook.org
www.cssresearch.org
CSS provides consumers with information to help them get high-quality services and products at the best possible prices. The organization publishes *Consumers' Checkbook* so that consumers can evaluate the quality and prices of service firms and stores in their local area.

Coalition Against Insurance Fraud
www.insurancefraud.org
The Coalition is an alliance of consumer groups, government agencies, and insurance companies dedicated to combating all forms of insurance fraud through advocacy and public information.

Consumer Action
221 Main St., Suite 480
San Francisco, CA 94105
415-777-9635 (Consumer Complaints)
TTY: 415-777-9456
✉: info@consumer-action.org
www.consumer-action.org
An education and advocacy organization specializing in credit, finance, and telecommunications issues, Consumer Action offers a multi-lingual consumer complaint hotline and consumer education materials in as many as eight languages. Community-based organizations can request these free publications in bulk.

Consumer Federation of America (CFA)
1620 I St., NW, Suite 200
Washington, DC 20006
202-387-6121
✉: cfa@consumerfed.org
www.consumerfed.org
CFA is a consumer advocacy and education organization. It represents consumer interests on issues such as telephone service, insurance and financial services, product safety, indoor air pollution, health care, product liability, and utility rates. It develops and distributes studies of various consumer issues, as well as printed consumer guides.

Consumers Union (CU)
101 Truman Ave.
Yonkers, NY 10703-1057
914-378-2000
914-378-2455 (Consumer Policy Institute)
Toll free: 1-800-879-9848 (*Consumer Reports* magazine)
Toll free: 1-866-208-9427 (ConsumerReports.org)
www.consumersunion.org
www.consumerreports.org
CU, publisher of *Consumer Reports*, is an independent, non-profit testing and information organization serving only consumers. CU is a comprehensive source for unbiased advice about products and services, personal finance, health and nutrition, and other consumer concerns. CU tests products, informs the public, and protects consumers. CU's Advocacy Offices provide tools to consumers to make their concerns heard by government and industry. Its Consumer Policy Institute conducts research and education projects on such issues as pesticides, toxic air pollution, and community right-to-know laws.

Families USA
1201 New York Ave., NW
Suite 1100
Washington, DC 20005
202-628-3030
✉: info@familiesusa.org
www.familiesusa.org
A national, nonprofit membership organization committed to affordable, high quality health care, Families USA creates materials to educate and mobilize consumers on health care issues.

Funeral Consumers Alliance (FCA)
33 Patchen Rd.
South Burlington, VT 05403
802-865-8300
Toll free: 1-800-765-0107
✉: info@funerals.org
www.funerals.org
FCA protects a consumer's right to choose a dignified, meaningful, affordable funeral. In addition to informing the public about its options and rights, FCA will assist in mediating complaints. Local affiliates around the country conduct funeral price surveys and counsel members and the general public.

Jump$tart Coalition for Personal Financial Literacy
919 18th St., NW, Suite 300
Washington, DC 20006
202-466-8604
Toll free: 1-888-453-3822
✉: info@jumpstartcoalition.org
www.jumpstart.org
The Coalition encourages curriculum enrichment to ensure that basic personal financial management skills are attained during the K–college educational experience.

Kids in Danger (KID)
116 W. Illinois St., Suite 5E
Chicago, IL 60654
312-595-0649
✉: email@kidsindanger.org
www.kidsindanger.org
KID is dedicated to educating parents, training engineers, designers, and manufacturers, and advocating for improvements in the safety of children's products.

The Medicare Rights Center
520 Eighth Ave.
North Wing, 3rd Floor
New York City, NY 10018
212-869-3850
Toll free: 1-800-333-4114
✉: info@medicarerights.org
www.medicarerights.org
The Medicare Rights Center works to ensure access to affordable health care for older adults and people with disabilities through counseling and advocacy, educational programs, and public policy initiatives. It works with clients nationwide through phone hotlines, Internet services, a large volunteer network, and community programs.

National Community Reinvestment Coalition (NCRC)
727 15th St., NW, Suite 900
Washington, DC 20005-2112
202-628-8866
✉: member@ncrc.org
www.ncrc.org
NCRC works to end discriminatory banking practices and increase the flow of private capital and credit into underserved communities across the country. It also offers a housing counseling network to help prospective and current homeowners.

National Consumer Law Center (NCLC)
Seven Winthrop Square
Boston, MA 02110-1245
617-542-8010
✉: consumerlaw@nclc.org
www.consumerlaw.org
NCLC is an advocacy and research organization focusing on the needs of low-income and other disadvantaged consumers. It concentrates on working for fairness in financial services, wealth building and financial health, ending predatory lending and consumer fraud, and the protection of basic energy and utility services. Limited resources prevent the organization from responding to individual inquiries.

◆ *Provided financial support for the publication of the Consumer Action Handbook.*

The National Consumer Protection Technical Resource Center
Senior Medicare Patrol Resource Center
PO Box 388
Waterloo, IA 50704-0388
Toll free: 1-877-808-2468
✉: info@smpresource.org
www.smpresource.org
The Center is funded by the U.S. Administration on Aging to support community-based Senior Medicare Patrol Programs (SMP). The SMP projects use the skills and expertise of retired professionals to help Medicare and Medicaid beneficiaries avoid, detect, and prevent health care fraud and abuse.

National Consumers League (NCL)
1701 K St., NW, Suite 1200
Washington, DC 20006
202-835-3323
www.nclnet.org
www.lifesmarts.org
www.fraud.org
www.fakechecks.org (Fake check scams)
The NCL provides government, businesses, and other organizations with the consumer's perspective on consumer issues and workplace concerns. The League sponsors the LifeSmarts competition to develop the consumer and marketplace knowledge of teenagers. NCL also works to provide consumers with the information they need to avoid becoming victims of telemarketing and Internet fraud and to help them communicate their complaints to law enforcement.

National Council on the Aging (NCOA)
1901 L St., NW, 4th Floor
Washington, DC 20036
202-479-1200
Toll free: 1-800-424-9046
TTY: 202-479-6674
✉: info@ncoa.org
www.ncoa.org
NCOA is a national voice for older adults — especially those who are vulnerable and disadvantaged — and the community organizations that serve them.

Society of Consumer Affairs Professionals International (SOCAP) ◆
675 N. Washington St., Suite 200
Alexandria, VA 22314
703-519-3700
✉: socap@socap.org
www.socap.org
SOCAP provides training, conferences, and publications to encourage and promote effective communication and understanding among business, government and consumers, and to define and advance the consumer affairs profession.

Contacting Your Local Consumer Protection Offices

State, county, and city consumer offices offer a variety of important services. They might mediate complaints, conduct investigations, prosecute offenders of consumer laws, license and regulate professionals, provide educational materials, and advocate in the consumer interest.

An advantage of contacting a city or county government office is that it is familiar with local businesses, ordinances, and state laws.

Other local consumer and non-profit organizations may provide consumer assistance and work with the state consumer office. Be sure to contact your state consumer protection office to get more information about other local resources.

Before sending a written complaint, call the office to confirm that it handles the type of complaint you have and determine whether complaint forms are provided. Many offices distribute consumer materials specifically geared to state laws and local issues. Ask whether any information is available regarding your problem.

Alabama

State Offices

Alabama Office of the Attorney General
Consumer Affairs Section
501 Washington Ave.
Montgomery, AL 36130
334-242-7335
Toll free: 1-800-392-5658 (AL)
www.ago.state.al.us

Alaska

State Offices

Office of the Attorney General
Consumer Protection Unit
1031 W. 4th Ave., Suite 200
Anchorage, AK 99501-5903
907-269-5100
Toll free: 1-888-576-2529
www.law.state.ak.us

Arizona

State Offices

Arizona Office of the Attorney General - Phoenix
Consumer Information and Complaints
1275 W. Washington St.
Phoenix, AZ 85007
602-542-5763
Toll free: 1-800-352-8431 (AZ, except Maricopa and Pima)
www.azag.gov

Arizona Office of the Attorney General - Tucson
Consumer Information and Complaints
South Bldg., Suite 315
400 W. Congress St.
Tucson, AZ 85701-1367
520-628-6504
Toll free: 1-800-352-8431 (AZ, except Maricopa and Pima)
✉: consumerinfo@azag.gov
www.azag.gov

Arkansas

State Offices

Arkansas Office of the Attorney General
Consumer Protection Division
323 Center St., Suite 200
Little Rock, AR 72201
501-682-2341 (Consumer Hotline)
501-682-2007 (Attorney General's Operator)
Toll free: 1-800-482-8982 (Consumer Hotline)
TTY: 1-800-482-8982
✉: consumer@arkansasag.gov
www.arkansasag.gov

California

State Offices

California Office of the Attorney General
Public Inquiry Unit
PO Box 944255
Sacramento, CA 94244-2550
916-322-3360
Toll free: 1-800-952-5225 (CA)
TTY: 1-800-735-2929
www.caag.state.ca.us

California Bureau of Automotive Repair
Department of Consumer Affairs
10240 Systems Parkway
Sacramento, CA 95827
Toll free: 1-800-952-5210 (Consumer Questions)
Toll free: 1-866-799-3811 (Complaint Intake)
✉: BAREditor@dca.ca.gov
www.autorepair.ca.gov

California Department of Consumer Affairs
Consumer Information Division
1625 N. Market Blvd., Suite N 112
Sacramento, CA 95834
916- 445-1254
Toll free: 1-800-952-5210
TTY: 916-928-1227; 1-800-326-2297
✉: dca@dca.ca.gov
www.dca.ca.gov

Contractors State License Board
9821 Business Park Dr.
Sacramento, CA 95827
916-255-3900 (Headquarters)
916-255-2924 (Northern CA)
562-345-7600 (Southern CA)
Toll free: 1-800-321-2752
www.cslb.ca.gov

County Offices

Contra Costa County District Attorney's Office
Special Operations Division
Consumer Fraud
900 Ward St., 4th Floor
Martinez, CA 94553
925-957-8604
www.co.contra-costa.ca.us

Fresno County District Attorney's Office
Consumer and Environmental Protection Division
929 L St.
Fresno, CA 93721
559-600-3156
✉: damail@co.fresno.ca.us
www.co.fresno.ca.us

Kern County District Attorney's Office
Consumer Protection Unit
Justice Building
1215 Truxtun Ave., 4th Floor
Bakersfield, CA 93301
661-868-7600
✉: investigation@co.kern.ca.us
www.co.kern.ca.us/da

Los Angeles County Department of Consumer Affairs
500 W. Temple St., Room B-96
Los Angeles, CA 90012-2722
213-974-1452
Toll free: 1-800-593-8222 (L.A. County)
TTY: 213-626-0913
✉: dca@dca.lacounty.gov
www.dca.lacounty.gov

Marin County District Attorney's Office
Consumer Protection Unit
3501 Civic Center Dr.
Hall of Justice, Room 130
San Rafael, CA 94903
415-499-6450
✉: consumer@co.marin.ca.us
www.co.marin.ca.us

Monterey County District Attorney's Office
Consumer Protection Division
1200 Aguajito Rd., Room 301
Monterey, CA 93940
831-755-5073 (Salinas)
831-647-7770 (Monterey)
831-385-8373 (King City)
www.co.monterey.ca.us

Napa County District Attorney's Office
Environmental Management
Consumer Protection Division
931 Parkway Mall
Napa, CA 94559
707-253-4059 (Hotline)
www.countyofnapa.org

Orange County District Attorney's Office
Consumer Protection Unit
401 Civic Center Dr., W
Santa Ana, CA 92701
714-648-3600
✉: consumercomplaint@ da.ocgov.com
orangecountyda.com

San Diego County District Attorney's Office
Consumer Protection Unit
330 W. Broadway
San Diego, CA 92101
619-531-4040
619-531-3507 (Hotline)
www.sdcda.org

San Francisco County District Attorney's Office
Consumer and Environmental Protection Unit
732 Brannan St.
San Francisco, CA 94102
415-551-9595 (Hotline)
www.sfdistrictattorney.org

San Luis Obispo County District Attorney's Office
Economic Crime Unit
Consumer Fraud Department
1050 Monterey St., Room 223
County Courthouse Annex
San Luis Obispo, CA 93408
805-781-5856
www.slocounty.ca.gov

San Mateo County District Attorney's Office
Consumer and Environmental Protection Unit
400 County Center, 3rd Floor
Hall of Justice and Records
Redwood City, CA 94063
650-363-4651
650-363-4636 (Bureau of Investigation)
www.co.sanmateo.ca.us

Santa Barbara County District Attorney's Office
Consumer Protection Unit
312-D E. Cook St.
Santa Maria, CA 93454
805-346-7632
www.countyofsb.org/da

Santa Clara County District Attorney's Office
Consumer Protection Unit
70 W. Hedding St., West Wing
San Jose, CA 95110
408-792-2880
✉: consumer_mediation@ da.sccgov.org
www.santaclara-da.org

Santa Cruz County District Attorney's Office
Consumer Affairs Unit
701 Ocean St., Room 200
Santa Cruz, CA 95060
831-454-2050
TTY: 831-454-2123
✉: dao@co.santa-cruz.ca.us
www.co.santa-cruz.ca.us

Solano County District Attorney's Office
Department of Resource Management
Consumer Protection Unit
675 Texas St., Suite 5500
Fairfield, CA 94533
707-784-6765
✉: RMHelp@solanocounty.com
www.co.solano.ca.us/depts/da

Stanislaus County District Attorney's Office
Consumer Protection Unit
832 12th St., Suite 300
Modesto, CA 95354
209-525-5550
www.stanislaus-da.org

Ventura County District Attorney's Office
Consumer Mediation Section
800 S. Victoria Ave.
Ventura, CA 93009
805-654-3110
Toll free: 1-800-660-5474 ext. 3110
da.countyofventura.org

City Offices

Los Angeles City Attorney's Office
Consumer Protection Unit
200 N. Main St., Room 500 CHE
Los Angeles, CA 90012
213-978-8070
TTY: 212-978-8310
www.atty.lacity.org

San Diego City Attorney's Office
Consumer and Environmental Protection Unit
1200 Third Ave., #1620
San Diego, CA 92101
619-533-5600
TTY: 619-702-7198
✉: cityattorney@sandiego.gov
www.sandiego.gov/ cityattorney

Santa Monica City Attorney's Office
Consumer Protection Unit
1685 Main St., 3rd Floor
Santa Monica, CA 90401
310-458-8336
TTY: 310-458-8696
✉: consumer.mailbox@smgov.net
www.smgov.net/atty

Colorado

State Offices

Colorado Office of the Attorney General
Consumer Protection Division
1525 Sherman St., 7th Floor
Denver, CO 80203
303-866-5189
Toll free: 1-800-222-4444 (CO)
✉: stop.fraud@state.co.us
www.coloradoattorneygeneral. gov

County Offices

Fourth Judicial District Attorney's Office
Economic Crimes Division
El Paso and Teller Counties
105 E. Vermijo Ave.
Colorado Springs, CO 80903
719-520-6000
www.4thjudicialda.com

Weld County District Attorney's Office
PO Box 1167
915 10th St.
Greeley, CO 80632-1167
970-356-4010
www.co.weld.co.us

Pueblo County District Attorney's Office
701 Court St.
Pueblo, CO 81003
719-583-6030
www.co.pueblo.co.us

City Offices

Denver District Attorney's Office
Economic Crimes Unit
201 W. Colfax Ave.
Denver, CO 80202
720-913-9179
✉: info@denverda.org
www.denverda.org

Connecticut

State Offices

Connecticut Office of the Attorney General
55 Elm St.
Hartford, CT 06106
860-808-5318
www.ct.gov/ag

Department of Consumer Protection
165 Capitol Ave.
Hartford, CT 06106-1630
860-713-6100 (Consumer Information/Complaints)
Toll free: 1-800-842-2649
TTY: 860-713-7240
✉: trade.practices@ct.gov
www.ct.gov/dcp

City Offices

Middletown Office of Consumer Protection
150 William St.
Middletown, CT 06457
860-344-3491
TTY: 860-344-3521
www.cityofmiddletown.com

Delaware

State Offices

Delaware Department of Justice
Consumer Protection Division
820 N. French St., 5th Floor
Wilmington, DE 19801
302-577-8600
Toll free: 1-800-220-5424
✉: consumer.protection@state. de.us
www.attorneygeneral. delaware.gov

District of Columbia

Department of Consumer and Regulatory Affairs
Government of the District of Columbia
1100 4th St., SW
Washington, DC 20024
202-442-4400
TTY: 202-123-4567
✉: dcra@dc.gov
www.dcra.dc.gov
www.consumer.dc.gov

Office of the Attorney General
Consumer Protection and Antitrust
441 4th St., NW
Washington, DC 20001
202-442-9828 (Hotline)
✉: consumer.protection@dc.gov
www.oag.dc.gov
www.consumer.dc.gov

Florida

State Offices

Florida Department of Agriculture and Consumer Services
Division of Consumer Services
2005 Apalachee Parkway
Terry Lee Rhodes Building
Tallahassee, FL 32399-6500
850-488-2221
Toll free: 1-800-435-7352 (FL)
Toll free: 1-800-352-9832 (in Spanish)
www.800helpfla.com

Florida Office of the Attorney General
PL-01 The Capitol
Tallahassee, FL 32399-1050
850-414-3990
Toll free: 1-866-966-7226 (FL)
Toll free: 1-800-203-3099 (Seniors vs. Crime)
TTY: 1-800-955-8771
myfloridalegal.com
www.seniorsvscrime.com

Regional Offices

Ft. Lauderdale Branch - Office of the Attorney General
Economic Crimes Division
110 S.E. 6th St., 9th Floor
Fort Lauderdale, FL 33301-5000
954-712-4600
www.myfloridalegal.com

Jacksonville Branch - Office of the Attorney General
Economic Crimes Division
1300 Riverplace Blvd., Suite 405
Jacksonville, FL 32207
904-348-2720
www.myfloridalegal.com

Orlando Branch - Office of the Attorney General
Economic Crimes Division
135 W. Central Blvd., Suite 1000
Orlando, FL 32801
407-999-5588
www.myfloridalegal.com

Tampa Branch - Office of the Attorney General
Economic Crimes Division
3507 E. Frontage Rd., Suite 325
Concourse Center 4
Tampa, FL 33607-1795
813-287-7950
www.myfloridalegal.com

West Palm Beach Branch - Office of the Attorney General
Economic Crimes Division
1515 N. Flagler Dr., Suite 900
West Palm Beach, FL 33401
561-837-5000
www.myfloridalegal.com

County Offices

Broward County Permitting, Licensing & Consumer Protection Division
One N. University Dr., Mailbox 302
Plantation, FL 33324
954-765-4400
✉: consumer@broward.org
www.broward.org/ permittingandlicensing

Hillsborough County Consumer Protection Agency
1101 E. 139th Ave.
Tampa, FL 33613
813-903-3430
www.hillsboroughcounty.org/ consumerprotection

Miami-Dade County Consumer Services Department
Consumer Protection Section
140 West Flagler St., Suites 901-904
Miami, FL 33130
305-375-3677
✉: consumer@miamidade.gov
www.miamidade.gov/csd

Office of the State Attorney for Miami-Dade County
Economic Crime Division
1350 N.W. 12th Ave.
Miami, FL 33136-2111
305-547-0671
www.miamisao.com

Orange County Consumer Fraud Unit
PO Box 1673
415 N. Orange Ave.
Orlando, FL 32802
407-836-2490
✉: fraudhelp@sao9.org
www.orangecountyfl.net

Palm Beach County Consumer Affairs Division
50 S. Military Tr., Suite 201
West Palm Beach, FL 33415
561-712-6600
Toll free: 1-888-852-7362 (Boca/ Delray/Glades)
www.pbcgov.com/consumer

Pinellas County Office of Consumer Protection
631 Chestnut St.
Clearwater, FL 33756
727-464-6200
TTY: 727-464-6088
✉: consumer@pinellascounty.org
www.pinellascounty.org/ consumer

Georgia

State Offices

Georgia Governor's Office of Consumer Affairs
Two Martin Luther King, Jr. Dr., SE
Suite 356
Atlanta, GA 30334-4600
404-651-8600
Toll free: 1-800-869-1123 (GA)
www.consumer.georgia.gov

Hawaii

State Offices

Hawaii Department of Commerce and Consumer Affairs - Hilo
Office of Consumer Protection
345 Kekuanaoa St., Suite 12
Hilo, HI 96720
808-933-0910
808-587-3222 (Consumer Resource Center)
✉: ocp@dcca.hawaii.gov
www.hawaii.gov/dcca

Hawaii Department of Commerce and Consumer Affairs - Honolulu (Main Location)
Office of Consumer Protection
235 S. Beretania St., Suite 801
Honolulu, HI 96813
808-586-2630
808-587-3222 (Consumer Resource Center)
✉: ocp@dcca.hawaii.gov
www.hawaii.gov/dcca/ocp

Hawaii Department of Commerce and Consumer Affairs - Wailuku
Office of Consumer Protection
1063 Lower Main St., Suite C-216
Wailuku, HI 96793
808-984-8244
808-587-3222 (Consumer Resource Center)
✉: ocp@dcca.hawaii.gov
www.hawaii.gov/dcca/ocp

Idaho

State Offices

Idaho Attorney General's Office
Consumer Protection Division
PO Box 83720
954 W. Jefferson, 2nd Floor
Boise, ID 83720-0010
208-334-2424
Toll free: 1-800-432-3545 (ID)
www.ag.idaho.gov

Illinois

State Offices

Illinois Office of the Attorney General - Carbondale
Consumer Fraud Bureau
1001 E. Main St.
Carbondale, IL 62901
618-529-6400
Toll free: 1-800-243-0607 (Fraud Hotline, IL)
Toll free: 1-866-310-8398 (in Spanish)
TTY: 1-877-675-9339 (IL)
✉: ag_consumer@atg.state.il.us
www.illinoisattorneygeneral. gov

Illinois Office of the Attorney General - Chicago
Consumer Fraud Bureau
100 W. Randolph St., 12th Floor
Chicago, IL 60601
312-814-3000
Toll free: 1-800-386-5438 (Fraud Hotline, IL)
Toll free: 1-866-310-8398 (in Spanish)
TTY: 1-800-964-3013 (IL)
✉: ag_consumer@atg.state.il.us
www.illinoisattorneygeneral. gov

Illinois Office of the Attorney General - Springfield
Consumer Fraud Division
500 S. 2nd St.
Springfield, IL 62706
217-782-1090
Toll free: 1-800-243-0618 (Fraud Hotline, IL)
Toll free: 1-866-310-8398 (in Spanish)
TTY: 1-877-844-5461 (IL)
✉: ag_consumer@atg.state.il.us
www.illinoisattorneygeneral. gov

Regional Offices

Chicago South Regional Office of the Attorney General
7906 S. Cottage Grove Ave.
Chicago, IL 60619
773-488-2600
TTY: 1-866-717-8798
www.illinoisattorneygeneral. gov

Chicago West Regional Office of the Attorney General
306 N. Pulaski Rd.
Chicago, IL 60624
773-265-8808
TTY: 1-866-717-8804
www.illinoisattorneygeneral. gov

East Central Illinois Regional Office of the Attorney General
1776 E. Washington St.
Urbana, IL 61802
217-278-3366
TTY: 217-278-3371
www.illinoisattorneygeneral. gov

Metro East Illinois Regional Office of the Attorney General
201 W. Pointe Dr., Suite 7
Belleville, IL 62226
618-236-8616
TTY: 618-236-8619
www.illinoisattorneygeneral. gov

Northern Illinois Regional Office of the Attorney General
200 S. Wyman St., Suite 307
Zeke Giorgi Center
Rockford, IL 61101
815-967-3883
TTY: 815-967-3891
www.illinoisattorneygeneral. gov

West Central Illinois Regional Office of the Attorney General
628 Maine St.
Quincy, IL 62301
217-223-2221
TTY: 217-223-2254
www.illinoisattorneygeneral. gov

County Offices

Cook County State Attorney's Office
Consumer Fraud Unit
69 W. Washington St., Suite 3130
Chicago, IL 60602
312-603-8600
312-603-8700 (Consumer Line)
✉: consumer@cookcountygov. com.
www.statesattorney.org/ index2/consumer_fraud.html

City Offices

Chicago Division of Business Affairs and Consumer Protection
City Hall, Room 800
121 N. LaSalle St.
Chicago, IL 60602
312-744-6060
TTY: 312-744-0254
www.cityofchicago.org/ ConsumerServices

Des Plaines Consumer Protection Office
1420 Miner St., Suite 401
Des Plaines, IL 60016
847-391-5303
✉: consumerprotection@ desplaines.org
www.desplaines.org

Indiana

State Offices

Office of the Attorney General
Consumer Protection Division
302 W. Washington St., 5th floor
Indianapolis, IN 46204
317-232-6330
Toll free: 1-800-382-5516
(Consumer Hotline)
www.indianaconsumer.com

Iowa

State Offices

Iowa Office of the Attorney General
Consumer Protection Division
1305 E. Walnut St.
Des Moines, IA 50319
515-281-5926
Toll free: 1-888-777-4590 (IA)
✉: consumer@ag.state.ia.us
www.IowaAttorneyGeneral.org

Kansas

State Offices

Office of Kansas Attorney
Consumer Protection & Antitrust Division
120 S.W. 10th St., Suite 430
Topeka, KS 66612-1597
785-296-3751
Toll free: 1-800-432-2310 (KS)
✉: cprotect@ksag.org
www.ksag.org

County Offices

Douglas County District Attorney's Office
Consumer Protection Division
111 E. 11th St.
Lawrence, KS 66044
785-330-2849 (Consumer Hotline)
785-841-0211 (Main)
✉: districtattorney@douglas-county.com
www.douglas-county.com/ depts/da/da_cpu.aspx

Johnson County District Attorney's Office
Consumer Fraud Unit
PO Box 728
Olathe, KS 66051
913-715-3003 (Consumer Hotline)
da.jocogov.org

Sedgwick County District Attorney's Office
Consumer Fraud and Economic Crime Unit
1900 E. Morris St.
Wichita, KS 67211
316-660-3600
Toll free: 1-800-432-6878 (KS)
✉: consumer@sedgwick.gov
www.sedgwickcounty.org/da

Kentucky

State Offices

Kentucky Office of the Attorney General
Consumer Protection Division
1024 Capital Center Dr.
Frankfort, KY 40601
502-696-5389
Toll free: 1-888-432-9257 (Hotline)
✉: consumer.protection@ag.ky. gov
www.ag.ky.gov/cp

Kentucky Office of the Attorney General - Louisville
Consumer Protection Division
310 Whittington Parkway, Suite 101
Louisville, KY 40222
502-429-7134
Toll free: 1-888-432-9257 (Hotline)
✉: consumer.protection@ag.ky.gov
www.ag.ky.gov

Kentucky Office of the Attorney General - Prestonsburg
361 N. Lake Dr.
Prestonsburg, KY 41653
606-889-1821
✉: consumer.protection@ag.ky.gov
www.ag.ky.gov/cp

Louisiana

State Offices

Louisiana Office of the Attorney General
Consumer Protection Section
1885 N. 3rd St.
Baton Rouge, LA 70802
225-326-6465
Toll free: 1-800-351-4889
✉: ConsumerInfo@ag.state.la.us
www.ag.state.la.us

Parish Offices

Jefferson Parish District Attorney's Office
Economic Crime Unit
200 Derbigny St.
Gretna, LA 70053-5894
504-361-2920
www.jpda.us

Maine

State Offices

Maine Attorney General's Office
Consumer Information and
Mediation Service
Six State House Station
Augusta, ME 04333
207-626-8849
Toll free: 1-800-436-2131
(Consumer Protection)
✉: consumer.mediation@maine.gov
www.maine.gov/ag

Bureau of Consumer Credit Protection
35 State House Station
Augusta, ME 04333-0035
207-624-8527
Toll free: 1-800-332-8529 (ME)
TTY: 1-888-577-6690
www.credit.maine.gov

Maryland

State Offices

Maryland Office of the Attorney General
Consumer Protection Division
200 Saint Paul Pl.
Baltimore, MD 21202
410-528-8662 (Consumer Complaints)
410-576-6550 (Consumer Information)
410-528-1840 (Medical Billing Complaints)
Toll free: 1-888-743-0023
Toll free: 1-877-261-8807 (Health plan decision appeals)
TTY: 410-576-6372 (MD)
✉: consumer@oag.state.md.us
www.oag.state.md.us/consumer

Regional Offices

Maryland Attorney Generals' Office - Western Maryland
Consumer Protection Division
44 N. Potomac St., Suite 104
Hagerstown, MD 21740
301-791-4780
TTY: 410-576-6372 (Baltimore office)
✉: consumer@oag.state.md.us
www.oag.state.md.us/consumer

Maryland Attorney General's Office - Southern Maryland
PO Box 745
Hughesville, MD 20637
301-274-4620
Toll free: 1-866-366-8343
TTY: 410-576-6372 (Baltimore office)
✉: consumer@oag.state.md.us
www.oag.state.md.us/consumer

Maryland Attorney General's Office - Eastern Shore
Consumer Protection Division
201 Baptist St., Suite 30
Salisbury, MD 21801-4976
410-713-3620
Toll free: 1-888-743-0023 (Baltimore office)
TTY: 410-576-6372
✉: consumer@oag.state.md.us
www.oag.state.md.us/consumer

County Offices

Howard County Office of Consumer Affairs
Box 220
6751 Columbia Gateway Dr.
Columbia, MD 21046
410-313-6420
TTY: 410-313-6401
✉: consumer@howardcountymd.gov
www.howardcountymd.gov/CA/CS_ConsumerAffairs.htm

Montgomery County Office of Consumer Protection
100 Maryland Ave., Suite 330
Rockville, MD 20850
240-777-3636
240-777-3681 (Anonymous Consumer Tip Line)
TTY: 240-773-3556
✉: ConsumerProtection@montgomerycountymd.gov
www.montgomerycountymd.gov/consumer

Massachusetts

State Offices

Massachusetts Office of the Attorney General
Public Information and Assistance Center
One Ashburton Pl.
Boston, MA 02108-1518
617-727-8400 (Consumer Hotline)
TTY: 617-727-4765
✉: ago@state.ma.us
www.mass.gov/ago

STATE & LOCAL

Office of Consumer Affairs and Business Regulation
10 Park Plaza, Suite 5170
Boston, MA 02116
617-973-8700 (General Information)
Toll free: 1-888-283-3757 (MA, Consumer Hotline)
TTY: 1-800-720-3480
www.mass.gov/Consumer

Regional Offices

Office of the Attorney General - Central Massachusetts Region
10 Mechanic St., Suite 301
Worcester, MA 01608
508-792-7600
TTY: 617-727-4765
✉: ago@state.ma.us
www.mass.gov/ago

Office of the Attorney General-Southern Massachusetts Region
105 William St., 1st Floor
New Bedford, MA 02740
508-990-9700
✉: ago@state.ma.us
www.mass.gov/ago

Office of the Attorney General - Western Massachusetts Region
1350 Main St., 4th Floor
Springfield, MA 01103
413-784-1240
TTY: 617-727-4765 (Boston office)
✉: ago@state.ma.us
www.mass.gov/ago

County Offices

Northwestern District Attorney's Office - Franklin County
Consumer Protection Unit
13 Conway St.
Greenfield, MA 01301
413-774-5102
northwesterndistrictattorney.org

Northwestern District Attorney's Office - Hampshire County
One Gleason Plaza
Northampton, MA 01060
413-586-9225
northwesterndistrictattorney.org

Norfolk District Attorney's Office
Consumer Protection Division
1515 Hancock St., 4th Floor
Quincy, MA 02169
617-769-6118 (Hotline)
www.mass.gov/da/norfolk

City Offices

Boston Consumer Affairs and Licensing
One City Hall Square, Room 817
Boston, MA 02201-2039
617-635-3834
✉: MOCAL@cityofboston.gov
www.cityofboston.gov/consumeraffairs

Cambridge Consumers' Council
831 Massachusetts Ave., 1st Floor
Cambridge, MA 02139
617-349-6150
TTY: 617-349-6112
✉: Consumer@cambridgema.gov
www.cambridgema.gov/consumercouncil.aspx

Newton-Brookline Consumer Office
1000 Commonwealth Ave.
Newton City Hall
Newton Centre, MA 02459
617-796-1292
TTY: 617-796-1089
✉: consumer@newtonma.gov
www.newtonma.gov

Revere Consumer Affairs Office
150 Beach St.
Revere, MA 02151
781-286-8114
www.revere.org

Springfield Mayor's Office of Consumer Information
36 Court St.
City Hall, Room 315
Springfield, MA 01103
413-787-6437
TTY: 413-787-6154
✉: moci@springfieldcityhall.com
www.springfieldcityhall.com

Michigan

State Offices

Office of the Attorney General
Consumer Protection Division
PO Box 30213

Lansing, MI 48909-7713
517-373-1140
Toll free: 1-877-765-8388
www.michigan.gov/ag

Michigan Department of Agriculture and Rural Development
Consumer Protection Section
Weights & Measures/ Motor Fuel Quality
940 Venture Ln.
Williamston , MI 48895
517-655-8202
Toll free: 1-800-632-3835
www.michigan.gov/wminfo

County Offices

Macomb County Consumer Protection Unit
Office of the Prosecuting Attorney
One S. Main St., 3rd Floor
Mt. Clemens, MI 48043
586-469-5350
www.macombcountymi.gov

City Offices

Detroit Consumer Advocacy Division
18100 Meyers Rd.
Detroit, MI 48235
313-224-6995
www.ci.detroit.mi.us

Minnesota

State Offices

Office of the Attorney General
Consumer Services Division
445 Minnesota St.
1400 Bremer Tower
St. Paul, MN 55101
651-296-3353
Toll free: 1-800-657-3787
TTY: 651-297-7206 or 1-800-366-4812
www.ag.state.mn.us

City Offices

Minneapolis Department of Regulatory Services
Division of Licenses and Consumer Services
350 S. 5th St.
City Hall, Room 1C
Minneapolis, MN 55415
612-673-2080
TTY: 612-673-2157
www.ci.minneapolis.mn.us/business-licensing/

Mississippi

State Offices

Mississippi Department of Agriculture and Commerce
Bureau of Regulatory Services
Consumer Protection
PO Box 1609
Jackson, MS 39215
601-359-1148
www.mdac.state.ms.us

Mississippi Office of the Attorney General
Consumer Protection Division
PO Box 22947
Jackson, MS 39225-2947
601-359-4230
Toll free: 1-800-281-4418 (MS)
www.ago.state.ms.us

Missouri

State Offices

Missouri Attorney General's Office
Consumer Protection Unit
PO Box 899
Jefferson City, MO 65102
573-751-3321
Toll free: 1-800-392-8222 (Hotline)
✉: consumer.help@ago.mo.gov
www.ago.mo.gov

Regional Offices

Missouri Attorney General's Office - St. Louis
Consumer Protection Division
815 Olive St., Suite 200
Old Post Office Building
St. Louis, MO 63101
314-340-6816
Toll free: 1-800-392-8222
✉: consumer.help@ago.mo.gov
www.ago.mo.gov

Montana

State Offices

Montana Office of Consumer Protection
PO Box 200151
2225 11th Ave.
Helena, MT 59620-0151
406-444-4500
Toll free: 1-800-481-6896
✉: contactocp@mt.gov
www.doj.mt.gov/consumer

Nebraska

State Offices

Nebraska Office of the Attorney General
Consumer Protection Division
2115 State Capitol
Lincoln, NE 68509
402-471-2682
Toll free: 1-800-727-6432 (NE)
Toll free: 1-888-850-7555 (in Spanish)
Toll free: 1-888-287-0778 (Senior Hotline)
www.ago.ne.gov

Nevada

State Offices

Nevada Department of Business and Industry
Fight Fraud Task Force
www.fightfraud.nv.gov

New Hampshire

State Offices

New Hampshire Office of the Attorney General
Consumer Protection and Antitrust Bureau
33 Capitol St.
Concord, NH 03301
603-271-3641
Toll free: 1-888-468-4454 (Consumer Protection Hotline)
TTY: 1-800-735-2964 (NH)
✉: DOJ-CPB@doj.nh.gov
www.doj.nh.gov/consumer

New Jersey

State Offices

Department of Law and Public Safety
Division of Consumer Affairs
124 Halsey St.
Newark, NJ 07102
973-504-6200
Toll free: 1-800-242-5846 (NJ)
TTY: 973-504-6588
✉: askconsumeraffairs@lps.state.nj.us
www.njconsumeraffairs.gov

County Offices

Bergen County Office of Consumer Protection
One Bergen County Plaza, 3rd Floor
Hackensack, NJ 07601-7076
201-336-6400
www.co.bergen.nj.us

Burlington County Office of Consumer Affairs/Weights & Measures
PO Box 6000
Mount Holly, NJ 08060-6000
609-265-5098 (Weights & Measures)
609-265-5054 (Consumer Affairs)
✉: consumer@co.burlington.nj.us
www.co.burlington.nj.us

Cape May County Consumer Affairs
Four Moore Rd., DN 310
Cape May Court House, NJ 08210-1601
609-463-6475
✉: consumer@co.cape-may.nj.us
www.capemaycountygov.net

Cumberland County Department of Consumer Affairs
788 E. Commerce St.
Bridgeton, NJ 08302
856-453-2203
www.co.cumberland.nj.us

Essex County Division of Consumer Services
50 S. Clinton St., Suite 3201
East Orange, NJ 07018
973-395-8350
www.essex-countynj.org

Gloucester County Office of Consumer Affairs and Weights & Measures
254 County House Rd.
Clarksboro, NJ 08020
856-384-6855
TTY: 856-232-9543
www.co.gloucester.nj.us/
Government/Departments/
ConsumerAffairs/main.cfm

Hudson County Division of Consumer Affairs
583 Newark Ave.
Jersey City, NJ 07306
201-795-6295 (Hotline)
www.hudsoncountynj.org

Hunterdon County Office of Consumer Affairs
PO Box 2900
Flemington, NJ 08822
908-806-5174
**www.co.hunterdon.nj.us/
consumeraffairs.htm**

Mercer County Office of Consumer Affairs
PO Box 8068
640 S. Broad St.
Trenton, NJ 08650-0068
609-989-6671
www.mercercounty.org

Middlesex County Consumer Affairs
75 Bayard St., 2nd Floor, Room 290
Middlesex County Administration Building
New Brunswick, NJ 08901
732-745-3875
✉: consumer@co.middlesex.nj.us
**www.co.middlesex.nj.us/
consumeraffairs/index.asp**

Monmouth County Department of Consumer Affairs
One E. Main St.
Hall of Records Annex
Freehold, NJ 07728-1255
732-431-7900
www.visitmonmouth.com

Ocean County Department of Consumer Affairs
1027 Hooper Ave., Building #2
Toms River, NJ 08754-2191
732-929-2105
✉: ConsumerAffairs@co.ocean.nj.us
www.co.ocean.nj.us

Passaic County Department of Consumer Protection/Weights & Measures
Department of Law
1310 Route 23 N
Wayne, NJ 07470
973-305-5881 (Consumer Protection)
973-305-5750 (Weights & Measures)
www.passaiccountynj.org

Somerset County Division of Consumer Protection
PO Box 3000
20 Grove St.
Somerville, NJ 08876-1262
908-203-6080
✉: consumerprotection@co.somerset.nj.us
www.co.somerset.nj.us

Union County Division of Consumer Affairs
Department of Public Safety
300 North Ave., E
Westfield, NJ 07090
908-654-9840
www.unioncountynj.org

City Offices

Nutley Consumer Affairs
c/o Department of Public Affairs
149 Chestnut St.
Nutley, NJ 07110
973-284-4975
www.nutleynj.org

Plainfield Action Services
510 Watchung Ave.
City Hall Annex, 1st Floor
Plainfield, NJ 07061
908-753-3519
**www.plainfield.com/
plainfieldactionservices.htm**

Secaucus Department of Consumer Affairs
1203 Patterson Plank Rd.
Municipal Government Center
Secaucus, NJ 07094
201-330-2008

Union Consumer Affairs Office
1976 Morris Ave.
Union, NJ 07083
908-851-5477
www.uniontownship.com

New Mexico

State Offices

Office of Attorney Generral
Consumer Protection Division
PO Drawer 1508
Santa Fe, NM 87504-1508
505-827-6060
Toll free: 1-800-678-1508
www.nmag.gov

New York

State Offices

New York State Department of State
Division of Consumer Protection
Five Empire State Plaza, Suite 2101
Albany, NY 12223
518-474-8583
Toll free: 1-800-697-1220
✉: webmaster@consumer.state.ny.us
www.nysconsumer.gov

New York State Department of State - New York City Office
Division of Consumer Protection
1740 Broadway, 15th Floor
New York City, NY 10019
518-474-8583
Toll free: 1-800-697-1220
✉: webmaster@consumer.state.ny.us
www.nysconsumer.gov

Office of the Attorney General - Albany Office
Bureau of Consumer Frauds and Protection
State Capitol
Albany, NY 12224-0341
518-474-5481
Toll free: 1-800-771-7755 (NY)
TTY: 1-800-788-9898
www.ag.ny.gov

Office of the Attorney General - New York City Office
Bureau of Consumer Frauds and Protection
120 Broadway, 3rd Floor
New York, NY 10271-0332
212-416-8000
Toll free: 1-800-771-7755 (Hotline)
TTY: 1-800-788-9898
www.ag.ny.gov

Regional Offices

Binghamton Regional Office of the Attorney General
44 Hawley St.
State Office Building, 17th Floor
Binghamton, NY 13901
607-721-8771
Toll free: 1-800-771-7755 (Consumer Hotline)
TTY: 1-800-788-9898
www.ag.ny.gov

Brooklyn Regional Office of the Attorney General
55 Hanson Place, Suite 1080
Brooklyn, NY 11217
718-722-3949
Toll free: 1-800-771-7755
(Consumer Hotline)
TTY: 1-800-788-9898
www.ag.ny.gov

Buffalo Regional Office of the Attorney General
350 Main St.
Main Place Tower, Suite 300A
Buffalo, NY 14202
716-853-8400
Toll free: 1-800-771-7755
(Consumer Hotline)
TTY: 1-800-788-9898
www.ag.ny.gov

Harlem Regional Office of the Attorney General
163 W. 125th St., Suite 1324
New York, NY 10027
212-961-4475
Toll free: 1-800-771-7755
(Consumer Hotline)
TTY: 1-800-788-9898
www.ag.ny.gov

Nassau Regional Office of the Attorney General
200 Old Country Rd., Suite 240
Mineola, NY 11501
516-248-3302
Toll free: 1-800-771-7755
(Consumer Hotline)
TTY: 1-800-788-9898
www.ag.ny.gov

Plattsburgh Regional Office of the Attorney General
43 Durkee St., Suite 700
Plattsburgh, NY 12901-2958
518-562-3288
Toll free: 1-800-771-7755
TTY: 1-800-788-9898
www.ag.ny.gov

Poughkeepsie Regional Office of the Attorney General
235 Main St., 3rd Floor
Poughkeepsie, NY 12601-3194
845-485-3900
Toll free: 1-800-771-7755
(Consumer Hotline)
TTY: 1-800-788-9898
www.ag.ny.gov

Rochester Regional Office of the Attorney General
144 Exchange Blvd., Suite 200
Rochester, NY 14614-2176
585-546-7430
Toll free: 1-800-771-7755
(Consumer Hotline)
TTY: 1-800-788-9898
www.ag.ny.gov

Suffolk Regional Office of the Attorney General
300 Motor Parkway, Suite 205
Hauppauge, NY 11788
631-231-2424
Toll free: 1-800-771-7755
(Consumer Helpline)
TTY: 1-800-788-9898
www.ag.ny.gov

Syracuse Regional Office of the Attorney General
615 Erie Blvd. W, Suite 102
Syracuse, NY 13204
315-448-4800
Toll free: 1-800-771-7755
(Consumer Hotline)
TTY: 1-800-788-9898
www.ag.ny.gov

Utica Regional Office of the Attorney General
207 Genesee St., Room 508
Utica, NY 13501
315-793-2225
Toll free: 1-800-771-7755
(Consumer Hotline)
TTY: 1-800-788-9898
www.ag.ny.gov

Watertown Regional Office of the Attorney General
317 Washington St.
Dulles State Office Building
Watertown, NY 13601
315-785-2444
Toll free: 1-800-771-7755
(Consumer Hotline)
TTY: 1-800-788-9898
www.ag.ny.gov

Westchester Regional Office of the Attorney General
101 E. Post Rd.
White Plains, NY 10601-5008
914-422-8755
Toll free: 1-800-771-7755
(Consumer Helpline)
TTY: 1-800-788-9898
www.ag.ny.gov

County Offices

Albany County Department of Consumer Affairs
112 State St., Suite 1207-08
Albany, NY 12207
518-447-7581
✉: consumer_complaints@albanycounty.com
www.albanycounty.com

Erie County District Attorney's Office
Consumer Fraud Bureau
350 Main St., Suite 300A
Main Place Tower
Buffalo, NY 14202
716-853-8404
www.ag.ny.gov

Nassau County Office of Consumer Affairs
200 County Seat Dr.
Mineola, NY 11501
516-571-2600
www.nassaucountyny.gov

Orange County Department of Consumer Affairs
99 Main St.
Goshen, NY 10924
845-360-6700
www.co.orange.ny.us

Putnam County Department of Consumer Affairs
110 Old Route 6, Bldg. 3
Carmel, NY 10512
845-808-1618
www.putnamcountyny.com

Rockland County Office of Consumer Protection
18 New Hempstead Rd., 6th Floor
New City, NY 10956
845-708-7600
www.co.rockland.ny.us

Schenectady County Department of Consumer Affairs/Bureau of Weights & Measures
64 Kellar Ave.
Schenectady, NY 12306
518-356-7473 (Consumer Affairs)
518-356-6795 (Weights & Measures)
www.schenectadycounty.com

STATE & LOCAL

Ulster County Consumer Fraud Bureau
20 Lucas Ave.
Kingston, NY 12401-3708
845-340-3260
**www.ulstercountyny.gov/
consumerfraud**

**Westchester County
Department of Consumer
Protection**
112 E. Post Rd., 4th Floor
White Plains, NY 10601
914-995-2155
✉: conpro@westchestergov.com
consumer.westchestergov.com

City Offices

Mt. Vernon Office of Consumer Affairs
One Roosevelt Square, Room 11
City Hall
Mount Vernon, NY 10550
914-665-2433
www.cmvny.com

New York City Department of Consumer Affairs
42 Broadway
New York, NY 10004
212-639-9675
718-286-2296 (in Korean)
TTY: 212-487-2710
www.nyc.gov/consumers

Town of Colonie Consumer Protection Board
534 Loudon Rd.
Memorial Town Hall
Newtonville, NY 12128
518-783-2787
www.colonie.org

Yonkers Consumer Protection Bureau
87 Nepperhan Ave., Room 212
Yonkers, NY 10701
914-377-6808
914-377-3000 (Helpline)
www.yonkersny.gov

North Carolina

State Offices

North Carolina Department of Agriculture and Consumer Services
1001 Mail Service Center
Raleigh , NC 27699-1001
919-733-3000
**www.agr.state.nc.us/index.
htm**

North Carolina Office of the Attorney General
Consumer Protection Division
Mail Service Center 9001
Raleigh, NC 27699-9001
919-716-6000
Toll free: 1-877-566-7226 (NC)
www.ncdoj.gov

North Dakota

State Offices

Office of the Attorney General
Consumer Protection and
Antitrust Division
1050 E. Interstate Ave., Suite 200
Gateway Professional Center
Bismarck, ND 58503-5574
701-328-3404
Toll free: 1-800-472-2600
TTY: 1-800-366-6888
✉: ndag@nd.gov
www.ag.nd.gov

Ohio

State Offices

Ohio Attorney General's Office
Consumer Protection Section
30 E. Broad St., 14th Floor
Columbus, OH 43215-3400
614-466-4320
Toll free: 1-800-282-0515
www.ohioattorneygeneral.gov
www.speakoutohio.gov
(consumer website)

County Offices

Summit County Office of Consumer Affairs
175 S. Main St., Suite 209
Akron, OH 44308
330-643-2879
✉: consumeraffairs@summitoh.
net
**www.co.summit.oh.us/
conaffairs.htm**

Oklahoma

State Offices

Oklahoma Attorney General
Consumer Protection Unit
313 N.E. 21st St.
Oklahoma City, OK 73105
405-521-3921 (Oklahoma City)
918-581-2885 (Tulsa)
www.oag.ok.gov

Oklahoma Department of Consumer Credit
4545 N. Lincoln Blvd., Suite 164
Oklahoma City, OK 73105-3403
405-521-3653
Toll free: 1-800-448-4904
✉: webmaster@okdocc.state.
ok.us
www.okdocc.state.ok.us

Oregon

State Offices

Oregon Department of Justice
Financial Fraud/Consumer
Protection Section
1162 Court St., NE
Salem, OR 97301-4096
503-378-4320 (Salem)
503-229-5576 (Portland)
Toll free: 1-877-877-9392 (OR)
TTY: 1-800-735-2900
✉: consumer.hotline@doj.state.
or.us
www.doj.state.or.us

Pennsylvania

State Offices

Office of the Attorney General
Bureau of Consumer Protection
Strawberry Square, 14th Floor
Harrisburg, PA 17120
717-787-9707
Toll free: 1-800-441-2555 (PA)
Toll free: 1-888-520-6680 (Home
Improvement)
www.attorneygeneral.gov

Regional Offices

Erie Regional Office of the Attorney General
Bureau of Consumer Protection
1001 State St., 10th Floor
Erie, PA 16501
814-871-4371
www.attorneygeneral.gov

Philadelphia Regional Office of the Attorney General
Bureau of Consumer Protection
21 S. 12th St., 2nd Floor
Philadelphia, PA 19107
215-560-2414
www.attorneygeneral.gov

Pittsburgh Regional Office of the Attorney General

Bureau of Consumer Protection
564 Forbes Ave.
Manor Complex, 6th Floor
Pittsburgh, PA 15219
412-565-5135
Toll free: 1-800-441-2555
www.attorneygeneral.gov

Scranton Regional Office of the Attorney General

Bureau of Consumer Protection
101 Penn Ave.
100 Samter Building
Scranton, PA 18503
570-963-4913
www.attorneygeneral.gov

County Offices

Bucks County Department of Consumer Protection

50 N. Main St.
Doylestown, PA 18901
215-348-7442
✉: consumerprotection@
co.bucks.pa.us
www.buckscounty.org

Delaware County Consumer Affairs

201 W. Front St.
Government Center Building
Media, PA 19063
610-891-4865
**www.co.delaware.pa.us/
consumeraffairs**

Puerto Rico

State Offices

Department de Asuntos Del Consumidor

Minillas Station
Apartado 41059
Santurce, PR 00940
787-722-7555
Toll free: 1-866-520-3226 (PR)
www.daco.gobierno.pr

Rhode Island

State Offices

Rhode Island Department of the Attorney General

Consumer Protection Unit
150 S. Main St.
Providence, RI 02903
401-274-4400
✉: contactus@riag.ri.gov
www.riag.state.ri.us

South Carolina

State Offices

South Carolina Department of Consumer Affairs

PO Box 5757
3600 Forest Dr., 3rd Floor
Columbia, SC 29250
803-734-4200
Toll free: 1-800-922-1594 (SC)
✉: scdca@scconsumer.gov
www.scconsumer.gov

South Dakota

State Offices

South Dakota Office of the Attorney General

Consumer Protection
1302 E. Highway 14, Suite 3
Pierre, SD 57501
605-773-4400
Toll free: 1-800-300-1986 (SD)
TTY: 605-773-6585
✉: consumerhelp@state.sd.us
www.state.sd.us/atg

Tennessee

State Offices

Tennessee Office of the Attorney General

Consumer Advocate and
Protection Division
PO Box 20207
Nashville, TN 37202-0207
615-741-1671
**www.attorneygeneral.state.
tn.us**

Tennessee Department of Commerce and Insurance

Division of Consumer Affairs
500 James Robertson Parkway
12th Floor
Nashville, TN 37243-0600
615-741-4737
Toll free: 1-800-342-8385 (TN)
✉: consumer.affairs@tn.gov
www.tn.gov/consumer

Texas

State Offices

Texas Office of the Attorney General

Consumer Protection Division
PO Box 12548
Austin, TX 78711-2548
512-463-2185
Toll free: 1-800-621-0508
www.oag.state.tx.us

Regional Offices

Office of the Attorney General - Dallas Region

Consumer Protection Division
1412 Main St., Suite 810
Dallas, TX 75202
214-969-7639
Toll free: 1-800-621-0508 (TX)
www.oag.state.tx.us

Office of the Attorney General - El Paso Region

Consumer Protection Division
401 E. Franklin Ave., Suite 530
El Paso, TX 79901
915-834-5800
www.oag.state.tx.us

Office of the Attorney General - Houston Region

Consumer Protection Division
808 Travis St., Suite 1520
Houston, TX 77002-
713-223-5886
Toll free: 1-800-621-0508 (TX)
www.oag.state.tx.us

Office of the Attorney General - Lubbock Region

Consumer Protection Division
4630 50th St., Suite 500
Lubbock, TX 79414
806-747-5238
Toll free: 1-800-621-0508 (TX)
www.oag.state.tx.us

Office of the Attorney General - McAllen Region

Consumer Protection Division
3201 N. McColl Rd., Suite B
McAllen, TX 78501
956-682-4547
Toll free: 1-800-621-0508 (TX)
www.oag.state.tx.us

STATE & LOCAL

Office of the Attorney General - San Antonio Region
Consumer Protection Division
115 E. Travis St., Suite 925
San Antonio, TX 78205
210-224-1007
Toll free: 1-800-621-0508 (TX)
www.oag.state.tx.us

County Offices

Dallas County District Attorney's Office
Check Division/ID Fraud
133 N. Industrial Blvd., LB 19
Dallas, TX 75207
214-653-3672
www.dallasda.com

Harris County District Attorney's Office
Consumer Protection Section
1201 Franklin St., Suite 600
Houston, TX 77002-1923
713-755-5836
app.dao.hctx.net

Utah

State Offices

Utah Department of Commerce
Division of Consumer Protection
PO Box 146704
160 E. 300 S, 2nd Floor
Salt Lake City, UT 84114-6704
801-530-6601
Toll free: 1-800-721-7233
✉: consumerprotection@utah.gov
www.consumerprotection.utah.gov

Vermont

State Offices

Vermont Office of the Attorney General
Consumer Assistance Program
146 University Pl.
Burlington, VT 05405
802-656-3183
Toll free: 1-800-649-2424 (VT)
✉: consumer@uvm.edu
www.atg.state.vt.us

Vermont Agency of Agriculture, Food, and Markets
Food Safety and Consumer Protection
116 State St.
Montpelier, VT 05620
802-828-2436
www.vermontagriculture.com

Virgin Islands

State Offices

Virgin Islands Department of Licensing and Consumer Affairs
3000 Golden Rock Shopping Center, Suite 9
St. Croix, VI 00820
340-773-2226
www.dlca.gov.vi

Virgin Islands Department of Licensing and Consumer Affairs
8201 Sub Base, Suite 1
Property and Procurement Bldg.
St. Thomas, VI 00802
340-774-3130
www.dlca.gov.vi

Virginia

State Offices

Virginia Department of Agriculture and Consumer Services
Office of Consumer Affairs
102 Governor St.
Richmond, VA 23219
804-786-2042
Toll free: 1-800-552-9963 (VA)
TTY: 1-800-828-1120
✉: webmaster.vdacs@vdacs.virginia.gov
www.vdacs.virginia.gov

County Offices

Fairfax County Department of Cable Communications and Consumer Protection
12000 Government Center Parkway, Suite 433
Fairfax, VA 22035
703-222-8435
TTY: 711
www.fairfaxcounty.gov/consumer.htm

City Offices

Office of Consumer Affairs
301 King St.
City Hall, Room 1900
Alexandria, VA 22313
703-746-4350
www.alexandriava.gov/citizen

Office of the Commonwealth's Attorney
Consumer Affairs Division
2425 Nimmo Parkway
Judicial Center, Building 10B
Virginia Beach, VA 23456
757-385-6373
✉: OCACAAdmin@vbgov.com
www.vbgov.com/dept/oca/

Washington

State Offices

Washington Office of the Attorney General
Toll free: 1-800-551-4636
TTY: 1-800-833-6384
www.atg.wa.gov

Regional Offices

Bellingham Office of the Attorney General
Consumer Protection Division
(Island, San Juan, Skagit and Whatcom Counties)
103 E. Holly St., Suite 308
Bellingham, WA 98225-4728
360-676-2037
Toll free: 1-800-551-4636 (WA)
TTY: 1-800-833-6384
www.atg.wa.gov

Seattle Office of the Attorney General
Consumer Protection Division
(N. King, Snohomish, Clallam and Jefferson Counties and Bainbridge Island)
800 5th Ave., Suite 2000
Seattle, WA 98104
206-464-7744
Toll free: 1-800-551-4636 (WA)
TTY: 1-800-833-6384
www.atg.wa.gov

Spokane Office of the Attorney General
Consumer Protection Division
(Eastern Washington)
1116 W. Riverside Ave.
Spokane, WA 99201-1194
509-456-3123
Toll free: 1-800-551-4636 (WA)
TTY: 1-800-833-6384
www.atg.wa.gov

Tacoma Office of the Attorney General
Consumer Protection Division
(Pierce, Mason, Grays Harbor
Kitsap, and South King Counties)
1250 Pacific Ave.
Tacoma, WA 98402
253-593-5243
Toll free: 1-800-551-4636 (WA)
TTY: 1-800-833-6384
www.atg.wa.gov

Vancouver Office of the Attorney General
Consumer Protection Division
(Clark, Cowlitz, Pacific, Skamania,
Wahkiakum, Lewis, and Thurston
Counties)
1220 Main St., Suite 549
Vancouver, WA 98660-2964
360-759-2100
Toll free: 1-800-551-4636 (WA)
TTY: 1-800-833-6384
www.atg.wa.gov/consumer

West Virginia

State Offices

Office of the Attorney General
Consumer Protection Division
PO Box 1789
Charleston, WV 25326-1789
304-558-8986
Toll free: 1-800-368-8808 (WV)
✉: consumer@wvago.gov
www.wvago.gov

Wisconsin

State Offices

Wisconsin Department of Agriculture, Trade and Consumer Protection
Bureau of Consumer Protection
2811 Agriculture Dr.
PO Box 8911
Madison, WI 53708-8911
608-224-4949
Toll free: 1-800-422-7128 (WI)
TTY: 608-224-5058
✉: hotline@datcp.state.wi.us
www.datcp.state.wi.us

Wyoming

State Offices

Office of the Attorney General
Consumer Protection Unit
200 W. 24th St.
123 State Capitol
Cheyenne, WY 82002
307-777-7841
TTY: 307-777-5351
attorneygeneral.state.wy.us

STATE & LOCAL

Contacting Your Local Banking Authority

The officials listed below regulate and supervise state-chartered banks. Many of them handle or refer problems and complaints about other types of financial institutions as well. Some also answer general questions about banking and consumer credit. If you are dealing with a federally chartered bank, check "Federal Agencies" on page 96. Also see the chart in the "Banking" section on page 3.

Alabama

State Banking Department
PO Box 4600
Montgomery, AL 36103-4600
334-242-3452
Toll free: 1-866-465-2279
www.banking.alabama.gov

Alaska

Department of Commerce, Community and Economic Development
Division of Banking and Securities
PO Box 110807
Juneau, AK 99811-0807
907-465-2521
Toll free: 1-888-925-2521
TTY: 907-465-5437
✉: dbsc@commerce.state.ak.us
www.commerce.state.ak.us/bsc/home.htm

Arizona

Department of Financial Institutions
2910 N. 44th St., Suite 310
Phoenix, AZ 85018
602-771-2800
Toll free: 1-800-544-0708
✉ consumeraffairs@azdfi.gov
www.azdfi.gov

Arkansas

State Bank Department
400 Hardin Rd., Suite 100
Little Rock, AR 72211
501-324-9019
✉ asbd@banking.state.ar.us
www.arkansas.gov/bank

California

State Department of Financial Institutions
45 Fremont St., Suite 1700
San Francisco, CA 94105-2219
415-263-8500
916-322-0622 (Consumer Services)
Toll free: 1-800-622-0620 (CA)
✉: consumer@dfi.ca.gov
www.dfi.ca.gov

Colorado

Department of Regulatory Agencies
Division of Banking
1560 Broadway, Suite 975
Denver, CO 80202
303-894-7575
✉: banking@dora.state.co.us
www.dora.state.co.us/banking

Connecticut

Connecticut Department of Banking
Government Relations and Consumer Affairs
260 Constitution Plaza
Hartford, CT 06103
860-240-8299
Toll free: 1-800-831-7225
www.state.ct.us/dob

Delaware

Office of the State Bank Commissioner
555 E. Loockerman St., Suite 210
Dover, DE 19901
302-739-4235
www.banking.delaware.gov

District of Columbia

Department of Insurance, Securities and Banking
Attn: Consumer Protection Advocate
810 1st St., NE, Suite 701
Washington, DC 20002
202-727-8000
✉: disb@dc.gov
www.disb.dc.gov

Florida

Office of Financial Regulation
Division of Financial Institutions
200 E. Gaines St.
Tallahassee, FL 32399-0371
850-410-9800
Toll free: 1-800-848-3792 (FL)
✉: ofr@flofr.com
www.flofr.com

Georgia

Department of Banking and Finance
2990 Brandywine Rd., Suite 200
Atlanta, GA 30341-5565
770-986-1633
Toll free: 1-888-986-1633 (GA)
www.dbf.georgia.gov

Hawaii

Department of Commerce and Consumer Affairs
Division of Financial Institutions
PO Box 2054
Honolulu, HI 96805
808-586-2820
808-984-2400, 6-2820# (Maui)
808-974-4000, 6-2820# (Hawaii)
808-274-3141 (Kauai)
Toll free: 1-800-468-4644 (Lanai and Molokai)
✉: dfi@dcca.hawaii.gov
www.hawaii.gov/dcca/dfi

Idaho

Department of Finance
Financial Institutions Bureau
PO Box 83720
Boise, ID 83720-0031
208-332-8005
Toll free: 1-888-346-3378 (ID)
✉: finance@finance.idaho.gov
www.finance.idaho.gov

Illinois

Department of Financial and Professional Regulation
320 W. Washington St.
Springfield, IL 62786
217-782-3000
Toll free: 1-800-532-8785
TTY: 217-524-6644
www.idfpr.com

Indiana

Department of Financial Institutions
30 S. Meridian St., Suite 300
Indianapolis, IN 46204
317-232-3955
Toll free: 1-800-382-4880 (IN)
www.in.gov/dfi

Iowa

Division of Banking
200 E. Grand Ave., Suite 300
Des Moines, IA 50309-1827
515-281-4014
www.idob.state.ia.us

Kansas

Office of the State Bank Commissioner
700 S.W. Jackson St., Suite 300
Topeka, KS 66603-3714
785-296-2266
Toll free: 1-877-387-8523
(Consumer Helpline)
✉: complaints@osbckansas.org
www.osbckansas.org

Kentucky

Department of Financial Institutions
1025 Capitol Center Dr., Suite 200
Frankfort, KY 40601
502-573-3390
Toll free: 1-800-223-2579
✉: kfi@ky.gov
www.kfi.ky.gov

Louisiana

Office of Financial Institutions
PO Box 94095
Baton Rouge, LA 70804-9095
225-925-4660
✉: ofila@ofi.la.gov
www.ofi.state.la.us

Maine

Bureau of Financial Institutions
36 State House Station
Augusta, ME 04333-0036
207-624-8570
Toll free: 1-800-965-5235
www.maine.gov/pfr/ financialinstitutions

Maryland

Commissioner of Financial Regulation
500 N. Calvert St., Suite 402
Baltimore, MD 21202
410-230-6077
Toll free: 1-888-784-0136 (MD)
TTY: 410-767-2117
✉: CFRComplaints@dllr.state.md.us
www.dllr.state.md.us/finance

Massachusetts

Division of Banks
1000 Washington St., 10th Floor
Boston, MA 02110-6400
617-956-1500
Toll free: 1-800-495-2265 (MA)
TTY: 617-956-1577
✉: dobconsumer.assistan@state.ma.us
www.mass.gov/dob

Michigan

Office of Financial and Insurance Regulation
PO Box 30220
Lansing, MI 48909-7720
517-373-0220
Toll free: 1-877-999-6442 (MI)
✉: ofir-fin-info@michigan.gov
www.michigan.gov/ofir

Minnesota

Department of Commerce
Financial Examinations Division
85 7th Pl. E., Suite 500
St. Paul, MN 55101
651-296-2135
TTY: 651-296-2860
✉: financial.commerce@state.mn.us
www.commerce.state.mn.us

Mississippi

Department of Banking and Consumer Finance
501 N. West St.
901 Woolfolk Building, Suite A
Jackson, MS 39201
601-359-1031
Toll free: 1-800-844-2499 (MS)
www.dbcf.state.ms.us

Missouri

Department of Finance
301 W. High St., Room 630
PO Box 716
Jefferson City, MO 65102
573-751-3242
✉: finance@dof.mo.gov
www.finance.mo.gov

Montana

Division of Banking and Financial Institutions
PO Box 200546
301 S. Park Ave., Suite 316
Helena, MT 59620
406-841-2920
Toll free: 1-800-914-8423
TTY: 406-444-1421
www.banking.mt.gov

Nebraska

Department of Banking and Finance
PO Box 95006
Lincoln, NE 68509-5006
402-471-2171
Toll free: 1-877-471-3445
www.ndbf.ne.gov

Nevada

Department of Business and Industry
Financial Institutions Division
2785 E. Desert Inn Rd.
Las Vegas, NV 89121
702-486-4120
Toll free: 1-866-858-8951 (NV)
✉: FIDMaster@fid.state.nv.us
www.fid.state.nv.us

New Hampshire

State Banking Department
53 Regional Dr., Suite 200
Concord, NH 03301
603-271-3561
Toll free: 1-800-437-5991
TTY: 1-800-735-2964
✉: NHBD@Banking.State.NH.US
www.nh.gov/banking

New Jersey

Department of Banking and Insurance
Division of Banking
PO Box 040
Trenton, NJ 08625
609-292-7272
Toll free: 1-800-446-7467
www.state.nj.us/dobi

New Mexico

Regulation and Licensing Department
Financial Institutions Division
2550 Cerrillos Rd., 3rd Floor
Santa Fe, NM 87505
505-476-4885
✉: rld.fid@state.nm.us
www.rld.state.nm.us/FID

New York

Banking Department
Consumer Help Unit
One State St.
New York, NY 10004-1417
212-709-3530
Toll free: 1-877-226-5697 (NY)
✉: consumer@banking.state.ny.us
www.banking.state.ny.us

North Carolina

Commissioner of Banks
4309 Mail Service Center
Raleigh, NC 27699-4309
Toll free: 1-888-384-3811
www.nccob.org

North Dakota

Department of Financial Institutions
2000 Schafer St., Suite G
Bismarck, ND 58501-1204
701-328-9933
TTY: 1-800-366-6888 (ND)
✉: dfi@nd.gov
www.nd.gov/dfi

Ohio

Department of Commerce
Division of Financial Institutions
Consumer Complaints
77 S. High St., 21st Floor
Columbus, OH 43215-6120
614-728-8400
Toll free: 1-866-278-0003
TTY: 1-800-750-0750
✉: webdfi-cf@com.state.oh.us
www.com.ohio.gov/fiin

Oklahoma

State Banking Department
2900 N. Lincoln Blvd.
Oklahoma City, OK 73105
405-521-2782
www.osbd.state.ok.us

Oregon

Department of Consumer and Business Services
Division of Finance and Corporate Securities
PO Box 14480
Salem, OR 97309-0405
503-378-4140
Toll free: 1-866-814-9710
✉: dcbs.dfcsmail@state.or.us
dfcs.oregon.gov

Pennsylvania

Department of Banking
17 N. Second St., Suite 1300
Harrisburg, PA 17101-2290
717-787-2665
Toll free: 1-800-722-2657
TTY: 1-800-679-5070
www.banking.state.pa.us

Puerto Rico

Oficina del Comisionado de Instituciones Financieras
PO Box 11855
San Juan, PR 00910-3855
787-723-3131
www.ocif.gobierno.pr

Rhode Island

Department of Business Regulation
Division of Banking
1511 Pontiac Ave.
Cranston, RI 02920
401-462-9503
✉: bankinquiry@dbr.state.ri.us
www.dbr.state.ri.us

South Carolina

Office of the Commissioner of Banking
1205 Pendleton St., Suite 305
Columbia, SC 29201
803-734-2001
www.banking.sc.gov

South Dakota

Department of Labor and Regulation
Division of Banking
217 1/2 W. Missouri Ave.
Pierre, SD 57501-4590
605-773-3421
✉: drr.banking.info@state.sd.us
www.dlr.sd.gov/reg/bank

Tennessee

Department of Financial Institutions
Consumer Resources Division
414 Union St., Suite 1000
Nashville, TN 37219
615-253-2023
Toll free: 1-800-778-4215
✉: TDFI.ConsumerResources@state.tn.us
www.tennessee.gov/tdfi

Texas

Department of Banking
2601 N. Lamar Blvd., Suite 201
Austin, TX 78705
512-475-1300
Toll free: 1-877-276-5554
(Consumer Hotline)
✉: consumer.complaints@
banking.state.tx.us
www.banking.state.tx.us

Utah

**Department of Financial
Institutions**
PO Box 146800
Salt Lake City, UT 84114-6800
801-538-8830
www.dfi.utah.gov

Vermont

**Department of Banking,
Insurance, Securities and
Health Care Administration**
Division of Banking
89 Main St., Drawer 20
Montpelier, VT 05620-3101
802-828-3301
Toll free: 1-888-568-4547
✉: BISHCA-BNKConsumer@
state.vt.us
www.bishca.state.vt.us

Virgin Islands

**Office of the Lieutenant
Governor**
Division of Banking and Insurance
18 Kongens Gade
St. Thomas, VI 00802
340-774-7166
www.ltg.gov.vi

Virginia

State Corporation Commission
Bureau of Financial Institutions
PO Box 640
Richmond, VA 23218
804-371-9657
804-371-9705
Toll free: 1-800-552-7945 (VA)
TTY: 804-371-9206
✉: bfiquestions@scc.virginia.gov
www.scc.virginia.gov

Washington

**Department of Financial
Institutions**
PO Box 41200
Olympia, WA 98504-1200
360-902-8700
Toll free: 1-877-746-4334
TTY: 360-664-8126
www.dfi.wa.gov

West Virginia

Division of Banking
One Players Club Dr., Suite 300
Charleston, WV 25311
304-558-2294
www.wvdob.org

Wisconsin

**Department of Financial
Institutions**
Division of Banking
PO Box 7876
Madison, WI 53707-7876
608-261-7578
TTY: 608-266-8818
✉: askthesecretary@dfi.state.
wi.us
www.wdfi.org

Wyoming

Division of Banking
122 W. 25th St.
Herschler Building, 3rd Floor, E
Cheyenne, WY 82002
307-777-7797
audit.state.wy.us/banking

Contacting Your Local Insurance Regulator

The officials listed below enforce laws and regulations for each type of insurance. Many of these offices can also provide you with information to help you make informed insurance-buying decisions. See the "Insurance" section in Part I of this Handbook for advice (p. 27).

If you have a question or complaint about your insurance company's policies, contact the company before you contact your state insurance regulator.

Alabama

Department of Insurance
PO Box 303351
Montgomery, AL 36130-3351
334-241-4141 (Consumer Services)
334-269-3550
✉: ConsumerServices@insurance.alabama.gov
www.aldoi.gov

Alaska

Division of Insurance
Department of Commerce, Community and Economic Development
550 W. 7th Ave., Suite 1560
Robert B. Atwood Building
Anchorage, AK 99501-3567
907-269-7900
Toll free: 1-800-467-8725
TTY: 907-465-5437
✉: insurance@alaska.gov
www.dced.state.ak.us/insurance

Arizona

Department of Insurance
Consumer Affairs Division
2910 N. 44th St., Suite 210
Phoenix, AZ 85018-7269
602-364-2499
Toll free: 1-800-325-2548 (AZ)
✉: consumers@azinsurance.gov
www.id.state.az.us

Arkansas

Insurance Department
Consumer Services Division
1200 W. Third St.
Little Rock, AR 72201-1904
501-371-2640
Toll free: 1-800-852-5494
✉: insurance.consumers@arkansas.gov
www.insurance.arkansas.gov

California

California Department of Insurance
Consumer Services Division
300 S. Spring St., South Tower
Los Angeles, CA 90013
213-897-8921
Toll free: 1-800-927-4357 (CA)
TTY: 1-800-482-4833
www.insurance.ca.gov

Department of Managed Health Care, California HMO Help Center
980 9th St., Suite 500
Sacramento, CA 95814-2725
Toll free: 1-888-466-2219
TTY: 1-877-688-9891
✉: GenInfo@dmhc.ca.gov
www.hmohelp.ca.gov

Colorado

Division of Insurance
1560 Broadway, Suite 850
Denver, CO 80202
303-894-7490 (Consumer Information)
Toll free: 1-800-930-3745 (CO)
TTY: 711
✉: insurance@dora.state.co.us
www.dora.state.co.us/Insurance

Connecticut

Insurance Department
Consumer Affairs Division
PO Box 816
Hartford, CT 06142-0816
860-297-3900
Toll free: 1-800-203-3447 (CT)
✉: cid.ca@ct.gov
www.ct.gov/cid

Delaware

Delaware Insurance Department
841 Silver Lake Blvd.
Dover, DE 19904
302-674-7310
Toll free: 1-800-282-8611
✉: consumer@state.de.us
www.delawareinsurance.gov

District of Columbia

Department of Insurance, Securities and Banking
Attn: Consumer Protection Advocate
810 First St., NE, Suite 701
Washington, DC 20002
202-727-8000
✉: disb@dc.gov
www.disb.dc.gov

Florida

Office of Insurance Regulation
200 E. Gaines St.
Tallahassee, FL 32399
850-413-3140
Toll free: 1-877-693-5236
www.floir.com

Georgia

Insurance and Safety Fire Commissioner
Two Martin Luther King, Jr. Dr.
West Tower, Suite 716
Atlanta, GA 30334
404-656-2070
Toll free: 1-800-656-2298 (GA)
TTY: 711
www.gainsurance.org

Hawaii

Department of Commerce and Consumer Affairs
Insurance Division
PO Box 3614
Honolulu, HI 96811
808-586-2790
✉: insurance@dcca.hawaii.gov
www.hawaii.gov/dcca/ins

Idaho

Department of Insurance
Consumer Affairs Bureau
PO Box 83720
700 W. State St.
Boise, ID 83720-0043
208-334-4250
Toll free: 1-800-721-3272 (ID)
www.doi.idaho.gov

Illinois

Division of Insurance - Springfield
320 W. Washington St.
Springfield, IL 62767-0001
217-782-4515
Toll free: 1-877-527-9431 (Office of Consumer Health Insurance)
Toll free: 1-866-445-5364 (Consumer Assistance Hotline)
TTY: 217-524-4872
✉: doi.director@illinois.gov
www.insurance.illinois.gov

Indiana

Department of Insurance
Consumer Services Division
311 W. Washington St., Suite 300
Indianapolis, IN 46204
317-232-2395
Toll free: 1-800-622-4461 (IN)
✉: consumerservices@idoi.in.gov
www.in.gov/idoi

Iowa

Division of Insurance
330 Maple St.
Des Moines, IA 50319-0065
515-281-6348
Toll free: 1-877-955-1212 (IA)
www.iid.state.ia.us

Kansas

Kansas Insurance Department
Consumer Assistance Division
420 S.W. 9th St.
Topeka, KS 66612
785-296-3071
Toll free: 1-800-432-2484 (KS)
TTY: 1-877-235-3151
✉: commissioner@ksinsurance.org
www.ksinsurance.org

Kentucky

Department of Insurance
Consumer Protection and Education Division
PO Box 517
Frankfort, KY 40602-0517
502-564-6034
Toll free: 1-800-595-6053
TTY: 1-800-648-6056
✉: doi.info@ky.gov
insurance.ky.gov

Louisiana

Department of Insurance
PO Box 94214
Baton Rouge, LA 70804-9214
225-342-5900
Toll free: 1-800-259-5300
www.ldi.state.la.us

Maine

Bureau of Insurance
34 State House Station
Augusta, ME 04333-0034
207-624-8475
Toll free: 1-800-300-5000 (ME)
TTY: 1-888-577-6690
✉: Insurance.PFR@maine.gov
www.maine.gov/insurance

Maryland

Insurance Administration
200 St. Paul Pl., Suite 2700
Baltimore, MD 21202
410-468-2000
Toll free: 1-800-492-6116
TTY: 1-800-735-2258
www.mdinsurance.state.md.us

Massachusetts

Division of Insurance
1000 Washington St., Suite 810
Boston, MA 02118-6200
617-521-7794
www.state.ma.us/doi

Michigan

Office of Financial and Insurance Regulation
PO Box 30220
Lansing, MI 48909-7720
517-373-0220
Toll free: 1-877-999-6442
✉: ofir-ins-info@michigan.gov
www.michigan.gov/ofir

Minnesota

Department of Commerce
Market Assurance Division
Suite 500
85 7th Place E
St. Paul, MN 55101
651-296-2488
Toll free: 1-800-657-3602 (MN)
✉: market.assurance@state.mn.us
www.insurance.mn.gov

Mississippi

Department of Insurance
PO Box 79
Jackson, MS 39205
601-359-3569
Toll free: 1-800-562-2957 (MS)
✉: consumer@mid.state.ms.us
www.mid.state.ms.us

Missouri

Missouri Department of Insurance, Financial, and Professional Registration
Consumer Affairs Division
PO Box 690
Jefferson City, MO 65102-0690
573-751-4126
Toll free: 1-800-726-7390 (MO)
TTY: 573-526-4536
✉: consumeraffairs@insurance.mo.gov
www.insurance.mo.gov

Montana

Montana State Auditor's Office
Insurance Division
840 Helena Ave.
Helena, MT 59601
406-444-2040
Toll free: 1-800-332-6148 (MT)
TTY: 406-444-3246
www.sao.mt.gov

Nebraska

Department of Insurance
941 O St., Suite 400
PO Box 82089
Lincoln, NE 68501-2089
402-471-0888
Toll free: 1-877-564-7323 (NE)
TTY: 1-800-833-7352
✉: DOI.ConsumerAffairs@nebraska.gov
www.doi.ne.gov

Nevada

Department of Business and Industry
Division of Insurance
788 Fairview Dr., Suite 300
Carson City, NV 89701
775-687-4270
Toll free: 1-888-872-3234
✉: cscc@doi.state.nv.us
www.doi.state.nv.us/

Department of Business and Industry
Division of Insurance
2501 E. Sahara Ave., #302
Las Vegas, NV 89104
702-486-4009
Toll free: 1-888-872-3234
✉: cnsmsvlv@doi.state.nv.us
www.doi.state.nv.us/

New Hampshire

Department of Insurance
21 S. Fruit St., Suite 14
Concord, NH 03301
603-271-2261
Toll free: 1-800-852-3416 (NH)
TTY: 1-800-735-2964 (NH)
✉: consumerservices@ins.nh.gov
www.nh.gov/insurance

New Jersey

Department of Banking and Insurance
Consumer Inquiries and Complaints
PO Box 471
Trenton, NJ 08625-0471
609-292-7272
Toll free: 1-800-446-7467
www.njdobi.org

New Mexico

Department of Insurance
PO Box 1269
Santa Fe, NM 87504-1269
505-827-4601
Toll free: 1-888-427-5772 (NM)
www.nmprc.state.nm.us

New York

Insurance Department
Consumer Services Bureau
One Commerce Plaza
Albany, NY 12257
518-474-6600
Toll free: 1-800-342-3736 (NY)
✉: consumers@ins.state.ny.us
www.ins.state.ny.us

Insurance Department
Consumer Services Bureau
25 Beaver St.
New York, NY 10004
212-480-6400
Toll free: 1-800-342-3736 (NY)
✉: consumers@ins.state.ny.us
www.ins.state.ny.us

North Carolina

Department of Insurance
1201 Mail Service Center
Raleigh, NC 27699-1201
919-807-6750 (Consumer Services)
Toll free: 1-800-546-5664 (NC, Consumer Services)
www.ncdoi.com

North Dakota

Insurance Department
State Capitol, 5th Floor
600 E. Boulevard Ave.
Bismarck, ND 58505-0320
701-328-2440
Toll free: 1-800-247-0560 (ND)
TTY: 1-800-366-6888
✉: insurance@nd.gov
www.nd.gov/ndins

Ohio

Department of Insurance
Office of Consumer Services
Suite 300
50 W. Town St., 3rd Floor
Columbus, OH 43215
614-644-2658
Toll free: 1-800-686-1526 (Consumer Hotline)
Toll free: 1-800-686-1527 (Fraud Hotline)
Toll free: 1-800-686-1578 (Senior Hotline)
TTY: 614-644-3745
www.insurance.ohio.gov

Oklahoma

Insurance Department
3625 N.W. 56th St., Suite 100
Five Corporate Plaza
Oklahoma City, OK 73112
405-521-2991
Toll free: 1-800-522-0071 (OK)
www.ok.gov/oid

Oregon

Insurance Division
PO Box 14480
Salem, OR 97309-0405
503-947-7984
Toll free: 1-888-877-4894 (OR)
✉: cp.ins@state.or.us
www.insurance.oregon.gov

Pennsylvania

Insurance Department
Bureau of Consumer Service
1209 Strawberry Square
Harrisburg, PA 17120
717-787-2317
Toll free: 1-877-881-6388
TTY: 717-783-3898
✉: ra-in-consumer@state.pa.us
www.insurance.state.pa.us

Puerto Rico

Office of the Commissioner of Insurance
B5 Calle Tabonuco, Suite 216 PMB 356
Guaynabo, PR 00968-3029
787-304-8686
Toll free: 1-888-722-8686
www.ocs.gobierno.pr

Rhode Island

Department of Business Regulation
Insurance Division
1511 Pontiac Ave.
Cranston, RI 02920
401-462-9520
✉: InsuranceInquiry@dbr.ri.gov
www.dbr.state.ri.us

South Carolina

Department of Insurance
Consumer Services
PO Box 100105
Columbia, SC 29202-3105
803-737-6180
Toll free: 1-800-768-3467 (SC)
✉: info@doi.sc.gov
www.doi.sc.gov

South Dakota

Department of Revenue and Regulation
Division of Insurance
445 E. Capital Ave.
Pierre, SD 57501
605-773-3563
✉: insurance@state.sd.us
www.sdjobs.org/reg/insurance

Tennessee

Department of Commerce and Insurance
Consumer Insurance Services
Davy Crockett Tower
500 James Robertson Parkway
Nashville, TN 37243
615-741-2218
Toll free: 1-800-342-4029 (TN)
✉: insurance.info@tn.gov
www.tn.gov/commerce

Texas

Department of Insurance
Consumer Protection (111-1A)
PO Box 149091
Austin, TX 78714-9091
512-463-6515
Toll free: 1-800-252-3439
TTY: 512 322-4238
✉: consumerprotection@tdi.state.tx.us
www.tdi.state.tx.us

Utah

Department of Insurance
State Office Building, Room 3110
Salt Lake City, UT 84114-6901
801-538-3800
Toll free: 1-800-439-3805 (UT)
TTY: 801-538-3826
www.insurance.utah.gov

Vermont

Department of Banking, Insurance, Securities and Health Care Administration
Insurance Division - Consumer Services
89 Main St.
Montpelier, VT 05620-3101
802-828-3301
802-828-2900   (Health Insurance)
Toll free: 1-800-964-1784
Toll free: 1-800-631-7788 (Health Insurance)
✉: consumercomplaints@state.vt.us
www.bishca.state.vt.us
www.vthealthinsurance.info

Virgin Islands

Division of Banking and Insurance
5049 Kongens Gade
St. Thomas, VI 00802
340-774-7166
www.ltg.gov.vi

Virginia

Bureau of Insurance
State Corporation Commission
PO Box 1157
Richmond, VA 23218
804-371-9741
Toll free: 1-800-552-7945 (VA)
TTY: 804-371-9206
✉: bureauofinsurance@scc.virginia.gov
www.scc.virginia.gov

Washington

Office of the Insurance Commissioner
Consumer Advocacy
PO Box 40256
Olympia, WA 98504-0256
360-725-7080
Toll free: 1-800-562-6900 (WA)
TTY: 360-586-0241
✉: cap@oic.wa.gov
www.insurance.wa.gov

West Virginia

Offices of the Insurance Commissioner
PO Box 50540
1124 Smith St.
Charleston, WV 25305-0540
304-558-3386
Toll free: 1-888-879-9842 (WV)
TTY: 1-800-435-7381
✉: consumer.service@wvinsurance.gov
www.wvinsurance.gov

Wisconsin

Office of the Commissioner of Insurance
PO Box 7873
Madison, WI 53707-7873
608-266-0103
Toll free: 1-800-236-8517 (WI)
TTY: Dial 711 and ask for 608-266-3586
✉: ocicomplaints@wisconsin.gov
oci.wi.gov

Wyoming

Department of Insurance
Consumer Affairs Section
106 E. 6th Ave.
Cheyenne, WY 82002
307-777-7402
Toll free: 1-800-438-5768 (WY)
insurance.state.wy.us

Contacting Your Local Securities Administrator

State securities regulators protect the investing public. Each state has its own laws and regulations for securities brokers and securities, including stocks, mutual funds, commodities, real estate, etc. The agencies listed below enforce these laws and regulations; they also license securities professionals, register securities, and investigate consumer complaints. While these agencies do not provide investment advice, many of them offer educational resources so investors can make informed investment decisions.

If you have a question or complaint about an investment, call the company or bank involved. If you are not satisfied with the response you get, call your state securities agency. See the "Investing" section in Part I of this Handbook for additional advice and sources of assistance (p. 35).

Alabama

Securities Commission
PO Box 304700
Montgomery, AL 36130-4700
334-242-2984
Toll free: 1-800-222-1253 (AL)
✉: asc@asc.alabama.gov
www.asc.state.al.us

Alaska

Department of Commerce, Community and Economic Development
Division of Banking and Securities
PO Box 110807
Juneau, AK 99811-0807
907-465-2521
Toll free: 1-888-925-2521 (AK)
TTY: 907-465-5437
✉: dbsc@alaska.gov
www.commerce.state.ak.us

Arizona

Arizona Corporation Commission
Securities Division
1300 W. Washington St., 3rd Floor
Phoenix, AZ 85007
602-542-4242
Toll free: 1-866-837-4399 (AZ)
✉: info@azinvestor.gov
www.azinvestor.gov

Arkansas

Arkansas Securities Department
201 E. Markham St.
Heritage West Building, Suite 300
Little Rock, AR 72201-1692
501-324-9260
Toll free: 1-800-981-4429
✉: info@securities.arkansas.gov
www.securities.arkansas.gov

California

Department of Corporations
Consumer Services Office
1515 K St., Suite 200
Sacramento, CA 95814
Toll free: 1-866-275-2677
TTY: 1-800-735-2966
www.corp.ca.gov

Colorado

Department of Regulatory Agencies
Division of Securities
1560 Broadway, Suite 900
Denver, CO 80202
303-894-2320
TTY: 1-800-659-2656
✉: securities@dora.state.co.us
www.dora.state.co.us/securities

Connecticut

Department of Banking
Securities and Business
Investments Division
260 Constitution Plaza
Hartford, CT 06103-1800
860-240-8230
Toll free: 1-800-831-7225
www.ct.gov/dob

Delaware

Department of Justice
Division of Securities
820 N. French St., 5th Floor
State Office Building
Wilmington, DE 19801
302-577-8424
TTY: 302-577-5783
www.state.de.us/securities

District of Columbia

Deparment of Insurance, Securities and Banking
Attn: Consumer Protection Advocate
810 1st St., NE, Suite 701
Washington, DC 20002
202-727-8000
✉: disb@dc.gov
disb.dc.gov

Florida

Office of Financial Regulation
Division of Securities
200 E. Gaines St.
Attn: Securities Area Financial Manager
Tallahassee, FL 32399-0374
850-410-9500
Toll free: 1-800-848-3792 (FL)
✉: ofr@flofr.com
www.flofr.com

Georgia

Office of the Secretary of State
Division of Securities and Business Regulation
237 Coliseum Dr.
Macon, GA 31217-3858
404-656-3920
Toll free: 1-888-733-7427
✉: securities@sos.state.ga.us
www.sos.ga.gov/securities

Hawaii

Department of Commerce and Consumer Affairs
Securities Enforcement Branch
Business Registration Division
PO Box 40
Honolulu, HI 96810
808-586-2744
Toll free: 1-877-587-2267
✉: seb@dcca.hawaii.gov
www.hawaii.gov/dcca/sec

Idaho

Department of Finance
Securities Bureau
PO Box 83720
Boise, ID 83720-0031
208-332-8000
Toll free: 1-888-346-3378 (ID)
✉: finance@finance.idaho.gov
finance.idaho.gov

Illinois

Secretary of State
Securities Department
300 W. Jefferson St., Suite 300A
Jefferson Terrace
Springfield, IL 62702
217-782-2256
Toll free: 1-800-628-7937 (IL)
www.sos.state.il.us

Indiana

Office of the Secretary of State
Securities Division
302 W. Washington St., Room
E-111
Indianapolis, IN 46204
317-232-6681
Toll free: 1-800-223-8791 (IN)
www.state.in.us/sos/securities

Iowa

Securities Bureau
340 Maple St.
Des Moines, IA 50319-0066
515-281-5705
Toll free: 1-877-955-1212 (IA)
✉: iowasec@iid.state.ia.us
www.iid.state.ia.us

Kansas

Office of the Securities Commissioner
109 S.W. 9th St., Suite 600
Topeka, KS 66612
785-296-3307
Toll free: 1-800-232-9580 (KS)
✉: ksc@ksc.ks.gov
www.ksc.ks.gov

Kentucky

Department of Financial Institutions
Division of Securities
1025 Capitol Center Dr., Suite 200
Frankfort, KY 40601-3868
502-573-3390
Toll free: 1-800-223-2579
✉: kfi@ky.gov
www.kfi.ky.gov

Louisiana

Office of Financial Institutions
Securities Division
PO Box 94095
Baton Rouge, LA 70804
225-925-4660
✉: ofila@ofi.louisiana.gov
www.ofi.state.la.us

Maine

Office of Securities
121 State House Station
Augusta, ME 04333-0121
207-624-8551
Toll free: 1-877-624-8551 (ME)
TTY: 1-888-577-6690
www.maine.gov/pfr/securities

Maryland

Office of the Attorney General
Securities Division
200 Saint Paul Pl.
Baltimore, MD 21202-2020
410-576-6360
Toll free: 1-888-743-0023 (MD)
TTY: 410-576-6372
✉: securities@oag.state.md.us
www.oag.state.md.us

Massachusetts

Office of the Secretary of the Commonwealth
Securities Division
One Ashburton Pl., 17th Floor,
Room 1701
Boston, MA 02108
617-727-3548
Toll free: 1-800-269-5428 (MA)
TTY: 617-878-3889
✉: securities@sec.state.ma.us
www.sec.state.ma.us/sct

Michigan

Office of Financial and Insurance Regulation
Securities Division
PO Box 30220
Lansing, MI 48909
517-373-0220
Toll free: 1-877-999-6442
✉: ofir-sec-info@michigan.gov
www.michigan.gov/ofis

Minnesota

Department of Commerce
Market Assurance Division
85 7th Pl. E, Suite 600
St. Paul, MN 55101
651-296-4973
Toll free: 1-800-657-3602 (MN)
TTY: 651-296-2860
✉: securities.commerce@state.
mn.us
www.commerce.state.mn.us

Mississippi

Secretary of State's Office
Securities Division
Business Regulation and
Enforcement
PO Box 136
Jackson, MS 39205-0136
601-359-1048
Toll free: 1-888-236-6167
www.sos.ms.gov

Missouri

Office of the Secretary of State
Securities Division
600 W. Main St.
Jefferson City, MO 65101-1276
573-751-4136
Toll free: 1-800-721-7996 (MO)
✉: securities@sos.mo.gov
www.sos.mo.gov

Montana

Montana State Auditor's Office
Securities Division
840 Helena Ave.
Helena, MT 59601
406-444-2040
Toll free: 1-800-332-6148 (MT)
✉: stateauditor@mt.gov
www.sao.mt.gov

Nebraska

Department of Banking and Finance
Bureau of Securities
PO Box 95006
Lincoln, NE 68509-5006
402-471-3445
Toll free: 1-877-471-3445
www.ndbf.ne.gov

Nevada

Office of the Secretary of State
Securities Division
555 E. Washington Ave., Suite 5200
Las Vegas, NV 89101
702-486-2440
✉: nvsec@sos.nv.gov
www.sos.state.nv.us

New Hampshire

Bureau of Securities Regulation
107 N. Main St., #204
Concord, NH 03301
603-271-1463
Toll free: 1-800-994-4200
✉: securities@sos.nh.gov
www.sos.nh.gov/securities

New Jersey

Department of Law and Public Safety
Bureau of Securities
PO Box 47029
Newark, NJ 07101
973-504-3600
Toll free: 1-866-446-8378 (NJ)
✉: Askbureauofsecurities@dca.lps.state.nj.us
www.njsecurities.gov

New Mexico

Regulation & Licensing Department
Securities Division
2550 Cerrillos Rd., 3rd Floor
Santa Fe, NM 87505
505-476-4580
Toll free: 1-800-704-5533 (NM)
www.rld.state.nm.us/securities

New York

Office of the Attorney General
Investor Protection Bureau
120 Broadway, 23rd Floor
New York, NY 10271
212-416-8200
www.oag.state.ny.us

North Carolina

Securities Division
PO Box 29622
Raleigh, NC 27626-0622
919-733-3924
Toll free: 1-800-688-4507 (Investor Hotline)
✉: secdiv@sosnc.com
www.sosnc.com

North Dakota

Securities Department
600 E. Boulevard Ave.
State Capitol, 5th Floor
Bismarck, ND 58505-0510
701-328-2910
Toll free: 1-800-297-5124 (ND)
✉: ndsecurities@nd.gov
www.ndsecurities.com

Ohio

Division of Securities
77 S. High St., 22nd Floor
Columbus, OH 43215-6131
614-644-7381
Toll free: 1-800-788-1194 (Investor Protection Hotline)
✉: securitiesgeneral.questions@com.state.oh.us
www.com.ohio.gov/secu

Oklahoma

Department of Securities
120 N. Robinson Ave., Suite 860
First National Center
Oklahoma City, OK 73102
405-280-7700
✉: general@securities.state.ok.gov
www.securities.ok.gov

Oregon

Department of Consumer and Business Services
Division of Finance and Corporate Securities
PO Box 14480
Salem, OR 97309-0405
503-378-4140
Toll free: 1-866-814-9710
TTY: 503-378-4100
✉: cp.ins@state.or.us
www.dfcs.oregon.gov

Pennsylvania

Securities Commission
Office of the Secretary
1010 N. 7th St.
Eastgate Office Building, 2nd Floor
Harrisburg, PA 17102-1410
717-787-8061
Toll free: 1-800-600-0007 (PA)
✉: pscwebmaster@state.pa.us
www.psc.state.pa.us

Puerto Rico

Office of the Commissioner of Financial Institutions
Securities Division
PO Box 11855
San Juan, PR 00910-3855
787-723-3131
✉: valores@ocif.gobierno.pr
www.ocif.gobierno.pr

Rhode Island

Department of Business Regulation
Securities Division
1511 Pontiac Ave.
Cranston, RI 02920
401-462-9527
✉: securitiesinquiry@dbr.ri.gov
www.dbr.state.ri.us

South Carolina

Office of the Attorney General
Securities Division
PO Box 11549
Columbia, SC 29211-1549
803-734-9916
www.scag.gov/scsecurities

South Dakota

Department of Labor and Regulation
Division of Securities
445 E. Capitol Ave.
Pierre, SD 57501-3185
605-773-4823
✉: drr.securities@state.sd.us
www.dlr.sd.gov/securities

Tennessee

Department of Commerce and Insurance
Securities Division
500 James Robertson Parkway
Davy Crockett Tower, Suite 680
Nashville, TN 37243-0575
615-741-2947
Toll free: 1-800-863-9117 (TN)
✉: Securities.1@tn.gov
www.state.tn.us/commerce/ securities

Texas

State Securities Board
PO Box 13167
Austin, TX 78711-3167
512-305-8300
www.ssb.state.tx.us

Utah

Department of Commerce
Division of Securities
PO Box 146760
Salt Lake City, UT 84114-6760
801-530-6600
Toll free: 1-800-721-7233 (UT)
✉: securities@utah.gov
www.securities.utah.gov

Vermont

Department of Banking, Insurance, Securities, & Health Care Administration
Securities Division
89 Main St.
Montpelier, VT 05620-3101
802-828-3301
www.vermontsecurities.info

Virginia

State Corporation Commission
Division of Securities and Retail Franchising
PO Box 1197
Richmond, VA 23218
804-371-9051
Toll free: 1-800-552-7945 (VA)
TTY: 804-371-9206
✉: SRF_General@scc.virginia. gov
www.scc.virginia.gov/srf

Washington

Department of Financial Institutions
Division of Securities
PO Box 41200
Olympia, WA 98504-1200
360-902-8760
Toll free: 1-877-746-4334
TTY: 360-664-8126
✉: investorcomplaints@dfi. wa.gov
www.dfi.wa.gov

West Virginia

State Auditor's Office
Securities Commission
Building 1, Room W-100
1900 Kanawha Blvd.
Charleston, WV 25305
304-558-2251
✉: securities@wvsao.gov
www.wvsao.gov/ securitiescommission

Wisconsin

Department of Financial Institutions
Division of Securities
PO Box 1768, 4th Floor
Madison, WI 53701-1768
608-266-1064
TTY: 608-266-8818
www.wdfi.org

Wyoming

Office of the Secretary of State
Compliance Division
200 W. 24th St.
State Capitol Building
Cheyenne, WY 82002-0020
307-777-7370
✉: compliance@wyo.gov
soswy.state.wy.us

Contacting Your Local Utilities Commission

State utilities commissions regulate services and rates for gas, electricity, and telephones in your state. In some states, the utility commissions regulate other services such as water, transportation, and the moving of household goods. Rates for utilities and services provided between states are regulated by the federal government.

Many utility commissions handle consumer complaints. Sometimes, if they receive a number of complaints about the same utility matter, they will conduct investigations.

Alabama

Public Service Commission
Consumer Services
PO Box 304260
Montgomery, AL 36130
334-242-5025
Toll free: 1-800-392-8050 (AL)
www.psc.state.al.us

Alaska

Regulatory Commission of Alaska
Consumer Protection Department
701 W. 8th Ave., Suite 300
Anchorage, AK 99501-3469
907-276-6222
Toll free: 1-800-390-2782
TTY: 907-276-4533
✉: rca.mail@alaska.gov
rca.alaska.gov

Arizona

Arizona Corporation Commission
Utilities Division
Consumer Services Section
1200 W. Washington St.
Phoenix, AZ 85007-2996
602-542-4251
Toll free: 1-800-222-7000 (AZ)
✉: mailmaster@azcc.gov
www.cc.state.az.us

Arkansas

Public Service Commission
Consumer Services Division
PO Box 400
Little Rock, AR 72203-0400
501-682-2051
Toll free: 1-800-482-1164 (AR)
TTY: 1-800-682-2698
✉: consumerissues@psc.state.ar.us
www.arkansas.gov/psc

California

Public Utilities Commission
Consumer Affairs Branch
505 Van Ness Ave., Room 2250
San Francisco, CA 94102
415-703-2782
Toll free: 1-800-649-7570 (CA)
TTY: 1-800-229-6846
✉: public.advisor@cpuc.ca.go
www.cpuc.ca.gov

Colorado

Public Utilities Commission
Consumer Protection Division
1560 Broadway, Suite 250
Denver, CO 80202
303-894-2070
Toll free: 1-800-456-0858 (CO)
✉: puc@dora.state.co.us
www.dora.state.co.us/puc

Connecticut

Department of Energy and Environmental Protection
Public Utilities Regulatory Authority
10 Franklin Square
New Britain, CT 06051
860-827-1553
Toll free: 1-800-382-4586 (CT)
TTY: 860-827-2837
✉: dpuc.information@po.state.ct.us
www.state.ct.us/dpuc

Delaware

Public Service Commission
861 Silver Lake Blvd.
Cannon Building, Suite 100
Dover, DE 19904
302-736-7500
Toll free: 1-800-282-8574 (DE)
www.depsc.delaware.gov

District of Columbia

DC Public Service Commission
Office of Consumer Services
1333 H St., NW, Suite 600
Washington, DC 20005
202-626-5120
www.dcpsc.org

Florida

Florida Public Service Commission
2540 Shumard Oak Blvd.
Tallahassee, FL 32399-0850
850-413-6100
Toll free: 1-800-342-3552 (FL)
TTY: 1-800-955-8771
✉: contact@psc.state.fl.us
www.floridapsc.com

Georgia

Public Service Commission
Consumer Affairs Division
244 Washington St., SW
Atlanta, GA 30334
404-656-4501
Toll free: 1-800-282-5813 (GA)
✉: gapsc@psc.state.ga.us
www.psc.state.ga.us

Hawaii

Public Utilities Commission
465 S. King St., Room 103
Honolulu, HI 96813
808-586-2020
✉: Hawaii.puc@hawaii.gov
www.puc.hawaii.gov

Idaho

Public Utilities Commission
Consumer Assistance Section
PO Box 83720
Boise, ID 83720-0074
208-334-0369
Toll free: 1-800-432-0369 (ID)
www.puc.idaho.gov

Illinois

Commerce Commission
Consumer Affairs
527 E. Capitol Ave.
Springfield, IL 62701
217-782-2024
Toll free: 1-800-524-0795 (IL)
TTY: 1-800-858-9277
www.icc.illinois.gov

Indiana

Utility Regulatory Commission
Consumer Affairs Division
101 W. Washington St., Suite 1500E
Indianapolis, IN 46204
317-232-2712
Toll free: 1-800-851-4268 (IN)
TTY: 317-232-8556
www.in.gov/iurc

Iowa

Utilities Board
Customer Service Group
1375 E. Court Ave., Room 69
Des Moines, IA 50319-0069
515-725-7300
Toll free: 1-877-565-4450 (IA)
✉: iub@iub.iowa.gov
www.state.ia.us/iub

Kansas

Corporation Commission
Office of Public Affairs and
Consumer Protection
1500 S.W. Arrowhead Rd.
Topeka, KS 66604
785-271-3140
Toll free: 1-800-662-0027 (KS)
TTY: 1-800-766-3777
✉: public.affairs@kcc.ks.gov
www.kcc.state.ks.us

Kentucky

Public Service Commission
PO Box 615
211 Sower Blvd.
Frankfort, KY 40602
502-564-3940
Toll free: 1-800-772-4636
TTY: 1-800-648-6056
www.psc.state.ky.us

Louisiana

Public Service Commission
602 N. Fifth St., Galvez Building
12th Floor
PO Box 91154
Baton Rouge, LA 70821-9154
225-342-4404
Toll free: 1-800-256-2397 (LA)
www.lpsc.org

Maine

Public Utilities Commission
Consumer Assistance Division
18 State House Station
Augusta, ME 04333-0018
207-287-3831
Toll free: 1-800-452-4699 (ME)
TTY: 1-800-437-1220
✉: maine.puc@maine.gov
www.state.me.us/mpuc

Maryland

Public Service Commission
Six St. Paul St., 16th Floor
Baltimore, MD 21202
410-767-8000
Toll free: 1-800-492-0474
TTY: 1-800-201-7165
www.psc.state.md.us

Massachusetts

Department of Public Utilities
Consumer Division
One South Station
Boston, MA 02110
617-737-2836
Toll free: 1-877-886-5066
TTY: 1-800-974-6006
✉: DPUConsumer.Complaints@
state.ma.us
www.mass.gov/dpu

Michigan

Public Service Commission
PO Box 30221
Lansing, MI 48909
517-241-6180
Toll free: 1-800-292-9555 (MI)
✉: mpsc_commissioners@
michigan.gov
www.michigan.gov/mpsc

Minnesota

Public Utilities Commission
Consumer Affairs Office
121 7th Pl. E, Suite 350
St. Paul, MN 55101-2147
651-296-0406
Toll free: 1-800-657-3782
✉: consumer.puc@state.mn.us
www.puc.state.mn.us

Mississippi

Public Service Commission
P.O. Box 1174
Woolfolk Building
Jackson, MS 39215
601-961-5430 (Central District)
601-961-5440 (Southern District)
601-961-5450 (Chairman &
Northern District)
Toll free: 1-800-356-6430 (Central
District)
Toll free: 1-800-356-6429 (Southern
District)
Toll free: 1-800-356-6428
(Chairman & Northern District)
www.psc.state.ms.us

Missouri

Public Service Commission
Consumer Services Department
PO Box 360
200 Madison St.
Jefferson City, MO 65102-0360
573-751-3234
Toll free: 1-800-392-4211 (MO)
TTY: 573-22-9061
✉: pscinfo@psc.mo.gov
www.psc.mo.gov

Montana

Public Service Commission
PO Box 202601
Helena, MT 59620-2601
406-444-6199
Toll free: 1-800-646-6150 (MT)
TTY: 406-444-4212
www.psc.mt.gov

Nebraska

Public Service Commission
1200 N St., Suite 300
Lincoln, NE 68508
402-471-3101
Toll free: 1-800-526-0017 (NE)
TTY: 402-471-0213
www.psc.state.ne.us

Nevada

Public Utilities Commission
Consumer Division
1150 E. William St.
Carson City, NV 89701-3109
775-684-6100
702-486-2600 (Las Vegas)
Toll free: 1-800-992-0900 ext. 46101
(NV)
pucweb1.state.nv.us/pucn

New Hampshire

Public Utilities Commission
21 S. Fruit St., Suite 10
Concord, NH 03301-2429
603-271-2431
Toll free: 1-800-852-3793 (NH)
TTY: 1-800-735-2964 (NH)
✉: puc@puc.nh.gov
www.puc.state.nh.us

New Jersey

Board of Public Utilities
Division of Customer Assistance
Two Gateway Center, 8th Floor
Newark, NJ 07102
973-648-2350
Toll free: 1-800-624-0241 (NJ)
Toll free: 1-800-624-0331 (Cable Complaint)
www.bpu.state.nj.us

New Mexico

Public Regulation Commission
Utilities Division
Consumer Relations Division
PO Box 1269
Santa Fe, NM 87504-1269
505-827-4592
Toll free: 1-888-427-5772
TTY: 505-827-6911
✉: crd.complaints@state.nm.us
www.nmprc.state.nm.us

New York

Department of Public Service
Office of Consumer Services
3 Empire State Plaza
Albany, NY 12223
518-474-7080
Toll free: 1-800-342-3377 (NY - General Complaints)
Toll free: 1-888-342-3355 (Termination)
www.askpsc.com

North Carolina

NC Utilities Commission
Consumer Services
4325 Mail Service Center
Raleigh, NC 27699-4325
919-733-9277
Toll free: 1-866-380-9816
✉: consumer.services@psncuc.nc.gov
www.ncuc.commerce.state.nc.us/

North Dakota

Public Service Commission
600 E. Boulevard Ave., Dept. 408
Bismarck, ND 58505-0480
701-328-2400
Toll free: 1-877-245-6685
TTY: 1-800-366-6888 (ND)
✉: ndpsc@nd.gov
www.psc.nd.gov

Ohio

Ohio Consumers' Counsel
10 W. Broad St., Suite 1800
Columbus, OH 43215-3485
614-466-8574 (outside OH)
Toll free: 1-877-742-5622
✉: occ@occ.state.oh.us
www.pickocc.org

Public Utilities Commission
180 E. Broad St.
Columbus, OH 43215
614-466-3292
Toll free: 1-800-686-7826 (OH)
TTY: 1-800-686-1570 (OH)
www.puco.ohio.gov

Oklahoma

Corporation Commission
Consumer Services Division
PO Box 52000
Oklahoma City, OK 73152-2000
405-522-0478
Toll free: 1-800-522-8154 (OK)
TTY: 405-521-3513
www.occeweb.com

Oregon

Public Utility Commission
Consumer Services Division
PO Box 2148
550 Capitol St., NE, Suite 215
Salem, OR 97308-2148
503-378-6600
Toll free: 1-800-522-2404
TTY: 1-800-648-3458 (OR)
✉: puc.consumer@state.or.us
www.puc.state.or.us

Pennsylvania

Office of the Attorney General
Pennsylvania Office of Consumer Advocate
5th Floor, Forum Place
555 Walnut St.
Harrisburg, PA 17101-1923
717-783-5048
Toll free: 1-800-684-6560 (PA)
✉: consumer@paoca.org
www.oca.state.pa.us

Public Utility Commission
Bureau of Consumer Services
PO Box 3265
Harrisburg, PA 17105-3265
Toll free: 1-800-692-7380
www.puc.state.pa.us

Puerto Rico

Public Service Commission
Hato Rey Station
PO Box 190870
San Juan, PR 00907-3981
787-756-1919

Rhode Island

Public Utilities Commission
Consumer Section
89 Jefferson Blvd.
Warwick, RI 02888
401-780-9700
✉: consumer.section@ripuc.org
www.ripuc.org

South Carolina

Consumer Services Division
Office of Regulatory Staff
1401 Main St., Suite 900
Columbia, SC 29201
803-737-5230
Toll free: 1-800-922-1531 (SC)
TTY: 1-800-334-2217 (SC)
www.regulatorystaff.sc.gov

South Dakota

Public Utilities Commission
Consumer Affairs
500 E. Capitol Ave.
Pierre, SD 57501-5070
605-773-3201 (General)
Toll free: 1-800-332-1782
✉: PUCConsumerInfo@state.sd.us
www.puc.sd.gov

Tennessee

Tennessee Regulatory Authority
Consumer Services Division
460 James Robertson Parkway
Nashville, TN 37243-0505
615-741-2904
Toll free: 1-800-342-8359
(Consumer Services)
TTY: 1-888-276-0677
www.state.tn.us/tra

Texas

Public Utility Commission
Customer Protection
PO Box 13326
1701 N. Congress Ave.
Austin, TX 78711-3326
512-936-7120
Toll free: 1-888-782-8477
TTY: 1-800-735-2988
✉: customer@puc.state.tx.us
www.puc.state.tx.us

Utah

Division of Public Utilities
160 East 300 South
Salt Lake City, UT 84114-6751
801-530-6716
Toll free: 1-800-874-0904 (UT)
TTY: 801-530-6769
✉: psc@utah.gov
www.psc.utah.gov

Vermont

Public Service Board
112 State St., 4th Floor
Montpelier, VT 05620-2701
802-828-2358
TTY: 1-800-253-0191 (VT)
✉: psb.clerk@state.vt.us
www.psb.vermont.gov

Virginia

State Corporation Commission
Bureau of Public Utilities
PO Box 1197
Richmond, VA 23218
804-371-9611
Toll free: 1-800-552-7945 (VA)
TTY: 804-371-9206
✉: EnergyReg@scc.virginia.gov
www.scc.virginia.gov

Washington

Utilities and Transportation Commission
PO Box 47250
Olympia, WA 98504
360-664-1160
Toll free: 1-888-333-9882
TTY: 1-800-416-5289
✉: consumer@utc.wa.gov
www.utc.wa.gov

West Virginia

Public Service Commission
Customer Assistance
201 Brooks St.
PO Box 812
Charleston, WV 25323
304-340-0300
Toll free: 1-800-642-8544
www.psc.state.wv.us

Consumer Advocate Division
Union Building, Suite 700
723 Kanawha Blvd., E
Charleston, WV 25301
304-558-0526
www.cad.state.wv.us

Wisconsin

Public Service Commission
Consumer Affairs Unit
PO Box 7854
Madison, WI 53707-7854
608-266-2001
Toll free: 1-800-225-7729
TTY: 608-267-1479
www.psc.wi.gov

Wyoming

Public Service Commission
2515 Warren Ave., Suite 304
Cheyenne, WY 82002
307-777-7427
Toll free: 1-888-570-9905 (WY)
✉: wpsc_complaints@state.
wy.us
psc.state.wy.us

Contacting Trade & Professional Organizations

Companies that manufacture similar products or offer similar services often belong to an industry association. These associations help resolve problems between their member companies and consumers. Most also provide consumer information through publications and websites.

If you have a problem with a company and cannot resolve it by working directly with that firm, ask whether the company is a member of an association. Then check this section to see whether the association is listed. If the association is not included here, your local library has reference materials to help you find the appropriate contact.

AFSA Education Foundation (AFSAEF) ◆
919 18th St., NW Suite 300
Washington, DC 20006-5517
202-466-8611
Toll free: 1-888-400-7577
✉: info@afsaef.org
www.afsaef.org
The AFSAEF mission is to educate all consumers about the benefits of responsible money management so they can make informed financial decisions, understand the credit process, and seek help if credit problems occur. Its MoneySKILL® program educates young adults on personal finance concepts in the areas of income, expenses, assets, liabilities, and risk management to empower them to make sound financial decisions.

American Arbitration Association
1633 Broadway, 10th Floor
New York, NY 10019
Toll free: 1-800-778-7879
www.adr.org
This is a not-for-profit public service organization committed to the resolution of disputes through arbitration, mediation, conciliation, and other voluntary procedures.

American Bankers Association (ABA)
1120 Connecticut Ave., NW
Washington, DC 20036
Toll free: 1-800-226-5377
www.aba.com
ABA represents the concerns of banks and their employees. It provides consumer education materials on request.

American Bar Association
321 N. Clark St.
Chicago, IL 60654-7598
312-988-5000
✉: askaba@abanet.org
www.abanet.org
The Bar Association publishes a directory of state and local alternative dispute resolution programs and provides consumer information on request.

American Cleaning Institute® (ACI) ◆
1331 L St., NW, Suite 650
Washington, DC 20005
202-347-2900
✉: info@cleaninginstitute.org
www.cleaninginstitute.org
The American Cleaning Institute® (formerly the Soap and Detergent Association) has been providing consumers with accurate information about cleaning products since 1926. ACI is the consumer source for free/low-cost educational materials designated to help individuals, families, and communities stay clean, safe and healthy at home, work, and school.

American Council of Life Insurers
101 Constitution Ave., NW
Suite 700
Washington, DC 20001-2133
202-624-2000
www.acli.com
This association represents the interests of over 500 insurance companies that provide life insurance, pensions and annuities, long-term care, and disability income insurance.

American Health Care Association
1201 L St., NW
Washington, DC 20005
202-842-4444
www.ahca.org
This federation of affiliated state health organizations advocates for quality care and services for frail, elderly, and disabled Americans.

American Institute of Certified Public Accountants (AICPA)
220 Leigh Farm Rd.
Durham, NC 27707
919-402-4500
Toll free: 1-888-777-7077
(Ethics Hotline)
✉: service@aicpa.org
www.aicpa.org
AICPA ensures that accountancy gains respect as a profession and is practiced by ethical, competent professionals.

American Moving and Storage Association (AMSA)
1611 Duke St.
Alexandria, VA 22314
703-683-7410
Toll free: 1-888-849-2672
✉: info@moving.org
www.moving.org
AMSA is a national trade association offering a wealth of information on its consumer website, including a Mover Referral Service. It also sponsors a dispute settlement program to help consumers resolve loss and damage claims on interstate moves.

American Pharmacists Association (APhA)
2215 Constitution Ave., NW
Washington, DC 20037
202-628-4410
Toll free: 1-800-237-2742
www.pharmacist.com
The APhA empowers its members to improve medication use and advance patient care through information, education, and advocacy.

◆ Provided financial support for the publication of the Consumer Action Handbook.

American Society of Travel Agents, Inc. (ASTA)
Consumer Affairs
1101 King St., Suite 200
Alexandria, VA 22314
703-739-2782
✉: consumeraffairs@asta.org
www.astanet.com
ASTA is an association of travel industry professionals. It provides training and education to professionals and travel tips for consumers.

America's Health Insurance Plans (AHIP)
601 Pennsylvania Ave., NW
South Bldg., Suite 500
Washington, DC 20004
202-778-3200
www.ahip.org
AHIP is the national association representing nearly 1,300 member companies providing health insurance coverage to more than 200 million Americans. Member companies offer medical, long-term care, disability income, dental, supplemental, stop-loss insurance, and reinsurance to consumers, employers, and public purchasers.

Assisted Living Federation of America (ALFA)
1650 King St., Suite 602
Alexandria, VA 22314
703-894-1805
www.alfa.org
ALFA sets best practices for senior living. They also provide a directory of senior living communities and other materials to help consumers determine their assisted living needs.

Association of Credit and Collection Professionals (ACA)
PO Box 390106
Minneapolis, MN 55439-0106
952-926-6547
✉: aca@acainternational.org
www.acainternational.org
www.askdoctordebt.org
ACA International is the leading trade association for credit and collection companies. The Education Foundation arm of ACA educates consumers challenged by debt. It works to inform consumer of their rights when contacted by creditors

Association of Independent Consumer Credit Counseling Agencies (AICCCA)
11350 Random Hills Rd., Suite 800
Fairfax, VA 22030
Toll free: 1-866-703-8787
www.aiccca.org
www.credithelp4u.org
AICCCA represents non-profit credit counseling companies. AICCA sets industry standards to ensure that member companies provide quality service to consumers. The organization also provides information directly to consumers (budgeting tips and a searchable database to locate a credit counseling company) on their website.

Automotive Recyclers Association (ARA)
9113 Church St.
Manassas, VA 20110
571-208-0428
Toll free: 1-888-385-1005
www.a-r-a.org
ARA is dedicated to the efficient removal and reuse of automotive parts, and the safe disposal of inoperable motor vehicles.

Better Hearing Institute (BHI)
1441 I St. NW, Suite 700
Washington, DC 20005
202-449-1100
Toll free: 1-800-327-9355
✉: mail@betterhearing.org
www.betterhearing.org
BHI is a not-for-profit corporation that educates the public about hearing loss and what can be done about it.

Blue Cross and Blue Shield Association
Consumer Affairs
1310 G St., NW
Washington, DC 20005
202-626-4780
www.bluecares.com
BCBSA is a national federation of 39 independent, community-based and locally operated Blue Cross and Blue Shield companies.

Cellular Telecommunications and Internet Association (CTIA)
1400 16th St., NW, Suite 600
Washington, DC 20036
202-736-3200
www.ctia.org
CTIA oversees certification programs to ensure a high standard of quality for wireless consumers.

Certified Financial Planner Board of Standards, Inc. (CFP)
1425 K St., NW, Suite 500
Washington, DC 20005
202-379-2200
Toll free: 1-888-487-1497
✉: mail@cfpboard.org
www.cfp.net
Certified Financial Planner Board of Standards is a regulatory organization that fosters professional standards in personal financial planning. The CFP Board works to ensure that the public benefits from competent financial planning. The CFP Board certifies financial planners who meet its requirements by granting use of its trademarks.

Children's Advertising Review Unit (CARU)
70 W. 36th St., 12th Floor
New York, NY 10018
212-947-5137
Toll free:1-866-334-6272, ext. 111
✉: caru@caru.bbb.org
www.caru.org
CARU handles consumer complaints about truth and accuracy of advertising directed to children under 12 years of age.

Commission on Accreditation of Rehabilitation Facilities (CARF)
6951 E. Southpoint Rd.
Tucson, AZ 85756
Toll free: 1-888-281-6531
www.carf.org
CARF is an independent accrediting body of rehabilitation, addiction, substance abuse, and retirement living services. The organization provides an online search tools to find services that match your rehabilitation needs, as well as links to consumer resources.

Consumer Electronics Association (CEA)
1919 S. Eads St.
Arlington, VA 22202
703-907-7600
Toll free: 1-866-858-1555
✉: cea@ce.org
www.ce.org
CEA represents corporations involved in the design, development, manufacturing, and distribution of consumer electronics.

Credit Union National Association (CUNA)
5710 Mineral Point Rd.
Madison, WI 53705-0431
Toll free: 1-800-356-9655
www.cuna.org
CUNA provides representation, information, and public relations for more than 90% of credit unions through credit union leagues throughout the nation.

Direct Marketing Association (DMA)
Department of Corporate Responsibility
1615 L St., NW, Suite 1100
Washington, DC 20036
202-955-5030
✉: consumer@the-dma.org
www.dmachoice.org
The DMA is the trade association for organizations involved in direct marketing via direct mail, catalogs, the Internet, telemarketing, magazines, and newspaper and TV ads. DMA's consumer website offers consumers options (free of charge) to better manage their mail.

Direct Selling Association (DSA)
1667 K St., NW
Suite 1100
Washington, DC 20006
202-452-8866
✉: info@dsa.org
www.dsa.org
DSA is the trade association of firms that manufacture and distribute goods and services sold directly to consumers.

Distance Education and Training Council (DETC)
1601 18th St., NW, Suite 2
Washington, DC 20009
202-234-5100
www.detc.org
The DETC is a voluntary, non-governmental, educational organization that accredits distance education institutions.

Financial Industry Regulatory Authority (FINRA) ◆
Office of Dispute Resolution
1736 K St., NW
Washington, DC 20006
301-590-6500 (Call Center)
Toll free: 1-800-289-9999 (Broker Check Hotline)
www.finra.org
FINRA is the largest independent regulator for all securities firms doing business in the U.S. The organization operates the largest dispute resolution forum in the securities industry for disputes between investors and securities firms.

Financial Planning Association (FPA)
4100 E. Mississippi Ave., Suite 400
Denver, CO 80246-3053
Toll free: 1-800-322-4237
✉: fpa@fpanet.org
www.fpanet.org
The FPA is a leadership and advocacy organization connecting those who provide services with the consumers they serve. This organization is a resource for the public to find educational resources and financial planners to deliver advice using an ethical, objective, client-centered process.

Food Marketing Institute (FMI)
2345 Crystal Dr., Suite 800
Arlington, VA 22202
202-452-8444
www.fmi.org
FMI conducts programs in research, education, industry relations, and public affairs on behalf of grocery retailers and wholesalers.

Grocery Manufacturers Association (GMA)
1350 I St. NW, Suite 300
Washington, DC 20005
202-639-5900
Toll free: 1-800-355-0983
www.gmaonline.org
www.makingfoodbetter.com
GMA represents food, beverage, and consumer products companies. The Association helps to ensure the safety and security of consumer packaged goods.

Insurance Information Institute (III)
Consumer Affairs
110 William St.
New York, NY 10038
212-346-5500
✉: info@iii.org
www.iii.org
III is a non-profit, communications organization supported by the property/casualty insurance industry that works to improve public understanding of insurance.

International Association of Movers (IAM)
5904 Richmond Highway
Suite 404
Alexandria, VA 22303
703-317-9950
✉: info@iamovers.org
www.iamovers.org
IAM is a global association of movers and forwarders committed to providing customers with the highest level of service available.

International Cemetery, Cremation and Funeral Association (ICCFA)
107 Carpenter Dr.
Suite 100
Sterling, VA 20164
703-391-8400
Toll free: 1-800-645-7700
www.iccfa.com
ICCFA is the trade association dedicated to funerals and final resting places. It provides management guidance to members and advocates for consumer choice and dispute resolution in circumstances surrounding final arrangements.

◆ *Provided financial support for the publication of the Consumer Action Handbook.*

Joint Commission
One Renaissance Blvd.
Oakbrook Terrace, IL 60181
630-792-5000
www.jointcommission.org
The Joint Commission accredits
and certifies healthcare
organizations and programs.

LeadingAge ◆
2519 Connecticut Ave., NW
Washington, DC 20008-1520
202-783-2242
✉: info@aahsa.org
www.leadingage.org
LeadingAge is committed to
advancing the vision of healthy,
affordable, ethical aging services
for America. The association
represents not-for-profit nursing
homes, continuing care retirement
communities, assisted-living and
senior housing facilities, and
community service organizations.

**Mortgage Bankers Association
of America (MBA)**
1717 Rhode Island Ave., NW
Suite 400
Washington, DC 20036
202-557-2700
www.mbaa.org
The MBA is the national
association representing the
real estate finance industry,
including mortgage banking firms,
commercial banks, life insurance
companies, title companies, and
savings and loan associations.

**Mystery Shopping Providers
Association (MSPA)**
4230 LBJ Freeway, Suite 414
Dallas, TX 75244
www.mysteryshop.org
The MSPA is the largest
professional trade association
dedicated to improving service
quality using anonymous
resources.

**National Advertising Review
Council (NARC)**
National Advertising Division
70 W. 36th St., 13th Floor
New York, NY 10018
Toll free: 1-866-334-6272
www.narcpartners.org
www.nadreview.org
NARC fosters truth and accuracy
in national advertising through
voluntary self-regulation.

**National Association of
Attorneys General (NAAG)**
2030 M St., NW, 8th Floor
Washington, DC 20036
202-326-6000
www.naag.org
This organization facilitates
communication among attorneys
general, who are responsible
for enforcing civil laws in their
respective states. The AG offices
often oversee state government
regulation agencies and represent
the public interest.

**National Association of
Home Builders (NAHB)**
1201 15th St., NW
Washington, DC 20005
202-266-8200
Toll free: 1-800-368-5242
✉: info@nahb.com
www.nahb.org
NAHB's mission is to enhance
the climate for housing and the
building industry.

**National Association of
Insurance Commissioners
(NAIC)**
Executive Headquarters
2301 McGee St., #800
Kansas City, MO 64108
816-842-3600
Toll free: 1-866-470-6242
✉: webpost@naic.org
www.naic.org
www.InsureUonline.org
(consumer insurance information)
NAIC is a national organization
of insurance regulators. The
organization helps insurance
regulators facilitate the fair and
equitable treatment of insurance
consumers and promote
competitive markets.

**National Association
of Professional
Insurance Agents (PIA)**
400 N. Washington St.
Alexandria, VA 22314
703-836-9340
✉: piainfo@pianet.org
www.pianet.com
This association provides
practical advice about purchasing
personal insurance through its
national outreach program.

**National Association
of Realtors (NAR)**
430 N. Michigan Ave.
Chicago, IL 60611-4087
312-329-8200
Toll free: 1-800-874-6500
www.realtor.org
NAR, organization of real estate
agents, develops standards for
effective and ethical real estate
business practices.

**National Foundation for Credit
Counseling (NFCC)**
2000 M Street, NW, Suite 505
Washington, DC 20036
Toll free: 1-800-388-2227
www.nfcc.org
The NFCC promotes the national
agenda for financially responsible
behavior and builds capacity for
its members to deliver the highest-
quality financial education and
counseling services.

**National Funeral Directors
Association (NFDA)**
13625 Bishop's Dr.
Brookfield, WI 53005-6607
262-789-1880
Toll free: 1-800-228-6332
✉: nfda@nfda.org
www.nfda.org
NFDA helps consumers make
informed decisions about funeral
services and offers a third-party
dispute resolution program for
complaints regarding funeral
homes.

National Futures Association (NFA) ◆
300 S. Riverside Plaza, Suite 1800
Chicago, IL 60606-6615
312-781-1300
Toll free: 1-800-621-3570
✉: information@nfa.futures.org
www.nfa.futures.org
NFA is the industry-wide self-regulatory organization for the U.S. futures industry. NFA provides innovative and efficient regulatory programs and services that safeguard the integrity of the derivatives markets. Consumers should contact NFA regarding any firm or individual who solicits them for investments in futures, options on futures, or foreign currency.

National Institute for Automotive Service Excellence (ASE)
101 Blue Seal Dr., SE, Suite 101
Leesburg, VA 20175
703-669-6600
Toll free: 1-888-273-8378
✉: webmaster@ase.com
www.ase.com
ASE is an independent organization that works to improve the quality of automotive service and repair through the voluntary testing and certification of automotive repair professionals. ASE publishes several consumer publications about auto maintenance and repair.

North American Consumer Protection Investigators (NACPI)
✉: webmaster@nacpi.org
www.nacpi.org
NACPI provides training and support for consumer protection investigators in government agencies at all levels. NACPI does not investigate individual consumer complaints, but helps investigators share information of mutual concern.

North American Securities Administrators Association, Inc. (NASAA)
750 1st St., NE, Suite 1140
Washington, DC 20002
202-737-0900
✉: info@nasaa.org
www.nasaa.org
NASAA is an international organization devoted to investor protection. NASAA is the voice of the 50 state securities agencies responsible for grassroots investor protection, investor education, and efficient capital formation.

Tire Industry Association (TIA)
1532 Pointer Ridge Pl., Suite G
Bowie, MD 20716-1883
301-430-7280
Toll free: 1-800-876-8372
✉: info@tireindustry.org
www.tireindustry.org
TIA represents all members of the tire industry, including companies that manufacture, sell, recycle, or retread tires, along with their suppliers.

Toy Industry Association, Inc. (TIA)
1115 Broadway, Suite 400
New York, NY 10010
212-675-1141
✉: info@toyassociation.org
www.toy-tia.org
www.toyinfo.org
TIA is the not-for-profit trade association for producers and importers of toys and youth entertainment products sold in North America.

United States Tour Operators Association (USTOA)
275 Madison Ave., Suite 2014
New York, NY 10016
212-599-6599
✉: information@ustoa.com
www.ustoa.com
USTOA is comprised of companies that conduct business in the U.S. and offer tours and packages throughout the world.

◆ *Provided financial support for the publication of the Consumer Action Handbook.*

A

AARP
  contact information, 109
  retirement planning resource, 38
Adjustable-rate mortgages, 23, 24
Administration for Children and Families, 98
Administration on Aging, 99
Advance medical directives, 50
Advertisements
  fraudulent employment opportunity
    advertisements, 17
  green marketing claims, 20
Standard Directory of Advertisers, 71
Affordable Care Act, 28
AFSA Education Foundation, 142
Aging. See Elderly persons; Medicare;
    Retirement plans; specific organizations
AHA. See American Hospital Association
Air Force Community Readiness and Family
    Support, 59
Air travel
  airline fees, 47
  delayed or canceled flights, 47
  delayed or damaged baggage, 47
  lost baggage, 47
  overbooked flights, 47-48
  tarmac delays, 48
Airlines. See Air travel
Alternative fuels, 6
A.M. Best
  insurance company ratings, 28
AMA. See American Medical Association
American Arbitration Association, 142
American Association of Retired Persons.
    See AARP
American Bankers Association, 142
American Bar Association, 142
American Citizens Services and Crisis
    Management, 103
American Cleaning Institute, 19, 142
American Council of Life Insurers, 27, 142
American Council on Consumer Interests,
    109
American Council on Science and Health,
    109
American Health Care Association, 142
American Hospital Association, 21
American Institute of Certified Public
    Accountants, 142
American Medical Association, 20
American Moving and Storage Association,
    142
American Pharmacists Association, 142
American Savings Education Council, 38
American Society of Travel Agents, Inc., 143
Americans with Disabilities Act, information
    line, 102
America's Health Insurance Plans, 143
Annual Percentage Rate, 6, 10, 12, 15, 23, 60
Appliances, 50
Applications. See apps
Apps, 39, 40

This alphabetical index will help you find the right organization to contact for information or for assistance with your complaint. First, look for the specific topic, for example, Cars. Under this topic there will be one or more contacts, followed by the Handbook page number(s). Sometimes you will be directed to "See" another entry for information and a list of contacts. "See also" references direct you to other topics that might be related to your problem and may help you locate the right contact. For company names see the alphabetical listings under "Corporate Consumer Contacts" (p. 71), and "Automotive Manufacturers and Dispute Resolution Resources" (p. 63).

  GPS enabled
APR. See Annual Percentage Rate
Arbitration, for dispute resolution, 55
Armed forces. See Military personnel
ARMs. See Adjustable-rate mortgages
As is, 7
Assisted-living facilities, 21. See also Long-
    term care insurance; Nursing homes
Assisted Living Federation of America, 21,
    143
Association of Credit and Collection
    Professionals, 143
Association of Independent Consumer Credit
    Counseling Agencies, 14
ATM cards
  overdraft protections, 4
  reporting missing cards, 3-4
  using, 3-4
Attorneys. See Lawyers
Auctions, online, 44
Automobiles. See Cars
Automotive Recyclers Association, 143
Aviation Consumer Protection Division, 103

B

Baggage
  airline fees for, 47
  delayed or damaged, 47
  insurance coverage, 30
  lost bags, 47
Balloon mortgage, 24
Balloon payment, 7
Bankruptcy
  filing for, 14-15
  personal, 14
Banks and banking
  ATM/debit cards, 3-4
  checking accounts, 4-5
  FDIC insurance for, 5
  savings accounts, 4-5
  state banking authorities, 5, 126-129
Base mileage, 7
BBBs. See Better Business Bureaus
Better Business Bureaus
  BBB Auto Line, 65
  BBB Military Line, 59
  BBB OnLine, 66
  description of services, 54, 66
  state-by-state listing and contact
    information, 66-70
Better Hearing Institute, 143
Blind persons, services for, 59

Blue Cross and Blue Shield Association, 143
Bonds. See Investments
Brokers
  financial, 37
  real estate, 23
Bundling, 31
Bureau of the Public Debt, 104
Bus safety, 48

C

Cable TV service, 49
Call for Action consumer hotlines, 54
Caller ID spoofing, 38
Cars
  alternative fuels, 6
  balloon payment, 7
  base mileage, 7
  BBB Auto Line, 65
  buying tips, 6
  choosing a safe vehicle, 8
  dealer versus private-party purchases, 7
  dispute resolution programs, 65
  electric, 6
  financing, 7
  fuel economy, 6
  hybrid, 6
  insurance for, 28
  leasing, 8
  "lemon" laws, 7, 8-9, 65
  manufacturers, 63-64
  new, 6
  recalls, 8
  rentals, 9
  repairs, 9
  reporting safety hazards, 56
  repossessions, 9
  "secret warranties," 8-9
  tax incentives, 6
  used, 6-7
CDC. See Centers for Disease Control and
    Prevention
Cash top-up cards, 5
Cell phones
  apps, 39, 40
  services, 39
  smart phones, 40
Cellular Telecommunications and Internet
    Association, 143
Cemeteries. See also Funerals
  for veterans, 52
Center for Auto Safety, 7, 9, 109
Center for Food Safety and Applied Nutrition
    Information Linc, 100

Single copies of the current Consumer Action Handbook are available by writing: Handbook, Federal Citizen Information Center, Pueblo, CO 81009. The Handbook can also be viewed and ordered online at Publications.USA.gov.

The 2012 Consumer Action Handbook will be current through summer 2013. To place your name on a mailing list to receive the 2013 Handbook, please mail your request to the address listed above. For regularly updated consumer information, visit USA.gov.

We need your help to keep the Handbook up-to-date. Please report any changes to Handbook Update, Federal Citizen Information Center, 1275 First St, NE, 11th Floor, Washington, DC 20417 or e-mail action.handbook@gsa.gov.

www.ingramcontent.com/pod-product-compliance
Lightning Source LLC
Chambersburg PA
CBHW081451170526
45166CB00008B/2395